Newsmakers®

ISSN 0899-0417

Newsmakers®

The People Behind Today's Headlines

Louise Mooney
Editor

1993
Issue 3

Includes Nationality, Occupation,
Subject and Newsmaker Indexes

Gale Research Inc. • DETROIT • WASHINGTON, D.C. • LONDON

STAFF

Louise Mooney, *Editor*

L. Mpho Mabunda, *Associate Editor*

Marilyn O'Connell Allen, *Editorial Assistant*

Michael J. Tyrkus, *Assistant Editor*

Barbara Carlisle Bigelow, Victoria France Charabati, John P. Cortez, Harvey Dickson, Christine Ferran, Laurie Freeman, Simon Glickman, Joan Goldsworthy, Anne Janette Johnson, Mark Kram, Michael L. LaBlanc, Jeanne M. Lesinski, Glen Macnow, Carolyn C. March, Greg Mazurkiewicz, Donna Raphael, Sharon Rose, Isaac Rosen, Susan Salter, Virginia Knight Tyson, and David Wilkins, *Contributing Editors*

Peter M. Gareffa, *Senior Editor, Newsmakers*

Pamela A. Hayes and Keith Reed, *Permissions Associates*

Arlene Johnson and Barbara Wallace, *Permissions Assistants*

Catherine Kemp, *Production Assistant*

Cindy Baldwin, *Art Director*

Nicholas Jacubiak and C. J. Jonik, *Keyliners*

Reginald A. Carlton, Clare Collins, Andrew Guy Malonis, and Norma Sawaya, *Editorial Associates*

Rachel A. Dixon, Eva Marie Felts, Shirley Gates, and Sharon McGilvray, *Editorial Assistants*

Cover Photos: Eric Clapton (AP/Wide World Photos) and Whoopi Goldberg (Archive Photos/Darlene Hammond)

The paper used in this publication meets the minimum requirements of the American National Standard for Information Sciences–Permanence Paper for Printed Library Materials, ANSI Z39.48-1984.

ISBN 0-8103-8037-4 (this volume)
ISBN 0-8103-8034-X (complete 1993 set)
ISSN 0899-0417

Printed in the United States of America

Published simultaneously in the United Kingdom
by Gale Research International Limited
(An affiliated company of Gale Research Inc.)

The trademark **ITP** is used under license.

Contents

Obituaries

Introduction

Newsmakers provides informative profiles of the world's most interesting people in a crisp, concise, contemporary format. Make *Newsmakers* the first place you look for biographical information on the people making today's headlines.

Important Features

- **Attractive, modern page design** pleases the eye while making it easy to locate the information you need.

- **Coverage of all the newsmakers** you want to know about—people in business, education, technology, law, politics, religion, entertainment, labor, sports, medicine, and other fields.

- **Clearly labeled data sections** allow quick access to vital personal statistics, career information, major awards, and mailing addresses.

- **Informative sidelights essays** include the kind of in-depth analysis you're looking for.

- **Sources for additional information** provide lists of books, magazines, and newspapers where you can find out even more about *Newsmakers* listees.

- **Enlightening photographs** are specially selected to further enhance your knowledge of the subject.

- **Separate obituaries section** provides you with concise profiles of recently deceased newsmakers.

- **Publication schedule and price** fit your budget. *Newsmakers* is published in three paperback issues per year, each containing approximately 50 entries, and a hardcover cumulation, containing approximately 200 entries (those from the preceding three paperback issues *plus* an additional 50 entries), *all at a price you can afford!*

- And much, much more!

Indexes Provide Easy Access

Familiar and indispensable: The *Newsmakers* indexes! You can easily locate entries in a variety of ways through our four versatile, comprehensive indexes. The Nationality, Occupation, and Subject Indexes list names from the current year's *Newsmakers* issues. These are cumulated in the annual hardbound volume to include all names from the entire *Contemporary Newsmakers* and *Newsmakers* series. The Newsmakers Index is cumulated in all issues as well as the hardbound annuals to provide concise coverage of the entire series.

- **Cumulative Newsmaker Index**—Listee names, along with birth and death dates, when available, are arranged alphabetically followed by the year and issue number in which their entries appear.

- **Nationality Index**—Names of newsmakers are arranged alphabetically under their respective nationalities.

- **Occupation Index**—Names are listed alphabetically under broad occupational categories.

- **Subject Index**—Includes key subjects, topical issues, company names, products, organizations, etc., that are discussed in *Newsmakers*. Under each subject heading are listed names of newsmakers associated with that topic. So the unique Subject Index provides access to the information in *Newsmakers* even when readers are unable to connect a name with a particular topic. This index also invites browsing, allowing *Newsmakers* users to discover topics they may wish to explore further.

Suggestions Are Appreciated

The editors welcome your comments and suggestions. In fact, many popular *Newsmakers* features were implemented as a result of readers' suggestions. We will continue to shape the series to best meet the needs of the greatest number of users. Send comments or suggestions to:

The Editor
Newsmakers
Gale Research Inc.
835 Penobscot Bldg.
Detroit, MI 48226-4094

Or, call toll-free at 1-800-347-GALE

Newsmakers®

Jason Alexander

Actor

Born c. 1962 and raised in New Jersey; married; wife's name, Daena Title; children: one son. *Education:* Attended Boston University.

Addresses: *Home*—Los Angeles, CA. *Office*—c/o *Seinfeld*, NBC Television, 3000 West Alameda Ave., Burbank, CA 91523.

Career

Stage, film, and television actor. Began working at age 17 in a New York children's television program; landed first movie role two years later in *The Burning*, 1981; other films appearances include *Brighton Beach Memoirs, Mosquito Coast, Jacob's Ladder, White Palace, Pretty Woman,* and *I Don't Buy Kisses Any More.* Stage credits include *Jerome Robbins' Broadway, Merrily We Roll Along, Accomplice, Broadway Bound, The Rink,* the modern opera *The Making of the Representative for Planet 8,* and *Give 'Em Hell Harry,* a one-man play in which he portrayed Harry Truman. Television credits include numerous commercials and series *Everything's Relative* and *E.R.,* the mini-series *Favorite Son,* and the NBC comedy series *Seinfeld.*

Awards: Tony Award, Outer Critics Award, and Drama Desk Award, all 1989, all for best actor in musical *Jerome Robbins' Broadway;* Emmy Award, Golden Globe nomination, and two American Comedy Awards for best supporting actor, all for role in *Seinfeld.*

Photo by Chris Haston, ©NBC Photo.

Sidelights

Jason Alexander was already a fairly successful Broadway star when his neurotic George Costanza character on the *Seinfeld* sitcom caught the amused attention of TV fans and critics. The multi-faceted actor is also an accomplished singer and dancer who's charmed youngsters in children's shows and earned kudos as an operatic tenor. His hilariously idiosyncratic interpretation of George boosted Alexander-awareness to a national level and earned the actor an Emmy to add to his well-established award collection.

Seinfeld is the oddball NBC-TV comedy that has inched its way into the hit category. Its star, Jerry Seinfeld (see *Newsmakers 92*), is a stand-up comic who plays himself, introducing each show with a brief monologue before a make-believe nightclub audience. Material for his comic routines comes from his exaggerated misadventures with three sidekicks, one of whom is Alexander/Costanza, and the absurd humor of their everyday lives in New York's Upper West Side. The inability to find a parked car in a huge parking structure, the tedium of waiting for a table in a Chinese restaurant, and the inevitable, exhausting complications of thirty-something dating are all grist for Seinfeld's mill. The unique personalities of the four principals and their interaction sets the show several notches above ordinary.

Alexander plays Seinfeld's best friend, a short, slightly pudgy, self-doubting, self-absorbed, angst-ridden, and almost stereotypically Jewish young professional. Typically, he falls madly in love with a woman, then immediately suspects she's flawed for being attracted to him. He breaks the relationship off to pine obsessively over her loss. He renews the affair only to begin another round of doubts. He is every single white female's worst nightmare, his mercurial moods ranging from arrogance to depression, his motives always muddy, his methods often devious.

Alexander's portrayal of George is right on the mark. *Seinfeld* viewers are amused, attracted, shocked, repelled, and made to feel ultimately superior to George and his sometimes mean-spirited antics. Thankfully, Alexander the actor and person seems blessedly likable. His quick wit is more nice than nasty, and his self-doubt/self-confidence levels seem comfortably normal. He's enjoying the attention that critical acclaim brings, but is properly modest about his role, deferring to the talent of *Seinfeld* writers.

"We do not ad lib and we don't change," he said during an interview on the *Today* show. "Our writers are brilliant. They make it look so deceptively simple . . . . We have always just done our little show, and everybody said it's not going to work, and nobody was watching. We were amusing ourselves and now all of a sudden, a lot of people are watching and we're still amusing ourselves."

Alexander yearned for the stage as a youngster. He entertained his classmates by memorizing comedy albums and doing impressions. He considered his bar mitzvah, at age 13, to be his "first paid gig," and performed on a New York children's program, *The Pushcart Players: Feelings and Friends* at age 17. While studying drama at Boston University, he won the Harold C. Case Award for scholarship and service, and managed to launch his career with national commercials and a role in the critically booed 1981 horror film, *The Burning.*

Alexander's credits include a wide variety of work. Currently famous for a comic portrayal, he's impressed critics equally for performances in a modern opera, *The Making of the Representative for Planet 8,* and drama, as Richard Gere's villainous and lecherous lawyer in the 1990 hit *Pretty Woman.* In *Jerome Robbins' Broadway* he wrote the narration, guiding the audience through 20 years of Broadway musicals, singing and dancing his way to the 1989 Tony for best actor in a musical, as well as the Outer Critics and Drama Desk Awards for best actor in a musical. He has also tickled audiences as guest host of *Saturday Night Live* by launching into awkward flight but confident song for a *Peter Pan* spoof.

An attractive man with regular features and dark eyes, Alexander nevertheless doesn't fit into the standard leading-man slot. Such physical attributes as lack of stature and receding hairline are often the focus of *Seinfeld* jokes; *Today* show guest host Matt Lauer inquired about Alexander's reaction to this. "You know, Matt, I never had a good year. Never a good year," Jason responded with good humor. "I got braces when I was nine years old. I wore them until I was 18 years old and at age 18 the braces came off and the hair fell out. When I started losing my hair I cried about it for two years. And then I noticed that I was working a lot more and the tears ended and I remember, actually, one year I got a very fine toupee made, and I started wearing that all the time, and I stopped working altogether. So, uh, baldness has been a great asset. Baldness has been very good to me. And the rest of it, I would certainly like to be in my fit and prime, but it's the kind of thing where you do what the character says. If someone turned around and said to me, 'Sean Connery is out and you're going to be doing all his roles,' I would trim right down."

The success of George on *Seinfeld* has led to inevitable talk of a spin-off series. What if George were to take off on his own? "Doubtful," Alexander told Lauer on *Today.* "The magic of the *Seinfeld* show is actually its ensemble. It would be greatly diminished if anybody was gone, and I suppose we could stand on our own, but I don't think it would be the kind of success or the kind of fun that we have when the four of us are together."

In spite of his outgoing, energetic stage presence, Alexander is a very private person, granting few interviews. He lives in Los Angeles with his wife, actress/writer Daena Title, and their baby son, but misses the New York theater community and former home "terribly." Alexander hopes to direct theater someday, and is finishing work on an upcoming movie, *The Coneheads,* with Dan Aykroyd and *Seinfeld* co-star Michael Richards.

Sources

The Atlantic, December 1992.
Cosmopolitan, December 1990.
Mademoiselle, September 1991.
New York, February 27, 1989.
Today show videotape, April 1993.
Opera News, December 24, 1988.
TV Guide, September 19, 1992.

—Sharon Rose

Lloyd Bentsen

AP/Wide World Photos

U.S. Secretary of the Treasury

Born Lloyd Millard Bentsen, Jr., February 11, 1921, in Mission, TX; son of Lloyd Bentsen Sr. (a financier and rancher); married Beryl Ann Longino (a former model), 1945; children: Tina, Lan. *Education:* Law degree from University of Texas, 1942.

Addresses: *Home*—Houston, TX.

Career

Texas county judge (Hidalgo County), 1946-48; served in the U.S. House of Representatives, 1948-54; founder and president of Consolidated American Life Insurance Co., 1955-58; president of Lincoln Liberty Life Insurance Co., 1958-70; elected to U.S. Senate, 1970; served until 1933 when appointed secretary of the U.S. Treasury, 1992. *Military Service:* U.S. Army pilot, 1942-45; received Distinguished Flying Cross.

Sidelights

Treasury Secretary Lloyd Bentsen bridges the worlds of the corporate boardroom and the welfare tenement. He dresses and acts like a banker, is the oil industry's best friend in Washington, and supports many conservative causes. But, as a 22-year member of the Senate, he also guided through Congress a two-year string of bills to help poor mothers get medical care for their sick babies, to keep workers from being laid off without two-month's notice, and to ensure Medicare payments for the elderly sick.

He bristles at the idea that he represents big business. "I'm also friendly to farmers, the elderly. I've worked hard on Social Security," he told the *Dallas Morning News.* "I've offered legislation that extended Medicaid to prenatal and neonatal health care. So, I'm that too." Bentsen, who wears $500 suits and enjoys fine wines, was named Treasury secretary after President Bill Clinton's election in 1992 (see *Newsmakers 92* for profile on Clinton). It was the cap on a brilliant career that saw him rise from being a county judge at age 25, to a powerful member of the Senate, to a popular vice-presidential candidate in 1988. He is the ultimate Washington insider.

Bentsen was born into power and prestige. His great uncle was Henry Wilson, who served as a senator from Massachusetts and went on to serve as vice-president under Ulysses S. Grant, a Republican, from 1873 to 1875. Bentsen's father, Lloyd Sr., was one of the most powerful Anglos in heavily Hispanic and poverty-stricken South Texas. "Big Lloyd" emigrated from the Midwest to the Rio Grande Valley in 1920 with $1.50 in his pocket and built a $50 million ranching empire through sometimes controversial land-selling practices. He ran the family business until his death in a car accident at the age of 94 in 1989. Lloyd Jr. was born in 1921 and was put to work as a salaried farmhand at age six. His birthplace, which he described to the *Boston Globe* in 1988 as "a cottage alongside a dirt road down in South Texas," was actually a lovely small house with an elaborate stone chimney. The U.S.-Mexican border was open then, and Bentsen and his childhood friends used to swim across the Rio Grande River. He learned to speak Spanish fluently, which later proved to be an asset with his state's Hispanic voters.

Young Lloyd graduated from high school when he was only 15, and earned a law degree from the University of Texas in 1942, when he was just 21. He then enlisted as a private in the army, and quickly became a bomber pilot—the youngest in the European theater. Flying a B-24 nicknamed *Double Trouble*, Bentsen won the Distinguished Flying Cross for his 50 combat missions. He was shot down twice during his tour of duty; the second time he nearly died when the bomber he was piloting crashed into the Adriatic Sea.

After the war, Bentsen married Beryl Ann Longino, a Lubbock, Texas, beauty he had met during college and wooed in New York, where she had moved to pursue a modeling career. He also began his career in politics. At age 25 he was elected a judge, the top administrative job in his home of Hidalgo County. His slogan was "Beat the Machine." Two years later, he resigned the judgeship to run for the U.S. House of Representatives. His Democratic primary opponent, J.T. Ellis, portrayed him as a tool of big-money developers like his father, but Bentsen won the election. Just 27, he was the youngest member of Congress, and quickly captured the attention of House Speaker Sam Rayburn of Texas. Bentsen has often told reporters that in 1951 Rayburn sent him to persuade Dwight D. Eisenhower to run for president as a Democrat.

What is best known about Bentsen's first congressional stint is that he advocated that the United States threaten to drop an atomic bomb on North Korea, and also introduced a bill, which did not pass, to "eliminate communists from positions of influence in labor unions." Less known is that as early as 1949 he was among a handful of Southern members of Congress who voted to abolish the poll tax often used to deny minorities their voting rights. He also drew notice in 1951 when an immigration quota system prevented Bentsen from bringing his adopted Norwegian daughter into the United States. Bentsen then put a rider on a billion-dollar tax bill that enabled Tina Bentsen to enter the country.

By 1954 Bentsen was considered a rising star in the House. But tired of trying to raise a family on his $12,500 congressional salary, he went home to

Texas, intent on making his fortune. Bentsen told the *Boston Globe* that he bypassed his father's offer to join the family empire, instead moving to Houston, "to cut my own spurs and build my own business." He founded an insurance company, Consolidated American, with a $5 million nest egg from his father and his uncle. Despite the well-financed start-up, Bentsen still ran into some hard times. The company, with total capital of $7 million, got only $75,887 in insurance premiums in its first year. That year, the company lost $86,000 and Bentsen Jr. paid himself only $20,000.

Before the second year had ended, Bentsen was looking for deeper pockets to invest in him. He found them in Nebraska, and merged Consolidated American with the Lincoln Liberty Life Insurance Co. Bentsen soon got a controlling interest in Lincoln and became company president in 1958. He used the company's resources to expand; he bought the Texas

> *Bentsen is fiercely competitive in politics, in business, and on the tennis court. And he never denied a story that he won the down payment for his first house in a poker game.*

City National Bank, entered the mutual funds and stock investment businesses, and built a $15 million hotel in downtown Houston that became the first in the city to allow blacks as guests. As the overseer of hundreds of millions of dollars in investments, he was a Wall Streeter in Texas clothing, earning an annual salary of $500,000 by 1970.

Politics was still in his blood, however, and Bentsen was eager to get back into public life. In 1960 he served as statewide fund-raiser for the John Kennedy-Lyndon B. Johnson presidential ticket. In 1964 he had considered running for the U.S. Senate before Johnson talked him out of it. By 1970 Bentsen was intent on reviving his political career. He ran against incumbent U.S. Senator Ralph Yarborough in a bitter Democratic primary that is remembered two decades later for Bentsen's nasty television commercials. The controversial campaign ads linked the liberal Yarborough to the street disorders during the 1968 Democratic National Convention. "Lloyd knew the way to beat a liberal Democrat in the late 1960s was to run against hippies in the streets, the Chicago riots," David Shapiro, a Texas political consultant, later told the *Chicago Tribune.*

The strategy worked. The well-financed Bentsen ousted the incumbent Yarborough and went on to beat Republican challenger George Bush, who was then a congressman from Houston, in the general election. Bentsen succeeded at that time in depicting Bush as too liberal for Texas. For instance, Bush had missed a chance to vote against gun control because he was in the House gym, and the Bentsen camp quickly dubbed him "Gymnasium George."

After returning to Congress, Bentsen charted a careful course. He more often supported than opposed President Richard Nixon's legislative programs, but he also voted for bills to speed the American withdrawal from Vietnam, to enact an Equal Rights Amendment for women and to preserve federal funding for busing to overcome racial imbalance. He argued that abortion should be an issue solely for pregnant women to handle, with no government involvement.

As a senator from Texas, he represented the interests of the oil and gas industries by sponsoring favorable tax legislation. He pushed repeatedly for repeal of the windfall profits tax and other measures sought by the oil industry. Critics called him "Loophole Lloyd" for championing such tax breaks. On the other hand, he carefully nurtured his support, not just among wealthy Texas business leaders, but also in poor Hispanic neighborhoods. "He has always treated Hispanics with respect and he has always been responsive to Hispanic elected officials," Henry Munoz, a Democratic Party official from Bexar County told the *Chicago Tribune.* "Long ago he understood the importance of the Hispanic vote and he's been very sensitive to it."

That kind of universal appeal seemed perfect for the 1976 presidential race. Bentsen jumped in, casting himself as the moderate southern alternative, only to be bested by Jimmy Carter—the little-known Georgia governor with a similarly moderate image but a better campaign strategy. Despite being armed with a rich treasury and the endorsement of many establishment figures, Bentsen got just two percent of an early caucus vote in Mississippi and 10 percent in the neighboring oil state of Oklahoma. He quickly disbanded his operation.

Back in the Senate, his influence continued to grow. Bentsen organized his office like a corporation, with staffers submitting their ideas in writing for him to study privately. Bentsen is quiet and precise, and is more comfortable in confidential negotiations than he is stirring a crowd with oratory. Despite his cautious reserve, Bentsen is fiercely competitive in politics, in business, and on the tennis court. His friends say he considers himself a risk taker and an entrepreneur. And he never denied a story that he won the down payment for his first house in a poker game.

His politics are tougher to label. "Lloyd has spent most of his public life tracking a zigzag ridge of his own selection to avoid being labeled either liberal or conservative," *Texas Observer* publisher Ronnie Dugger told the *Philadelphia Inquirer.* Indeed, in a 1988 newspaper survey, 51 percent of Texans polled said that they were unsure whether Bentsen was liberal or conservative. Jane Macon, a Democratic activist in San Antonio, told the *Chicago Tribune,* "You can call him fiscally conservative but a social liberal. His support is widespread among Democrats and Republicans because once he makes a commitment, he stands by it."

In 1987 Bentsen was named chairman of the prestigious Senate Finance Committee, which handles the major trade, tax, welfare and health insurance legislation. In some ways, he seemed more of a Republican than a Democrat, pushing for big-business tax breaks and announcing that he did not intend "to participate in the dismemberment of industry in this country." But he also sponsored legislation requiring companies to give notice before shutting plants, reforming the welfare system and reviving tax deductibility of individual retirement accounts—all stands that are popular with liberal and middle-income voters. "Bentsen is known for a mild-mannered style and an ability to compromise, but he can be a tough negotiator," wrote the *Chicago Tribune's* Elaine S. Povich. "He is also a well-known friend to major business and Washington lobbyists. Nevertheless, he also has looked after the needs of the middle class."

Soon after becoming Finance Committee chairman, Bentsen made his biggest political gaffe. Early in 1987, he planned a series of breakfasts—which became known as "Eggs McBentsen"—at which lobbyists would pay $10,000 each for a morning meal with him. Once it was made public, Bentsen admitted he had made a "doozy" of a mistake, disbanded the group and returned the $92,500 that had already been collected. He survived the incident with just a minor smudge to his reputation. "He is a man of immense integrity," Senator Bill Bradley, a New Jersey Democrat, told the *Dallas Morning News* in Bentsen's defense. "He is very stable and comfortable with himself."

By the late 1980s Bentsen had come to be regarded as the senior statesman of the Democratic Party. Party pollster Geoff Garin told the *Dallas Morning News* that Bentsen "effectively serves as our Rock of Gibraltar." So when presidential nominee Michael Dukakis went looking for a running mate in 1988 who would balance him on age, geography, and ideology, Bentsen seemed an exceptional choice. Democrats hoped that the unlikely coupling of Massachusetts and Texas politicians would remind voters of the 1960 ticket of John F. Kennedy and Lyndon B. Johnson.

The choice of Bentsen was not universally applauded by Democrats. Not since 1924, when John W. Davis was the standard-bearer and pilloried as an agent of Wall Street, had the party offered a national candidate with as strong an alliance with big business. While Dukakis hoped that Bentsen's identification with wealth would broaden the party's base, others feared that he might undercut support for Dukakis among some members of the Democrats' traditional middle- and lower-income constituency.

Certainly, Dukakis and Bentsen differed on many issues, including gun control, *MX* missiles, contra aid, the death penalty, and proposals to levy fees on imported oil. During the 1988 campaign, Bentsen tried to turn their differences into an asset, telling the *Boston Globe* that Dukakis displayed "character and strength in picking someone who was no clone. Dukakis didn't want to be surrounded by a bunch of cheerleaders and yes men."

Certainly, picking Bentsen was the best move Dukakis made during an otherwise dreary campaign. Bentsen's sterling performance came during the vice-presidential debate, in which he skewered GOP nominee Dan Quayle (see *Newsmakers 89*) with the now-famous put-down, "Senator, you're no Jack Kennedy." "The choice of Bentsen was without doubt the single best decision in this campaign," Richard Moe, a Washington lawyer who was a top aide to Vice-President Walter F. Mondale, told the *Boston Globe* during the campaign. "The ticket would not be doing as well without Lloyd Bentsen as it is doing with him. He has clearly enhanced our prospects." The Democrats went down in defeat, but Bentsen had captured the national limelight. A CBS News-*New York Times* poll taken after the November 8 election found a three-to-one favorable rating for Bentsen, better than a two-to-one positive rating for Bush, and far better than the ratings given Dukakis and Quayle. "By the time he executed some of the

prettiest political knife work of the 1988 presidential campaign, carving up Dan Quayle, Lloyd Bentsen was already well on his way to a kind of Democratic Valhalla, a place of honor reserved for the select few," wrote the *Boston Globe*'s Peter G. Gosselin. "For the patrician senator from Texas, his role as vice-presidential candidate marked a final turn in the long road that he had traveled from the conservative hinterland of business-coddling, pork-wrestling, backroom-bargaining Texas politics to the moderate center of Washington policy-making."

No doubt Bentsen enjoyed the experience. "One of the happiest times I ever saw him was during the 1988 campaign," Jack Martin, a longtime Bentsen confidant remarked to the *Dallas Morning News.* "He relished the involvement with people all across the country, particularly the young people. He just seemed totally fascinated by being in a front-row seat in the American political process." After the election, Bentsen returned to the Senate, where he continued as head of the Finance Committee, often locking horns with the Bush Administration, and emerging as the Senate's foremost expert on financial, trade, and tax issues. Bentsen considered entering the 1992 presidential race, but instead threw his support behind Arkansas Governor Bill Clinton. The two men had worked together in the mid-1980s as founders of the Democratic Leadership Conference, a moderate group. And during the campaign Clinton sought Bentsen's advice on how to handle the issue of the North American Free Trade Agreement, which Bentsen supports and shepherded through the Finance Committee.

When Clinton was elected president few were surprised that Bentsen was the first person named to a Cabinet post. On December 9, 1992, Clinton appointed Bentsen as his Treasury secretary, declaring that the Texan has "the unique capacity to command the respect of Wall Street, while showing an unrelenting [concern] for the Americans who make their living on Main Street." Bentsen initially balked at the appointment, not eager to give up the power he had amassed in Congress. "But I am comforted by the fact that I will be representing the president in working for an economic policy to create jobs in this country, to have a more competitive economy, better able to create opportunity in our country," he told the *Dallas Morning News.*

Bentsen's appointment drew mixed reviews. Texas political columnist Molly Ivins told the *Boston Globe*, "He may be the respectable senior citizen of the Democratic Party, but he's been carrying water for the oil and gas industry for as long as I've known him." On the other hand, Lacy Hunt, the U.S. economist for the Hong Kong bank group in New York, told the *Dallas Morning News*, "The business community is certainly very comfortable with Mr. Bentsen."

Bentsen conceded that he is more conservative on financial issues than Clinton, but disagreed with the perception that his selection represented a business-as-usual choice of a political insider: "I've felt like an outsider for 12 years, and I'm tired of the gridlock." He said Democratic initiatives on issues ranging from crime to taxes were stymied by Republican administrations.

At the Treasury, Clinton has in Bentsen a well-known Washington figure with a commanding presence in economic circles who is known to favor business-stimulating tax policies. And he brings a strong international reputation to a president who is little known outside the United States.

Sources

Boston Globe, July 7, 1988; July 12, 1988; July 16, 1988; November 5, 1988; December 10, 1992.
Charlotte Observer, October 5, 1988.
Chicago Tribune, July 12, 1988; July 23, 1988; September 18, 1988; December 13, 1992.
Dallas Morning News, October 26, 1989; December 10, 1992; December 11, 1992.
Philadelphia Inquirer, October 5, 1988; December 10, 1992.

—Glen Macnow

Mayim Bialik

AP/Wide World Photos

Actress

Name pronounced "MY-im Bee-AH-lik"; born December 12, 1975, in San Diego, CA; raised in Los Angeles; daughter of Barry and Barbara Bialik; has one older brother, Isaac.

Career

Trained in dance, trumpet, piano and guitar; began acting career at age 12 with small role in the horror film *Pumpkin Head,* following up with guest roles on television shows *Beauty and the Beast* and *Facts of Life.* Additional film credits include *Beaches,* 1989; stage appearances include *The Wizard of Oz, Cats,* and *Hansel and Gretel;* star of NBC television series *Blossom,* c. 1990—. Additional television credits include roles on *Webster, Once a Hero, MacGyver, Murphy Brown, Empty Nest,* and *Molloy.*

Sidelights

Mayim Bialik is the smart and spunky teenager enjoying a successful acting career, which she's planned since the tender age of six. An energetic and multitalented mimic, she diligently practiced tap, ballet, jazz, piano, trumpet, guitar, and singing, while persuading her parents to back her attempts at stardom. Her television success as the title star in NBC's *Blossom* hasn't cancelled her interest in marine biology as an alternate career, however.

Bialik, whose first name means "water" in Hebrew, was raised in Los Angeles by parents who initially

tried to discourage their daughter's precocious ways. Father Barry, however, a high school drama teacher, and mother Barbara, a nursery school teacher, were eventually swayed by her hard work, persistence, and undeniable talent. Barbara quit her teaching job to help launch and oversee Mayim's career. She contacted local agents, billing her daughter as a Bette Midler/Barbra Streisand type, and accompanied her to auditions. Within a month, Mayim landed a five-line part in the horror film *Pumpkin Head.*

Her electric performance in the feature film *Beaches* caught the attention of the media. Her portrayal as a young C.C. Bloom, portrayed as an adult in the film by Bette Midler, was impressive, due in part to her study of Midler concert films shot during the 1960s. "I really don't know why they picked me," the green-eyed, brunette Bialik told *People Weekly.* "They changed my hair color [to red], they changed the color of my eyes, and they didn't like my singing voice. Beats me." However, the director's choice was backed up by reviewers' raves. *Seventeen* called her a "pint-size dynamo" and further touted her performance: "A murmur runs through the audience at the first sight of her onscreen: When she sings 'The Glory of Love' or taps her heart out, she so exactly captures the special, flamboyant essence of Midler it's uncanny. How did they find someone so perfect?"

Doors to the world of television started opening for Bialik. She appeared as a guest or part-timer on several sitcoms. In 1990 the Fox network cast her in the lead of their summer series, *Molloy*. The show flopped, but the young actress didn't suffer from it. *Newsweek* called her "an irresistible actress," and *People* said "she's a charmer, but she delivers every line with a verve that makes Ethel Merman look like a wallflower."

Within a year, Bialik was back in a lead role, this time in NBC's half-hour weekly comedy *Blossom*. She portrays a video-taping, diary-keeping teen who lives with her father and two brothers and copes with age-typical dilemmas. "The show is about a young woman, which is so rarely done," she told *TV Guide*. "I might as well try to be a positive role model. I don't want my character to be the typical bimbo who is just interested in shopping and boys. Basically, I want to break down the stereotypes." When scripts contain material Bialik finds objectionable, she airs her views with producers. "I'm a little feminist," she continued in the *TV Guide* interview. "So when it comes to things like that, you don't have to go along. Especially with the 'flat-chested' jokes. I think that's sexist. I think it was very insulting to me as a woman, and as a human being. I never make any compromises in my life. If there's something I believe in, I say it. I turn a lot of people off." Apparently she's not turning off the teen viewers who've tuned in faithfully for three seasons. *Blossom* is the third-rated series aimed at teenagers.

Bialik impresses reporters with her down-to-earth, unspoiled attitude. A high school senior, she takes school seriously and spends two or three hours a day working in a makeshift classroom on the *Blossom* set. She plans to attend college and is interested in marine biology. Bialik lives with her family, and apparently feels no need to rebel against parental authority. "People ask me, do I live at home, and they're totally serious," she told a reporter from *Sassy*. "And I say, my gosh, I'm 16. I've got so many years to live with my friends and buy my own milk. I mean, in this business you are dealing with a lot of adults, and you do get an adult side, but the fact is, I've only been alive 16 years. My parents are great people, and I live with them." In fact, Mayim is quite close to the older Bialiks, and says she respects them and trusts their judgment.

Along with school and acting, Bialik fits in personal hobbies such as video games, shopping, painting, and making jewelry. She sang at the 1989 Golden Globe Awards, tackled the National Anthem at Dodger Stadium, and performed the opening trapeze act for the CBS special *Circus of the Stars*. She also does the voices of male and female cartoon characters for Hanna-Barbera and ABC.

Outspoken in support of social and environmental causes, Mayim has demonstrated on behalf of the homeless and was the U.S. representative for the United Nations International School's program for better relations between nations. Bialik's informed, intelligent attitude has made her a popular talk-show guest.

Despite the attention *Blossom* receives, Mayim told *Seventeen* she considers herself to be "an employed actress, not a celebrity." She thrives on her hectic pace. "I like to be busy," she explained to *TV Guide*. "I'm not very patient as an actress. I love to be always working and I like being in every scene."

Sources

Newsweek, July 16, 1990.
People, February 6, 1989; July 30, 1990; January 21, 1991.
Sassy, November 1992.
Seventeen, April 1989; August 1992.
TV Guide, March 30, 1991.

—Sharon Rose

Barry Bonds

Professional baseball player

Born Barry Lamar Bonds, July 24, 1964, in Riverside, CA; son of Bobby (a professional baseball player and coach) and Patricia (Howard) Bonds; married; wife's name, Susann; children: Nikolai, Shikari. *Education:* Attended Arizona State University, 1982-85.

Addresses: *Home*—Murietta, CA. *Office*—c/o San Francisco Giants, Candlestick Park, San Francisco, CA 94124.

Career

Professional baseball player, 1985—. Outfielder for the Pittsburgh Pirates, 1986-92; outfielder for the San Francisco Giants, 1993—.

Selected awards: Named National League Most Valuable Player, 1990 and 1992; Rawlings Golden Glove Awards, 1990, 1991, and 1992.

Sidelights

Superstar leftfielder Barry Bonds is one of only a handful of players who have been named National League Most Valuable Player more than once. Bonds won the MVP honors in 1990 and 1992 as a member of the Pittsburgh Pirates. The special recognition helped him, as a free agent in 1993, to land a record-breaking six-year, $43.75 million contract to play for the San Francisco Giants. The son of a professional baseball player, Bonds has been around the big leagues most of his life. He therefore approaches baseball as a job—with its own pitfalls

and pleasures—and does little to enhance his personal image.

Bonds has been called uncooperative, arrogant, and selfish. He has quarreled openly with teammates, managers, and especially reporters who try to corner him for interviews. His image has suffered to such an extent that he has become a favorite target for fan abuse on the road—and an occasional target of scolding from fellow players. Nothing has swayed Bonds to become more tolerant or easygoing. He points to his awesome offensive numbers, his three Golden Glove awards for fielding, and his MVP honors, and says they speak for themselves. "I'm not a media person," he told the *San Francisco Examiner.* "I don't like to answer the same questions. I just like to play baseball. I'm not into the other stuff. I turn down a lot of interviews. It's the United States of America. I have freedom of choice. It's two different jobs—keeping the media happy, and keeping yourself and your family happy. It's too much for one man."

If Bonds is unpopular elsewhere, he is nothing less than a hero in Candlestick Park, home of the Giants. Since joining San Francisco in 1993 he has proved to be a major catalyst for improving the team's fortunes. *Philadelphia Inquirer* correspondent Sam Carchidi noted that since Bonds moved to San Francisco, the team "has made major strides, mainly because of him....Bonds is part of a metamorphosis in San Francisco." Indeed, Bonds has helped to energize a franchise that has not seen playoff action in years and has attracted new hometown fans at a time when the club needed it most.

You might say that Barry Lamar Bonds inherited a family business. He is the oldest son of baseball star Bobby Bonds and the godson of superstar Willie Mays. While other boys his age watched longingly from the bleachers, he used to shag fly balls in the Candlestick Park outfield with his dad and Mays. "I was too young to bat with them," Bonds told *Sports Illustrated*, "but I could compete with them in the field."

> "I just like to play baseball. I'm not into the other stuff. I turn down a lot of interviews. It's the United States of America. I have freedom of choice."

Bonds's father joined the Giants in 1968 and played there until 1974. Early in his career, Bobby Bonds was heralded as the successor to Willie Mays, especially since the two men were such good friends. Unfortunately, Bobby could never live up to the expectations heaped upon him by well-meaning but over-zealous fans. Even though he achieved the fabulous 30 home runs-30 stolen bases combination in five different seasons, his performance never satisfied the critics. He left the Giants in 1974 and played for a number of other major league teams, including the New York Yankees, the California Angels, the Chicago White Sox, the Texas Rangers, and the Cleveland Indians.

In the *San Francisco Examiner*, Larry Stone wrote: "The Bonds' have, well, bonds. They know what it's like to never do quite enough to satisfy the fans and the media. Bobby was supposed to be the next Willie Mays. Barry was supposed to be the next Bobby Bonds. With both, the story line was always potential, and how it wasn't being fulfilled." Barry Bonds seemed to echo these sentiments when asked about his father by *Sports Illustrated*. "No one gives my dad credit for what he did, and they want to put me in the same category," he said. "He did 30-30 five

times, and they say he never became the ballplayer he should have become. Ain't nobody else done 30-30 five times. Nobody. Zero. So I don't care whether they like me or they don't like me. I don't care."

The elder Bonds was an all-out competitor who liked to push his children to excel. Before he even attended school, young Barry could hit a Wiffle ball so hard it could break glass. He took to baseball naturally and learned from his father as well as his high school and college coaches. As a student at Sierra High School in San Mateo, California, he played baseball, basketball, and football. When he graduated in 1982, he was offered a contract with his father's former team, the San Francisco Giants. The money was significant—$75,000—but Bonds asked for more. The offer was withdrawn, and Bonds went to college instead.

At Arizona State University, Bonds played baseball for coach Jim Brock. The young outfielder's talent was evident from the outset, and by his junior year he had been named to the All-Pac 10 team three consecutive years. He hit 23 home runs as a junior and compiled a career .347 average, and he was chosen to the *Sporting News* All-American Team in 1985. Brock recalled his years coaching Bonds in *Sports Illustrated*: "I liked the hell out of Barry Bonds. Unfortunately, I never saw a teammate care about him. Part of it would be his being rude, inconsiderate and self-centered. He bragged about the money he turned down, and he popped off about his dad. I don't think he ever figured out what to do to get people to like him."

Bonds was drafted again in 1985, this time as the sixth pick in the first round. The team that won his services was the Pittsburgh Pirates. Bonds was sent to the minor leagues, where he played for the Prince William (Virginia) Pirates of the Carolina League. There he batted .299, hit 13 home runs, and was named League Player of the Month for July. The following season found him in Hawaii, where he batted .311 in just 44 games before being called up to Pittsburgh. All told, Bonds spent less than two years in the minor leagues. He was just 21 when he became a Pittsburgh Pirate.

Bonds quickly became the starting centerfielder and leadoff hitter for the Pirates. On his second day with the team he smacked a double, and less than a week later he had his first home run. By year's end he led the National League rookies in home runs, runs batted in, stolen bases, and walks. The Pittsburgh front office rejoiced—it was hoped that Bonds could help the team back into playoff contention.

In 1987 Bonds was switched to left field and moved to fifth in the batting order because he could hit to all fields. His batting average shot to .261, he hit 25 home runs, and he stole 32 bases. The following year a knee injury kept his stolen base total down but did nothing to his average (.283) or home run total (24).

Bonds came into his own in 1990, the year he won his first National League Most Valuable Player award. He hit 32 home runs and stole 52 bases—prompting further comparisons with his father—and he led the National League in slugging percentage with .565. Thanks in part to his outstanding season, the Pirates finished first in the National League East but could not win the league championship series.

In 1990, Pirate manager Jim Leyland told *Sports Illustrated:* "Barry's at the point in his career where he should be. If he handles himself the way he is capable of, he's going to be a consistent star for years." The *if* in Leyland's comment was important. Leyland recognized Bonds's talent but also found the young star temperamental and insensitive toward teammates. After he won the MVP award, Bonds asked for salary arbitration. He wanted a bigger raise than the Pirates were willing to give him. He lost.

Matters took a turn for the worse after the Pirates lost the 1990 National League Championship Series. Bonds joined a group of other star players for a goodwill tour of Japan. Associated Press reporter Alan Robinson claims that Bonds quit early in an exhibition game and then insulted his Japanese hosts by tossing aside a token gift during a post-game ceremony. Trouble followed Bonds back to America. During 1991 spring training in Florida, he engaged in a heated swearing match with Leyland and Pirates coach Bill Virdon after he refused to pose for photographs. Bonds and Leyland reconciled, both of them recognizing that they had a job to do for the Pirates. Once again the team advanced to the League Championship series, and Bonds hit .292 for the 1991 season. Bonds narrowly missed being voted League MVP again, finishing second to Terry Pendleton of the Atlanta Braves. In 1992 Bonds returned to the top of the heap with his second MVP award and a .311, 34-home run year.

San Francisco Giants hitting coach Bobby Bonds, left, instructs his son Barry during Giants' spring training in Scottsdale, Arizona, in 1993. AP/Wide World Photos.

It is especially rare for a team to trade a Most Valuable Player. Almost any club will try every avenue to keep such a star happy. The Pirates made little effort to court Bonds when he became a free agent at the end of the 1992 season. It was essentially a foregone conclusion that Bonds would leave the team, and everyone acted accordingly. For some time in the Fall of 1992 it looked like Bonds would sign with the New York Yankees. Then, in December, he received a more tempting offer.

The San Francisco Giants had narrowly escaped being sold and sent to St. Petersburg, Florida. New ownership had been found in the San Francisco area instead, and that ownership wanted to take the fifth-place team and make it a serious contender. The new owner/president, Peter Magowan, eyed Bonds as the most desirable free agent on the marketplace. Magowan offered Bonds a deal that would make him the best-paid player in baseball. Then the president sweetened the deal by adding Bonds's father, Bobby, as a Giants hitting coach. Recognizing Barry's solitary personality, Magowan even offered the star private hotel suite accommodations on the road. Bonds's average salary for *one year* of the six-year deal came to more money than his father and godfather earned—in their entire careers.

Together, Bobby and Barry Bonds hold the major league record for home runs from fathers and sons. Now they work side-by-side on the Giants, and they are closer than ever. If anyone understands Barry's unwillingness to talk to reporters and sign autographs, it is Bobby. "For them to say my son is moody is not right," the elder Bonds told the *San Francisco Examiner*. "How many days have they spent with my son? How many nights? They've met

him for a couple of minutes, and because he might be busy that day, or they don't know his business-like attitude at the ballpark, they say, 'My god, he's got an attitude.' And that's wrong."

For his own part, Barry Bonds has given up arguing about his attitude, his perceived lack of team spirit, his aloofness. He does not care if Giants fans like him or not—he just wants to win, just wants that World Series ring that has eluded him through three straight playoff losses with Pittsburgh. And he steadfastly refuses to discuss his record-breaking salary. "Money, money, money—why does everyone want to talk money?" he asked *Newsday*. Bonds added: "Look, no matter what happens, I'm going to get all of it—every last cent. Whether I hit .100 or .300, I'm going to the bank and cash that check. If I pass away, my kids get it. There's nothing y'all can do about it, so you might as well sit back and enjoy the show." And quite a show it is.

Sources

Associated Press wire report, March 6, 1991.
Daily News (New York), March 5, 1991.
Jet, December 10, 1990; August 17, 1992; December 28, 1992-January 4, 1993.
Los Angeles Times, November 19, 1992.
Newsday (Long Island, NY), April 4, 1993.
Philadelphia Daily News, February 25, 1993.
Philadelphia Inquirer, April 28, 1993.
San Francisco Examiner, October 8, 1990.
Sports Illustrated, June 25, 1990.
USA Today, June 19, 1991.

—*Mark Kram*

Ron Carey

Reuters/Bettmann

Union leader

Full name, Ronald Robert Carey; born March 22, 1936, in New York City; son of Joseph (a United Parcel Service driver) and Loretta Carey; married Barbara Murphy (a sales clerk), c. 1954; children: Ronald Jr., Sandra, Daniel, Barbara, and Pamela. *Education:* Graduated from Long Island City High School, 1953.

Addresses: *Office*—25 Louisiana Ave. NW, Washington, DC 20001.

Career

Driver for the United Parcel Service (UPS) in New York, 1955-67; president, Teamsters local 804, New York, 1967-91; president, International Brotherhood of Teamsters, Washington, DC, 1992—.

Sidelights

Ron Carey, the firebrand whose 1991 election as president of the International Brotherhood of Teamsters symbolized for many the triumph of democracy over corrupt tyranny, was not discouraged in the early 1960s, when he lost his first two bids for union officialdom. On his third try he won the presidency of his local union in an election that perfectly illustrated the spotlight he would shine, for years to come, on the dark side of organized labor. In the early days of his union activism, Carey was summoned to a meeting with his boss, who warned the young firebrand that unless he withdrew quietly from the union presidential race, his wife would receive evidence that he was having an affair. Carey, who had been tipped off about the meeting and about the manufactured allegations of infidelity, had a tape recorder running during this meeting with his boss. He later played the recording to rank and file members at campaign rallies, vowing that, if elected, he would never succumb to such intimidation and deceit.

Nearly 25 years later, Carey was making the same pledge to Teamsters across the country, men and women increasingly distressed by a union that bestowed limousines and jets on its leaders while it ignored the rank and file's modest wishes for higher wages and improved employment security. It was fitting that Carey was nominated for president at a convention at Florida's Disney World, a fantasy land offering hope and escape from a brutal and dispiriting reality. After his subsequent rise to the leadership of what was once called the most corrupt union in America, Carey told the *New York Times*, "If you read the fine print in our [union] constitution, you'll find an outrageous provision allowing the general president and a companion to vacation anywhere, any time, for any amount of time. At Teamster expense! To that special perk, I say, 'No thank you.' That is not how your hard earned money is going to be spent in the new Teamsters."

Ronald Robert Carey was born in 1936 in New York City, the second of five sons of Joseph and Loretta Carey. His father, a driver for United Parcel Service, was a die-hard union man who instilled in his children a strong work ethic. After graduating from Long Island City High School, young Ron, an outstanding athlete, turned down a swimming scholarship from St. John's University and enlisted in the Marines. Upon his discharge in 1955, he joined his father at UPS, delivering packages throughout the New York City borough of Queens. Having inherited his father's support of the union movement, Carey, in 1958, became a shop steward for local 804, which, at roughly 6000 members, was one of the largest UPS locals in the country, and also included the deliverymen and warehouse workers at many New York department stores. He took several labor relations courses and ran unsuccessfully for local trustee in 1962 and for recording secretary in 1965. Increas-

Carey's voice—the voice of a leader who had demonstrated his commitment to his workers—found a friendly audience in the rank and file fed up with a union gripped by corruption.

ingly disappointed with the union leadership's lack of concern for worker complaints, Carey ran for and won the local presidency. While his boss's backfired blackmail attempt certainly energized his supporters, his election was due mostly to the integrity, hard work, and selflessness that the workers perceived in him.

Carey would be reelected in landslides to eight three-year terms—a payback for his prodigious negotiating skills and a determination, so lacking in other union leaders, never to lose sight of the "grunts" whose support he sought to renew each day. He listened to workers, and fought management to resolve serious concerns about wages and working conditions, but he would not refrain from chastising workers who made frivolous complaints or used the grievance procedure to avoid work. Carey put a stop to the entrenched nepotism within the local, and abolished union credit cards, which shop officers had been using for personal use. A modest man whose grow-

ing power did not affect his material tastes, Carey took a cut in pay when the local union treasury ran low. Indeed, by the time he left the local, his salary was considerably lower than that of many members of his union. During his campaign for the Teamster presidency, supporters frequently made the telling point that Carey earned less than the Teamsters' French chef, whose elegant dishes were cooked up for union leaders at their fancy Washington headquarters. Seen as a common man, Carey would always enjoy the trust of the common folk.

Carey saw his first strike as local president just a few months after taking office, when he demanded retirement benefits for employees with 25 years of service, rather than 30 years. UPS rejected the policy change, and, in a surprise move, the national Teamsters leadership supported the company's position, concerned that other local leaders who had accepted the 30-year requirement would lose face if the young Carey succeeded where they had failed. For his efforts on this issue Carey received death threats, but pressed on, and after several months Teamsters president Frank Fitzsimmons ordered Carey to put a UPS counteroffer to a vote of the membership. In a glaring rebuke to the Teamsters throne, the majority backed Carey's rejection of the proposal, and the following day UPS agreed to the 25-year retirement clause.

The cost and seriousness of strikes became apparent in 1974, when Carey's drivers protested UPS's increased hiring of inexpensive, part-time workers over the benefit-laden union full-time workers. A compromise was reached—UPS would take on part-timers only to replace full-time workers who retired or quit—but not before a union trustee and friend of Carey's was killed when a driver at another local in New Jersey drove through the 804 picket.

In his first decade as local president, Carey negotiated contracts that doubled the wages of UPS drivers, but it was clear that the leaders at the top, notoriously corrupt and mob-influenced, would not hesitate to safeguard their own interests at the expense of the rank and file. In 1979 the local lost its longstanding right to negotiate its own contracts, and was forced to accept employment terms negotiated by a national team that did not include Carey, even though he had earned a solid reputation at the bargaining table. When the resulting contracts in 1982, 1985, and 1987 won wage increases as meager as two percent, Carey led a campaign against what he described as "sweetheart deals," but he lost these fights because of union bylaws that made ratification of these contracts nearly automatic.

In 1987 Carey filed a lawsuit against the union for its ratification provisions. Rather than face the possibility of an embarrassing adverse ruling, the executive board instituted the change that allowed a simple majority of members to reject a contract. It was at this time that Carey also began publicly decrying the excesses, greed, corruption, and the maniacal stranglehold on power of the national leadership. While violence and intimidation were seen as everyday, coercive tools of the Teamsters, the leadership retaliated peacefully against the increasingly prominent Carey. His name was expunged from union publications, and at a convention his microphone was turned off just as he was urging a reduction in dues. At a time of declining union membership and stagnant real wages, Carey's voice—the voice of a leader who had demonstrated his commitment to his workers—found a friendly audience in the rank and file fed up with a union gripped by corruption.

Carey's reformist calls were given greater weight following a suit brought by the U.S. government in 1988 charging that the executives of the 1.6 million-member Teamsters were in cahoots with the Mafia, which had consistently fixed the union's leadership elections, including that of the president. Teamsters president Jackie Presser and the entire executive board were charged. While the government sought to take control of the union, the Teamsters for a Democratic Union—a reformist group established in 1976—pushed a proposal, ultimately accepted, calling for the direct election of officers. The hope was that under strict government scrutiny, the union (whose last three out of five presidents, including Jimmy Hoffa, had gone to jail on charges of bribery and tampering with pension funds), could be cleansed and set on the path of legitimacy. With direct elections, Alan Black wrote in *New Statesman & Society*, "the rank and file would have the chance to bury the shameful past that had so badly damaged not just the Teamsters, but also the entire American labor movement."

Carey, supported by Teamsters for a Democratic Union, was one of three Teamsters nominated in June of 1991 to pursue the brass ring. Running against him were R. V. Durham, an International vice-president and the leading old-guard candidate, and Walter Shea, an executive assistant to the previous four Teamsters presidents. Tapping the prevailing political mood, Carey's opponents cast themselves as the vehicles of wholesale change. But both Durham's and Shea's electoral slates, featuring Teamsters who had run afoul of the law, reflected the dirty politics of the past. Carey emerged as the only candidate whose reformist zeal was not dis-

missed as pretense. And, as Aaron Bernstein wrote in *Business Week*, "since Carey is the only real outsider, his rivals are running scared."

Whereas his opponents relied on mid-level officials to get out the vote among the rank and file, Carey, as he had done as the local president, sought contact with the workers in the field. He crisscrossed the country in a beat-up station wagon, and at every stop he cut the figure of a dissident populist urging his colleagues, newly empowered with the right to vote, to take a stand against the elitist leaders who had sold the common workers down the river. "If you're happy with what you've got, then vote for the leaders you've got," he was quoted in *U.S. News & World Report* as saying. "But remember, you're the forgotten Americans."

While direct elections were new to the Teamsters, the candidates took to negative advertising with the expertise and ferocity of seasoned politicos. A Durham ad featured a close-up of Carey with the word "scab" scrawled across it. Carey's retaliation was an ad showing Durham arm in arm with a prison inmate and an armed gangster. Shea's contribution was a picture of Durham cast as a dog, being led on a leash by outgoing Teamsters president William McCarthy.

During the campaign, Carey was outspent by his opponents five to one, and it was not uncommon for workers who publicly endorsed his candidacy to suffer threats of lay-offs and injury. But in the largest union election in U.S. history, where rank and file members enjoyed secret balloting for the first time, it quickly became clear that Carey's message had been delivered. With government workers monitoring the ballots, Carey received 48 percent of the vote, Durham 33 percent, and Shea 18 percent. Carey's victory was hailed as a triumphant turnaround for a union that for years had been seen as inextricably corrupt, and a symbol of hope that other labor groups might democratize the process by which their leaders are selected. Among his first acts as International president was the cutting of his own salary from $225,000 to $175,000, and the selling off of union-owned limousines, jets, and a condominium in Puerto Rico. Shortly into his tenure, Carey succeeded in convincing a contingent of flight attendants not to abandon the Teamsters for another union and in spearheading a new contract for 16,000 car haulers. Although labor observers question whether Carey will be able to stem the shrinkage of union membership, and whether the Teamsters will ever again be blessed with the political clout of the old days, a Chicago janitor, as quoted in the *New York Times*, voiced the modest hope shared by many rank and file. "The honest people are firmly in control," he reportedly said. "There are going to be battles, but we're in a much better position to clean up the union."

Sources

Business Week, December 9, 1991.
New Statesman & Society, May 24, 1991.

Newsweek, December 16, 1991.
New York Times, December 10, 1991; December 15, 1991; February 2, 1992.
People, January 13, 1992.
Time, December 23, 1991.
U.S. News & World Report, November 25, 1991.
Wall Street Journal, November 12, 1990.

—Isaac Rosen

Eric Clapton

AP/Wide World Photos

Guitarist, singer, and songwriter

Name originally Eric Patrick Clapp; born March 30, 1945, in Ripley, Surrey, England; son of Patricia Clapp; raised by grandparents John and Rose Clapp; married Pattie Boyd Harrison, March 27, 1979 (divorced 1988); children: (with Lori Del Santo) Conor, born 1986 (died 1991). *Education:* Attended Kingston College of Art.

Career

Performing and recording artist, 1963—. Played with bands the Roosters, Casey and the Engineers, the Yardbirds, John Mayall's Bluesbreakers, Cream, Blind Faith, Delaney and Bonnie and Friends, Derek and the Dominos, 1963-73. Solo artist, 1974—. Appeared in films *Tommy* and *Water.*

Awards: World's Top Musician Award from *Melody Maker* magazine, 1969; *Guitar Player* magazine Reader's Poll, best in rock category, 1971-74, in overall category, 1973, in electric blues category, 1975 and 1980-82; co-winner of Grammy Award for album of the year for *The Concert for Bangla Desh,* 1972, for best historical collection for *Crossroads,* 1988; six Grammy Awards including album of the year and song of the year for *Unplugged* and "Tears in Heaven," 1993.

Sidelights

At the 1993 Grammy Awards ceremony, Eric Clapton barely had a chance to sit down. He received six trophies over the course of the evening for his single "Tears in Heaven" and for the album *Unplugged.* It was something of a valedictory for the veteran musician, who has been a star in the pop music firmament since the mid-1960s and who has weathered an astonishing number of tragedies and hardships—including drug addiction, alcoholism, romantic disaster, and the deaths of several loved ones—during his career. Through it all, however, he has maintained a singular grace and a devotion to the emotional truth music can convey. As B. B. King, a pioneer of electric blues guitar, said of Clapton to *Rolling Stone,* "You know it's the blues when he plays it."

Clapton's lifelong musical love has been the blues, and his life has often been the stuff of which the blues are made. Clapton was born illegitimately in Ripley, England, as World War II drew to a close. His mother left him to be raised by his grandparents, Rose and John Clapp, when he was a small child. He was brought up thinking they were his parents until his real mother returned home when he was nine years old. The family pretended that his mother was his sister, but he soon found out the truth from outside sources. "I went into a kind of ... shock, which lasted through my teens, really," he told *Musician,* "and started to turn me into the kind of person I am now ... fairly secretive, and insecure, and madly driven by the ability to impress people or be the best in certain areas."

As an adolescent, Eric first heard the sound of blues music from the United States and felt a profound and immediate connection to it. The "shatteringly intimate" voice of Delta bluesman Robert Johnson—as Clapton described it in a *Rolling Stone* interview—and, later, the electric blues of Muddy Waters and others motivated him to pick up the guitar; by his teens he was playing in coffee houses. He joined such groups as the Roosters and Casey Jones and the Engineers before finding his way into the Yardbirds in 1963. The group became a sensation for its guitar-fueled, bluesy rock, but Clapton left the Yardbirds after it became clear that greater success would come from pop hits like "For Your Love" rather than the heavy blues he loved.

Clapton first attracted real attention as a member of John Mayall's Bluesbreakers. Even then, *Rolling Stone*'s Robert Palmer noted, "he played the blues *authentically*, with a genuinely idiomatic feel." By this time the guitarist had worshippers—for whom the now-famous graffito "Clapton is God" formed the only gospel—and they would multiply after he began to perform and record with his next group, the legendary power trio Cream. With bassist-vocalist Jack Bruce and drummer Ginger Baker, Clapton helped take rock in a new direction: Cream fused heavy blues with psychedelic rock and jazzy improvisation. The result, as many critics have observed, laid the groundwork for much of the progressive rock and heavy metal that would follow. Clapton wrote the music for Cream's all-time greatest hit "Sunshine of Your Love" and sang a rollicking live version of Robert Johnson's "Crossroads"; both tracks have become "classic rock" standards. Clapton referred to Cream in a 1985 *Rolling Stone* interview as "three virtuosos, all of us soloing all the time."

Cream disintegrated in 1968; all three members had gotten into drugs, and the band chemistry was intense to begin with. Their farewell performance at London's Albert Hall is now legendary. The guitarist had in the meantime become close to Beatle George Harrison; Clapton co-wrote the late Cream hit "Badge" with him and had played a memorable solo on Harrison's "While My Guitar Gently Weeps" for 1968's *The Beatles*, known colloquially as "The White Album." Clapton's relationship with Harrison, though tempestuous, would be a constant in his life; he would also play live somewhat later with ex-Beatle John Lennon's Plastic Ono Band. Clapton and Baker joined keyboardist-vocalist Steve Winwood and bassist Rick Grech in forming another super-

group, Blind Faith. That band broke up after an album and a tour, and Clapton was never satisfied with its performance, though songs like "Presence of the Lord" and "Can't Find My Way Home" are widely regarded as classics more than two decades later.

Eric Clapton, the guitarist's first solo LP, hit the stores in 1970. He recorded the album with his friends from Delaney and Bonnie, the group that had opened for Blind Faith on its tour. Even as he honed his singing and songwriting, however, and publicly declared his Christianity, Clapton fell under the sway of two very demanding substances: cocaine and heroin. The situation did not improve even as he formed another short-lived but powerful group, Derek and the Dominos. The group recorded a passionate double-length album, *Layla and Other Assorted Love Songs*; it featured the late superlative guitarist Duane Allman, whose work challenged and inspired Clapton to new heights. "Layla," a driving, anguished rocker about his unrequited love for Harrison's wife Pattie, became one of the enduring anthems of the 1970s. Debilitated by rampant drug abuse and road fatigue, the group disbanded before making another album. Clapton was further devastated by the subsequent death of Allman in a motorcycle accident and friend and fellow guitar giant Jimi Hendrix's fatal barbiturate overdose. The idea of dying this way "didn't bother me," Clapton confessed to *Rolling Stone* years later. "When Jimi died, I cried all day because he'd left me behind."

The early 1970s were especially difficult for Clapton, though he reached his fans again with the highly publicized all-star Rainbow Concert, which yielded an album. For the most part he lived a reclusive life; it wasn't until 1974 that he quit heroin and put out a new album, the highly successful *461 Ocean Boulevard*. The record, which featured Clapton's hit version of Bob Marley's "I Shot the Sheriff," set the mood for much of his work during the next decade or so: relaxed and rootsy. Subsequent albums, like 1977's *Slowhand*, suggested Clapton was settling into a comfortable musical middle age; beneath the laid-back surface, however, storm clouds were gathering. Clapton had moved from heroin addiction to alcoholism, and would struggle with it for several more years. "Drink is very baffling and cunning," he told *Musician* years later. "It's got a personality of its own."

Clapton married Pattie Boyd—who had divorced Harrison some years earlier—in 1979 and the two would struggle to make their relationship work for nearly nine years; in the meantime, however, the alcohol was taking its toll. In 1981 he was forced to cancel a tour due to a severe ulcer; as a result he scaled back his drinking and improved his musical fortunes. He played a memorable benefit performance with fellow ex-Yardbirds Jeff Beck and Jimmy Page in 1983 and, over the next few years, released the variously regarded albums *Money and Cigarettes, Behind the Sun*—which contains the hit "Forever Man"—and *August*. Clapton also provided the scores for the *Lethal Weapon* films and the British television movie *Edge of Darkness*. Polygram's 1988 release of the four-CD hits package *Crossroads* provided exhaustive evidence of Clapton's massive contribution to rock music; the collection took the Grammy Awards for best historical album and best liner notes. Yet the same period saw what *Entertainment Weekly* called the "sad sight" of Clapton appearing on TV beer commercials, playing his version of "After Midnight"; it scarcely need be added that many found the choice of Clapton as a pitchman a tad ironic.

In 1988 he and Pattie Boyd divorced. In the meantime he had a son, Conor, with Italian model Lori Del Santo, and had for the most part turned his life around. His 1989 album *Journeyman* was quite successful, and his status as a rock institution was assured. The next couple of years, however, would bring him perhaps the most horrendous blows of all. First, esteemed guitarist Stevie Ray Vaughn and Clapton road crew members Colin Smythe and Nigel Browne—all close friends of Clapton's—were killed in a helicopter crash in August of 1990. Vaughn had himself recovered from alcoholism and was in peak form and on his way to major, widespread success at the time of his death. "There was no one better than him on this planet," Clapton noted in a 1991 *Rolling Stone* interview. Yet Eric and his whole crew—with whom Vaughn had been touring—voted to go on with the tour. The next show, he said, was an ordeal, but "it was the best tribute I thought we could make—to carry on and let everybody who was coming to see us know that it was in honor of their memory." Some of Clapton's live performances at Albert Hall were released on the 1991 collection *24 Nights*.

Fate dealt Eric Clapton an even more terrible blow a few months later. On March 20, 1991, his son Conor fell 49 stories to his death from a hotel window. "I went blank," he told *Rolling Stone*. "As Lori has observed, I just turned to stone, and I wanted to get away from everybody." With the help of Alcoholics Anonymous meetings and the support of friends like Rolling Stone Keith Richards (also in *Newsmakers 93*) and Genesis leader Phil Collins, he managed to take

a devastating crisis and transform it into art. The song "Tears in Heaven," described by *People* as "his sweet, sorrowful lullaby to Conor" and first recorded for the soundtrack of the film *Rush*, also appears on *Unplugged*, an album culled from a live acoustic performance on MTV. The album features a delicate rendering of "Layla" as well; both songs became massive hits and pushed *Unplugged* into the Top Ten.

Clapton was all over the musical map in 1992 and 1993. He reunited with his old mates from Cream for a blistering reunion set at the banquet commemorating the group's induction into the Rock and Roll Hall of Fame. Despite the power of the performance he downplayed rumors of a reunion album or tour. He also played an intimate night of the blues at his now-traditional Albert Hall concert; he disappointed some fans by completely avoiding his hits. *Rolling Stone's* David Sinclair concluded that the guitarist "may be this year's most exalted superstar, but no matter how

> "I try to look on every day now as being a bonus, really...life is very fragile, and that if you are given another twenty-four hours, it's a blessing. That's the best way to look at it."

the trophies stack up, the man still has a mean case of the blues." The trophies did stack up at the Grammies—Clapton won six of the nine for which he was nominated—and it seemed clear that Grammy voters and fans wanted both to compensate him for his crushing recent experiences and to thank him for a quarter-century or so of memorable music. Clapton's strength and poise in the face of tragedy, noted David Browne of *Entertainment Weekly*, "was optimism incarnate. In a simple unassuming way, it said that if he could get through this mess, then so could we." As Clapton told Palmer of *Rolling Stone*, "I try to look on every day now as being a bonus, really. And I try to make the most of it." He added, "the death of my son, the death of Stevie Ray, taught me that life is very fragile, and that if you are given another twenty-four hours, it's a blessing. That's the best way to look at it."

Selected discography

With the Yardbirds

Sonny Boy Williamson and The Yardbirds, Fontana, 1964.
For Your Love (includes "For Your Love"), Epic, 1965.

With John Mayall's Bluesbreakers

Bluesbreakers, Decca, 1966.

With Cream (On Atco except where noted)

Fresh Cream, 1966.
Disraeli Gears (includes "Sunshine of Your Love"), 1967.
Wheels of Fire, 1968.
Goodbye (includes "Badge"), 1969.
Cream Live, 1970.
Cream Live 2 (includes "Crossroads"), 1971.
Strange Brew: The Very Best of Cream, Polygram, 1983.

With Blind Faith

Blind Faith (includes "Presence of the Lord" and "Can't Find My Way Home"), Atco, 1969.

With Derek and the Dominos

Layla and Other Assorted Love Songs (includes "Layla"), Atco, 1971.
Derek and the Dominos—Live in Concert, RSO, 1973.

Solo albums

Eric Clapton's Rainbow Concert, RSO/Polygram/Polydor, 1973.
461 Ocean Boulevard (includes "I Shot the Sheriff"), RSO/Polygram/Polydor, 1974.
There's One in Every Crowd, RSO/Polygram/Polydor, 1975.
E.C. Was Here, RSO/Polygram/Polydor, 1975.
No Reason to Cry, RSO/Polygram/Polydor, 1976.
Slowhand, RSO/Polygram/Polydor, 1977.
Backless, RSO/Polygram/Polydor, 1978.
Just One Night, RSO/Polygram/Polydor, 1980.

Another Ticket, RSO/Polygram/Polydor, 1981.
Time Pieces: The Best of Eric Clapton, RSO/Polygram/Polydor, 1982.
Times Pieces II: Live in the Seventies, RSO/Polygram/Polydor, 1982.
Money and Cigarettes, Warner Bros./Reprise, 1983.
Behind the Sun (includes "Forever Man"), Warner Bros./Reprise, 1985.
August, Warner Bros./Reprise, 1986.
Crossroads, 1988.
Journeyman, Warner Bros./Reprise, 1989.
24 Nights, Warner Bros./Reprise, 1991.
Unplugged (includes "Tears in Heaven" and "Layla"), Warner Bros./Reprise, 1992.

With Other Artists

The Beatles, *The Beatles* (appears on "While My Guitar Gently Weeps"), Capitol, 1968.
Various Artists, *The Concert for Bangla Desh*, 1972.
Various Artists, *The Last Waltz*, 1976.
Lethal Weapon soundtrack, Warner Bros./Reprise, 1987.
Lethal Weapon II soundtrack, Warner Bros./Reprise, 1990.
Lethal Weapon III soundtrack, Warner Bros./Reprise, 1992.
Rush soundtrack (includes "Tears in Heaven"), Warner Bros./Reprise, 1992.

Sources

Commonweal, March 13, 1992.
Crawdaddy!, November 1975.
Entertainment Weekly, February 19, 1993.
Guitar Player, July 1985.
Musician, May 1992.
People, March 1, 1993.
Rolling Stone, October 17, 1991; October 15, 1992; April 15, 1993; April 29, 1993.

—Simon Glickman

Cindy Crawford

Supermodel

Born in 1966; grew up in De Kalb, IL; father worked as an electrician and glazier, mother as a homemaker; married Richard Gere (a movie actor), December 12, 1991. *Education:* Attended Northwestern University.

Career

Model since 1984; worked for Elite Models in New York, beginning in 1986; featured on over 200 magazine covers since 1986, including *Vogue, Glamour, Cosmopolitan, Mademoiselle,* and *Sports Illustrated;* cover model for Revlon cosmetics since 1989; has appeared in various television commercials, including for diet sodas; host of MTV's *House of Style* since 1989.

Sidelights

Even if you don't know Cindy Crawford by name, you most likely know her by face. Since her career exploded in 1986, she has attained nothing less than supermodel status, appearing on the cover of more than 200 magazines, ranging from *Vogue* to *Sports Illustrated.* Michael Gross of *New York* magazine described her as "an intelligent, olive-skinned, brown-eyed brunette with a full-blown figure and a distinctive beauty mark" who "has been cast as Everywoman precisely because she is so unlike the thin white-bread blonde models who once dominated modeling." Whether it has been about the mole above her lip, her spot as host for MTV's *House of Style,* or her marriage to movie actor Richard Gere,

Crawford has people talking. But she keeps her fame and good fortune in perspective, noting the fickle nature of the modeling industry. "I wouldn't have been a model ten years ago," she told Gross. "I would have been a freak."

The second of three daughters, Crawford was born in 1966 and grew up in De Kalb, Illinois. Her mother, a homemaker, divorced her father, an electrician and glazier, when Crawford was a freshman in high school. Even though the family "never had many extras," as she recalled to Gross, she was a straight-A student in school and had high career aspirations from the start. "First I wanted to be a doctor," Crawford told *Vogue.* "Then, in the seventh grade, I went to my state's capital and I heard about ERA [the Equal Rights Amendment] and I wore this ERA button all over the place. I was going to be the first woman president."

Crawford's introduction to modeling came her sophomore year in high school when a local clothing store asked her to appear in a fashion show with other girls from her school. She quit her minimum-wage job shucking corn and was hired by a local photographer to pose as "Co-Ed of the Week" for a college newspaper. From there, Crawford met a makeup artist who advised her to volunteer for a hairstyling demonstration sponsored by Clairol in Chicago. Attracted by the promise of having her expenses paid, she ventured to Chicago, where a Clairol representative helped her contact a local model agency.

The agency took test photographs of Crawford but decided that her mole hindered her from being model material. One of the photographs, however, was seen by Marie Anderson Boyd, who was just starting out as a model agent in 1982. Boyd contacted Crawford's parents and encouraged them to allow her to model. Their skepticism did not prevent them from lending support: "They gave me $500—all they could afford to lose," she told Gross. "I paid them back with my first check." Despite the suggestion by potential clients that she have her mole removed, Crawford, with Boyd's backing, refused to do it. Her decision paid off, and she was offered her first modeling job doing a lingerie ad for Marshall Field's department store. She arranged her school schedule so that she could drive to Chicago every afternoon and graduated as valedictorian of her high-school class.

Six months after she started at Field's, Crawford's agency merged with Elite, a large New York model firm. As a contestant in Elite's Look of the Year contest, she made it to the national finals in New York. "[Cindy] worked her ass off," Boyd noted in *New York*. "She was a pro from the beginning." After graduation, she was sent to Europe by Elite to see how she would fare as a model there. She began in Rome, working for Italian *Vogue*, where she was forced to get her long brown hair, another of her beauty trademarks, cut short and colored before her first photo shoot. From there, Crawford went to Paris, where, as she mentioned to Gross, "they put four girls who don't speak French in a tiny apartment and [left] them alone. I worked, but I had this short hair. I didn't know who I was." Though she was expected to return to New York afterward, Crawford went home and enrolled as a chemical engineering major at Northwestern University.

It was in Chicago that Crawford devoted herself full time to modeling and met her most important teacher—fashion photographer Victor Skrebneski. "He made me. He did. But you can't make something and keep it for yourself," she told Gross, in reference to the falling out she and Skrebneski had after two years of working together. In 1986 model agent Monique Pillard, who had seen Crawford at a Azzedine Alaia fashion show, convinced her to relocate to New York. Her appearance on the cover of *Vogue* in August of that year marked a career

explosion, and since then she has graced hundreds of magazine covers. Some of her more attention-getting poses have been as cover model for the celebrated *Sports Illustrated* annual swimsuit edition and in erotic layouts for *Playboy* and *GQ*. In 1989 Crawford signed a four-year contract with Revlon, estimated at $4 million. She now commands her profession's top dollar—$10,000 per day—and has explored other career avenues as well.

The words "Thanks for letting me talk," which, according to *Vanity Fair*, are inscribed on a picture of Crawford hanging in MTV producer Alisa Belletini's office, show her gratitude for another offer she got in 1989. The music-television network asked her to host their show *House of Style*, which airs six times a year and is devoted to fashion, beauty, and celebrity interviews. The venture worked out well on all sides: Crawford was eager to try something new, and Belletini found just what she wanted. "What's great about Cindy is her versatility," she told *People*. "She can do serious interviews, but she's not afraid to make fun of herself either." *New York Times* fashion writer Woody Hochswender, according to the same source, called her "a poised and articulate narrator" who possesses the "gentle cynicism of the insider." And Crawford herself identified the appeal of putting her talent to uses other than modeling: "The reason I love this show is I don't have to be the ice-perfect runway princess."

When she is not modeling or doing her MTV spot, Crawford spends as much time as she can with actor Richard Gere, her husband since 1991. The couple met in 1988 at a barbecue hosted by mutual friend and photographer, Herb Ritts. Though Crawford still maintains her own Manhattan apartment, she and Gere share a home in Los Angeles and a five-bedroom ranch house in New York's Westchester County. Her most recent interests include contemplating having children and a settled home life. "More than anything, I want a family, and Richard knew that," she told *People*. "I love kids and sort of feel that's the thing in my life I'm going to be best at, [being] a mother." But she will not forget the power she has as a celebrity to support more public causes. "It's only been fairly recently, since I became famous or whatever you call my celebrity status, that I really have been able to help and make people more aware," she said in the *Detroit Free Press*. "I must say, Richard has been instrumental in making me see that, as a public person, I have a voice and can make things happen!"

Sources

Detroit Free Press, March 15, 1993.
New York, October 30, 1989.
People, January 13, 1992; April 27, 1992.
Vanity Fair, April 1992.
Vogue, August 1991.

—*Carolyn C. March*

Faith Daniels

AP/Wide World Photos

Television newscaster and talk-show host

Born in 1958 in Pittsburgh, PA; adopted by Steven (a sheet-metal worker) and Mary (a hairstylist and homemaker) Skironsky; married Dean Daniels, 1981; children: Andrew, Alyx Rae. *Education:* Attended college in West Virginia.

Career

Reporter and weather forecaster in Wheeling, WV, Peoria, IL, Columbus, OH, and Pittsburgh, PA, in the early 1980s; news anchor at CBS News on *Sunday Morning, 48 Hours,* and *CBS This Morning* shows, 1985-90; news anchor at NBC News on *NBC News at Sunrise* and *Today* shows, 1990-92; host of *A Closer Look,* NBC, 1991-93.

Sidelights

Newscaster and talk-show host Faith Daniels has a personal stake in treating sensitive topics with grace and compassion. On the March 4, 1993 episode of her NBC talk show, *A Closer Look,* she moderated a discussion on women who become pregnant as a result of rape. Though she seemed dispassionate as she listened to the stories of her guests, Daniels, just before breaking for a commercial, made a startling disclosure. As *People* reported, she announced to panelists and audience alike: "There are many adoptees—including this one—who were conceived in the exact same way. It really doesn't matter how you were conceived. Only what you've become." While Daniels had mentioned her adoption before,

she had never talked in public of the circumstances behind it—that, as a teenager, her birth mother had become pregnant with her after being beaten and raped by the man she was dating.

Daniels has taken her own words—that what matters is what you become—to heart. She spent the first eight months of her life in a Catholic orphanage, until Steven Skironsky, a sheet-metal worker, and his wife, Mary, a hairstylist and homemaker, adopted her. The couple also adopted a nine-year-old boy from an Italian orphanage and raised the two children outside of Pittsburgh. If Daniels shocked viewers with her disclosure, she maintained, with characteristic composure, that people who share her situation should feel neither shame nor embarrassment and that her own adoptive parents gave her a good start in life. "[The circumstance of conception] isn't something that's a cross to carry or that I dwell on," she was quoted in *People* as saying. "Date rape is truly an awful thing. But if a child is the result, and is placed in a loving home, there should be no stigma."

Once she decided on a career as a news anchor, Daniels went from station to station reading local news. "At my first job, in Wheeling, West Virginia, I earned a hundred and fifty-five dollars a week, before taxes," she recalled in *Cosmopolitan*. "I had to do odd jobs to pay my bills. But it was the only way. You have to start small and hungry." Her second position was in Peoria, Illinois, where her station manager and producer argued over whether she should wear her hair in a bob, like now-deceased newscaster Jessica Savitch, or a ponytail, like anchor Jane Pauley. She was hired as a reporter but was forced, as she put it, to become a "weather bunny" when the regular forecaster left for a different station. "I purposely tried to do a terrible job," she told the same source, "because I thought if I screwed up, they would find someone else and put me back in news, where I belonged."

While Daniels continued to make intentional mistakes, viewers loved her, and the ratings soared. The station was so pleased that it ran a newspaper ad featuring her face under an umbrella that said, "Have Faith in Your Forecast." She quit the next day and worked as a reporter in Columbus, Ohio, and Pittsburgh. A career break came in 1985, when she was asked to join CBS News. In addition to her position as anchor on the morning news, she filed stories for the network's *Sunday* and *48 Hours* shows and anchored news segments on *CBS This Morning*.

For Daniels, 1985 was an important year for personal reasons as well. She had been married to Dean Daniels, an executive producer at WCBS, for four years, and decided it was time to speak to her birth mother, whose identity she had known since she was 21. "I was thinking about starting a family," she told *People*, "and I didn't know anything about my genes. I felt, 'If I'm ever going to do anything, I may as well do it now.'" Several months after an initial phone call, Daniels and her birth mother arranged to meet in a restaurant. Her birth mother told Daniels that she had later married twice but had never had another child as, *People* reported, "It just wasn't anything she wanted to repeat. It was too traumatic for her." Daniels assured her that she was very close to her adoptive parents and felt she had not missed out on anything as a child.

In 1990 Daniels moved from CBS to NBC, where she anchored *Sunrise*, read the news on the *Today* show, and filled in on weekend newscasts. She also presided over her own talk show, called *A Closer Look*, during which she worked 18-hour days and tackled such topics as teenage alcoholism, incompetent doctors, and children's fear of war. For her, the distinction between daily newscasts and a more topical show remains clear. "When I anchor regularly scheduled newscasts, we go on for 30 minutes about this problem and that problem, then at the end we smile and say goodnight," she told *New York*. "What we're

trying to do on *A Closer Look* is isolate stories where there is something that you can do and give you not only the problem but the solutions and options." The show allowed Daniels to combine three of her favorite activities—anchoring, reporting, and interviewing—and to get involved in human-interest stories.

What frustrates Daniels about her profession is that female anchors seem to face more criticism than male broadcasters on topics that have little to do with actual performance—namely, their appearance and dress. "More often than not when people stop me on the street they don't say, 'I really liked the way you reported the news out of the Middle East,'" she noted in *McCall's*. "It's usually, 'Boy, you had on a great outfit today.'" She also points to the recent trend in publicizing the college grade-point averages of women in the field, observing that men do not fall under the same scrutiny. It rankles her that different assumptions are made about how men and women earn their positions. "I think the assumptions people most often make about how a woman got to sit in that chair are different," she asserted in the same source. "They assume she got the job because of the way she looks or because somebody fancies her. These are the negative kinds of assumptions that female broadcasters have to fight."

While she sometimes feels pulled in two different directions, Daniels maintains that the best decision she ever made was having children. Her scant free time is spent caring for and playing with her young son, Andrew, and daughter, Alyx Rae. Yet she has not stopped moving forward in her career, and plans to host her own prime-time news magazine by the summer of 1993. She also intends to visit Bosnia, where she will look into adopting an orphaned child. "I'm certainly capable of having more children," she told *People*, "But it would be awfully nice if I could give an abandoned child a home first." Learning the story of her birth has not scarred her, Daniels claims, though it has left her with a legacy. She had always thought that the nuns in the orphanage had named her Faith. "But that was actually the name given to me by my biological mother," she mentioned in *People*. "She felt I would need it."

Sources

Cosmopolitan, January 1990.
McCall's, April 1991.
New York, March 4, 1991.
People, March 8, 1993.

—Carolyn C. March

Afonso Dhlakama

Reuters/Bettmann

Mozambique leader

Full name, Afonso Macacho Marceta Dhlakama; born January 1, 1953, in Chibabava, Sofala Province, Mozambique; son of Manguande (a chief); married; wife's name, Dona Rosaria; children: Isabel, Albertina, Henriques, and a fourth, name unknown. *Education:* Attended Catholic mission school, St. Francis of Assisi; attended Zobue Seminary, Tete Province; Industrial School, Beira, Sofala Province, 1969; took accounting course in Beira, 1975. *Politics:* Anti-Marxist. *Religion:* Roman Catholic.

Career

Portuguese army recruit, 1970-72; member of FRELIMO (Front for the Liberation of Mozambique) beginning in 1972 as commander in Niassa Province, becoming logistical commander for Sofala Province, 1974; member of RENAMO (Resistencia Nacional Mocambican), 1976—; commander-in-chief and president of RENAMO, 1980—.

Sidelights

On October 4, 1992, a peace agreement signed in Rome, Italy, ended a 16-year civil war that killed more than one million people in Mozambique. Lying on the southeast coast of Africa, Mozambique is one of the poorest countries in the world. At its outset, the war was between the Soviet-backed government in Maputo, the nation's capital, and a guerrilla group trained and supported by white military governments on Mozambique's borders— Rhodesia (now Zimbabwe) and South Africa. When

Mozambique became independent of Portugal in 1974, FRELIMO (the Front for the Liberation of Mozambique), Marxist-Leninist nationalists, assumed power. FRELIMO was sympathetic to the nationalist cause in neighboring Rhodesia and offered sancuary to the guerrillas trying to overthrow its government. FRELIMO also provided sanctuary to African National Congress (ANC) guerrillas trying to end minority rule in South Africa.

In the late 1970s the Rhodesian military created RENAMO (a Portuguese acronym for Resistancia Nacional Mocambican) to undermine the Mozambique government's ability to rule and to gather intelligence on Zimbabwe nationalists in Mozambique. After 1980, when the nationalists came to power in Zimbabwe, South African military operatives took over RENAMO, moving its base from Zimbabwe to South Africa.

With the end of the Cold War and the new political atmosphere in South Africa, RENAMO and its commander, Afonso Dhlakama, were abandoned by their former supporters and compelled to sign the 1992 peace treaty. Under the new accords, RENAMO and the governments agreed to allow the United Nations to supervise troop demobilization, to create a unified armed forces, and to hold nationwide multiparty elections. Dhlakama faces the challenge of transforming himself and his movement from a loosely organized guerrilla operation into a credible political organization that can successfully compete in nationwide elections.

Dhlakama comes from a subsistence farming area where his father was a chief. He received his elementary education at a Catholic mission school and briefly attended a seminary school but was forced to withdraw because of a lack of money. He told a British Broadcasting Corporation (BBC) radio reporter in March of 1992 that he had wanted to become a priest but, because he was the eldest of six children, he had to withdraw from the seminary and learn a commercial skill. He has spent all of his adult life in military service of some sort.

Dhlakama joined FRELIMO in March of 1972 and trained in Tanzania. He became commander of Niassa province in Mozambique and, after independence from Portugal, was made logistical officer in Sofala province. Before joining FRELIMO, he claims he was conscripted into the Portuguese army but he deserted. Dhlakama was recruited by Rhodesian agents while he was serving time in a FRELIMO reeducation camp. Freed by the Rhodesian forces, he fled to Rhodesia and became deputy to "Commander Andre"—Andre Matsangaissa—the first RENAMO commander.

Dhlakama, whose *nom de guerre* was Jacamo, succeeded Matsangaissa as leader of RENAMO after Matsangaissa was killed in a battle in October of 1979. The commander's death set off a major power struggle within RENAMO. Although Dhlakama was next in line to succeed Matsangaissa, Rhodesian military officials and black Mozambican recruits opposed him. Dhlakama owed his eventual succession to the intervention of a powerful white Portuguese, Orlando Cristina, and the "mysterious disappearance of the main challengers to [Dhlakama's] leadership," according to Alex Vines, author of *Renamo: Terrorism in Mozambique*. The Rhodesian military transferred responsibility for RENAMO to the South African Defense Forces just before the British colony of Rhodesia became the independent nation of Zimbabwe in April of 1980. The Rhodesian intelligence organization dismantled the entrie RENAMO operation, including the radio transmitter, and transported it to Phalaborwa in northern South Africa. There the South African Defense Forces reorgainzed and re-equipped RENAMO.

Although Dhlakama was the nominal head of RENAMO, RENAMO secretary general Orlando Cristina was the main go-between with the South African government. As second in command in the organization, Cristina took part in all important military planning and financial decisions. At the urging of the South African Military Intelligence, Cristina published in 1981 political tracts attributed to RENAMO's National Council that were designed to create a credible political presence within RENAMO acceptable to Western governments. In reality RENAMO lacked any political agenda other than being anti-Communist. Eleven years later, RENAMO hired United States lobbyist Bruce Fein to write a political platform and draw up a constitution.

In 1983 Cristina was assassinated in South Africa. The South Africans picked Evo Fernandes, a Mozambican lawyer born in Goa, to succeed Cristina. Unlike Cristina, Fernandes did not participate in military strategy and planning. He acted as go-between with South Africa and travelled in the West raising funds for RENAMO. Fernandes was assassinated in Lisbon in 1988, a victim of rivalry between South African interests and U.S. interests for control of RENAMO.

In the early 1980s RENAMO was no more than a front for the South African military and former Rhodesian military men. The South African Defence Forces themselves carried out some of the terrorist actions attributed to RENAMO. According to H. Ellert in *The Rhodesian Front War*, the South African Defense Forces attacked the rail line running from Mutare in Zimbabwe to the Mozambican port of Beira, Zimbabwe's main link to the sea. They also blew up Zimbabwe's oil storage tanks in Beira.

By mid-1982 RENAMO had extended its operations in Mozambique, operating as far afield as Gaza province in the south and Zambezia province in the north. RENAMO radio, *Voz da Africa Livre* (the Voice of Free Africa), resumed broadcasting from South Africa. At this time RENAMO had recruited about 10,000 men and boys who were operating in nine of Mozambique's ten provinces. "Recruitment was both semi-voluntary (from local villages in RENAMO-controlled areas and from FPLM [Mozambican army] deserters) and entirely forced (especially by abduction of military age civilians from communal villages)," according to a report compiled by Western governments.

The FRELIMO government was unable to stop the terrorism or protect its citizens. Dhlakama was half-jokingly referred to as "the circuit breaker" because RENAMO continually destroyed the pylons for the electric lines servicing Maputo and Beira. By 1990, of Mozambique's 16 million people, nearly two million rural people had been displaced because of RENAMO attacks and acts of sabotage. Another one million people had fled their homes and sought safety in refugee camps in Malawi and Zimbabwe.

In 1984, the South African government offered to end its support for RENAMO in exchange for Mozambique expelling the African National Congress (ANC) and its military wing from Mozambique territory. The ANC had been infiltrating guerrillas and arms into South Africa from Mozambique. The two governments signed the Nkomati Accord on March 16, 1984. But the South African military, given carte blanche by the government of P.W. Botha, reneged on its promises and continued to supply RENAMO. In a raid on Dhlakama's Casa Banana headquarters in 1985, a joint operation of Zimbabwean and Mozambican troops discovered documents confirming South Africa's continued involvement.

> "What has emerged in Mozambique is one of the most brutal holocausts against ordinary human beings since World War II....Renamo is waging a war of terror against innocent Mozambican civilians through forced labor, starvation, physical abuse and wanton killings."
> —Robert Gersony

United States relations with Mozambique President Machel's government improved as a result of the Nkomati Accord. But as bilateral relations improved, anti-Communist and anti-FRELIMO right-wing activities in the United States increased. The major catalyst for right-wing fund raising and lobbying was Machel's vist to the United States in 1985 at the invitation of the White House. U.S. lobbyists and some elements in the State Department compared RENAMO to the anti-Communist Contras in Nicaragua, Mujahedin in Afghanistan, and UNITA (the National Union for the Total Independence of Angola) forces in Angola. RENAMO sponsors provided Dhlakama with sophisticated communications equipment. Journalists held captive by RENAMO reported seeing a communications system that allowed RENAMO headquarters at Casa Banana to communicate

with all its provincial bases. The radio system also allowed RENAMO headquarters to communicate with its officials in Kenya and Malawi.

In one of the worst acts of brutality in the war, RENAMO attacked the city of Homoine in Gaza province in 1987, killing 424 civilians. Following that attack, the U.S. State Department commissioned Robert Gersony to provide a first-hand report on the actual conditions in Mozambique. In addition to the disturbing level of violence, the State Department was particularly alarmed at the image the right-wing was creating for RENAMO and by the possibilty the U.S. government might provide RENAMO with covert funding. Gersony's 1988 report compared the brutality of RENAMO to that of Pol Pot's Khmer Rouge in Cambodia, concluding that "100,000 civilians may have been murdered by RENAMO." Roy A. Stacy, deputy assistant of state for African affairs, told a press conference that: "What has emerged in Mozambique is one of the most brutal holocausts against ordinary human beings since World War II.... Renamo is waging a war of terror against innocent Mozambican civilians through forced labor, starvation, physical abuse and wanton killings." Complementing Stacy's remark was that of an old villager who described RENAMO as "the locust people." The old man said, "They eat everything, food, clothes and us, until we have no more. Then they go and eat elsewhere," reported Vines.

After the Gersony report was issued, Dhlakama was taken to a South African base where he was coached in social etiquette and public speaking. To improve his image with the public, he was taught how to speak, dress, and behave with journalists. According to *Africa Confidential*, "the South African secret servicemen teaching Dhlakama to be articulate and televisual have an uphill job since he is no genius."

When Dhlakama travelled to Portugal in 1991 he did not give a single interview to the press. A Portuguese newspaper, *Semanario*, described Dhlakama "as a strangely self-effacing man. He has none of the retinue of an African chief.... He exudes nothing of the cult of power, the taste for leadership, the immediate charisma, or the leonine narcissism of the UNITA leader [Jonas Savimbi in Angola]."

As the extent of RENAMO atrocities became known, right-wing support fell away, forcing RENAMO to become more resourceful. RENAMO developed an extensive and lucrative trade in ivory, as well as in gemstones. In a 1988 raid on RENAMO bases, the Mozambican army found 19,700 elephant tusks valued at $13 million. RENAMO also received protection money from Malawi and South Africa by promising not to attack rail and power lines in exchange for tribute, according to *Africa Confidential*.

The breakup of the Soviet Union and the eastern bloc countries in 1989 and 1990 suddenly deprived RENAMO of its raison d'etre—its image of freedom fighters against Communism. The Mozambique ruling party had also preempted RENAMO by officially abandoning Marxisim-Leninism and by adopting a constitution guaranteeing human rights, a multiparty system, and a free market economy. The coming to power of F.W. de Klerk in South Africa in 1989 also reduced South Africa's support for RENAMO. Evidence obtained from raids on RENAMO headquarters indicated that in the late 1980s Kenya replaced South Africa as RENAMO's logistical rear base of support.

RENAMO might have continued its low-scale chronic destabilization except for the drought of 1992. The drought in Mozambique and in the rest of southern Africa in 1991-92 was the most severe ever recorded. Traditionally, RENAMO troops forced villagers to supply them with food and to be their bearers. With the drought there was simply no food and no water. RENAMO troops resorted to raiding international food relief convoys and preventing food aid from going into some areas. Eventually, Dhlakama agreed to allow food into agreed-upon corridors, and eventually agreed to a cease fire. RENAMO troops also began receiving food aid.

Despite some violations, the cease-fire agreement held, demonstrating Dhlakama's ability to control his widespread organization. After some delay, RENAMO and the Mozambique government signed a peace treaty in Rome in October 1992. The timetable for the peace agreement was subsequently revised, partly because United Nations funding was delayed and because Dhlakama was reluctant to establish a residence in Maputo. Vines attributed his reluctance to come to Maputo to an incident in 1989 when Dhlakama narrowly escaped being killed or captured by Mozambique troops and "ever since ... Dhlakama has been pre-occupied with security."

Dhlakama may also be reluctant because "he is well aware that his position will become more vulnerable to being undermined by the wheeling and dealing that will take place with his other officials once the peace process takes root." Lacking a political ideology, RENAMO has a difficult time negotiating with any consistency or direction. Its goals are vague and undefined, although RENAMO officials are agreed on wanting to achieve positions of power and wealth.

The question of whether Dhlakama and RENAMO can make the transition from a guerrilla movement to legitimate political figures is crucial for peace and stability in Mozambique. The tortured image of Angola after rebel leader Jonas Savimbi went back to fighting because he did not like the October 1992 election results looms over Mozambique. Dhlakama bristles when the question is raised at a press conference, as quoted by *Mozambiquefile*: "That is a silly question. I am not Savimbi, President Chissano is not [President Eduardo] dos Santos, and Mozambique is not Angola." He pledged that "if we lose the election, we will accept that we are in opposition."

Sources

Books

Conspicuous Destruction: War, Famine and the Reform Process in Mozambique, Africa Watch, 1992.
Ellert, H., *The Rhodesian Front War*, Mambo (Gweru), 1989.
Gersony, Robert, *Summary of Mozambican Refugee Accounts of Principally Conflict-Related Experience in Mozambique*, U.S. State Department, 1988.
Hoile, David, *Mozambique: A Nation in Crisis*, Claridge Press, 1989.
Vines, Alex, *RENAMO: Terrorism in Mozambique*, Indiana University Press, 1991.

Periodicals

Africa Confidential, March 22, 1991; July 12,1991.
The Herald (Harare, Zimbabwe), March 11, 1993.
Mozambiquefile (Maputo, Mozambique), October 1992.
New African (London), August 1991.
O Jornal (Lisbon, Portugal), November 8, 1991.
Semanario (Lisbon), November 9, 1991.
The Star (Johannesburg, South Africa), February 18, 1988.

—*Virginia Knight Tyson*

Clint Eastwood

Actor and director

Full name, Clinton Eastwood, Jr.; born May 31, 1930, in San Francisco, CA; son of Clinton and Ruth Eastwood; married Maggie Johnson, 1953 (divorced); children: Kyle, Alison. *Education:* Attended Los Angeles City College. *Military service:* U.S. Army, Special Services, 1950-54.

Addresses: *Office*—c/o Warner Bros. Studios, 4000 Warner Blvd., Burbank, CA 91522.

Career

Actor, 1955—; film director, 1969—; founder and owner of Malpaso Productions, 1969—. Principal films include *A Fistful of Dollars*, 1964; *For a Few Dollars More*, 1967; *The Good, the Bad, and the Ugly*, 1967; *Hang 'em High*, 1968; *Coogan's Bluff*, 1968; *Paint Your Wagon*, 1969; *Kelly's Heroes*, 1970; *Two Mules for Sister Sara*, 1970; (and director) *Play Misty For Me*, 1971; *The Beguiled*, 1971; *Dirty Harry*, 1971; *Joe Kidd*, 1972; *Magnum Force*, 1973; (and director) *Breezy*, 1973; (and director) *High Plains Drifter*, 1973; *Thunderbolt and Lightfoot*, 1974; (and director) *The Eiger Sanction*, 1975; *The Enforcer*, 1976; (and director) *The Outlaw Josey Wales*, 1976; (and director) *The Gauntlet*, 1977; *Every Which Way but Loose*, 1978; *Escape from Alcatraz*, 1979; *Any Which Way You Can*, 1980; (and director) *Bronco Billy*, 1980; (and director, producer) *Firefox*, 1982; (and director, producer) *Honkytonk Man*, 1982; (and director, producer) *Sudden Impact*, 1983; *City Heat*, 1984; *Tightrope*, 1984; (and director, producer) *Pale Rider*, 1985; (and director, producer) *Heartbreak Ridge*, 1986; *White Hunter, Black Heart*, 1990; (and director) *Unforgiven*, 1992.

Reuters/Bettmann

Also director and producer of *Bird*, 1988, and director of *In the Line of Fire*, 1993. Appeared in television series *Rawhide*, CBS, 1959-66.

Selected awards: Chevalier des Arts et Lettres (France), 1985; numerous awards for *Unforgiven*, including Academy Awards for best director and best picture of 1992.

Sidelights

He seems chiseled out of stone: a cold, intimidating squint above high cheekbones and square jaw, a lanky, no-nonsense frame, and a mouth tailor-made to sneer at bad guys. He is Academy Award-winner Clint Eastwood, one of the most popular film actors in the world. Eastwood has been starring in movies since 1964 and has produced and directed them since 1970. Other filmmakers might have made more money here and there, but over the long run— with blockbuster after blockbuster to his credit— Eastwood has outworked and overshadowed all competitors. As a *Vogue* magazine contributor put it: "Eastwood has reworked and reinvented America's two most popular movie genres, cowboy and cop, into personal formulas and made himself a rumored $2 billion along the way." The actor-director has also overcome critical barbs to earn the industry's highest honors in America and abroad.

Eastwood forged his extraordinary career by portraying a series of antisocial heroes who pursue personal vendettas with little respect for the letter of the law. *Commentary* correspondent Richard Grenier noted that in a typical Eastwood vehicle, the star "kills a lot of people and never flinches once. They are all very bad people, of course, so there is no need to feel sorry for them. But [his] hand never trembles."

For years the actor offered variations on this ever-popular character, sometimes in westerns, sometimes in detective dramas. "His wince is an instrument of understatement," wrote the *Vogue* reporter. "Poor saps come at him six or 10 at a time, trying to brain him with meat hooks and crowbars. He's cornered into a chivalrous position: reluctantly he takes charge. He gits mad, plumb mad-dog mad, and the body count multiplies. Through clenched teeth he invites his victims to 'sit there and bleed awhile afore you git to taste real pain.' Then he says, 'I bin here way too long,' and rides back into the sunset, women running after him."

A number of actors have imitated the Eastwood concept, but what distinguishes Eastwood is his constant reassessment of the limitations of the human condition, his exploration of the dark side of his laconic heroes. "I've played winners, I've played losers who were winners, guys who are cool, but I like reality," Eastwood told *Premiere* magazine.

"And in reality, it's not all like that. There's sort of that frailty in mankind that's very interesting to explore. Heroics are so few and far between." Indeed, Eastwood never was a straightforward hero, and his recent movies paint vivid portraits of men who pay a steep emotional price for their supposed invulnerability. "I like playing people with a little bit of a chink in the armor," he told *Vogue*. "It's like they have some problems they're trying to overcome, other than the antagonist."

This refusal to settle for easy genre films has finally won Eastwood an enormous following among movie critics who at one time dismissed or openly berated his work. "Eastwood is above all a thoroughly American icon," wrote David Ansen in *Newsweek*. "The lonely, stubborn individualism—both brutal and elegant in its intransigence—is rooted in a tradition that goes back at least as far as James Fenimore Cooper.... [Eastwood rarely ventures] beyond certain histrionic perimeters. Within those borders, however, he's smashingly effective. Few actors have the charisma, or the bone structure, to

convey such a strong impact with such minimalist means."

Clinton Eastwood, Jr. was born in Depression-era California on May 31, 1930. His family moved from town to town throughout the state while his father pursued various temporary jobs. The Eastwoods were not poverty-stricken like many of the Dust Bowl immigrants to California. Their unsteady prosperity rested on Clinton, Sr.'s strong work ethic, which was passed on to Eastwood and his sister. The family relocated more than ten times while Eastwood was a youngster. "Since I was almost always the new boy on the block, I often played alone and in that situation your imagination becomes very active," the actor told *McCall's*. "You create little mythologies in your own mind."

Finally, the elder Eastwood obtained a permanent position with the Container Corporation of America in Oakland. Clint settled into Oakland Technical

---

Dirty Harry "caused an uproar. Eastwood was called a brute, a fascist, and worse."
—Richard Grenier

High School, where he played varsity basketball. "Nobody ever told him he was smart or promising," noted John Vinocur in the *New York Times Magazine*. Certainly, Eastwood had little inkling what lay in store for him career-wise. After graduating from high school, he went straight to work. He pumped gas, cut lumber, fought fires in Oregon, and even worked in a Texas blast furnace. In 1950 he was drafted. The Army sent him to Fort Ord in Monterey, California, where he taught other recruits how to swim. While at Fort Ord he became friends with a number of aspiring actors, including the late David Janssen. They encouraged him to try to break into the film business.

Following his discharge from the service, Eastwood moved to Los Angeles and took courses at Los Angeles City College. Once again he was rarely idle, pumping gas, digging swimming pool foundations, and even picking up garbage in order to make ends meet. In 1955 he was hired by Universal Studios as a contract player. His salary was $75 a week, and his assignments included bit parts in B-pictures such as

Revenge of the Creature, Francis in the Navy, and *Ambush at Cimarron Pass.* Eastwood told *Show* magazine: "I'd always play the young lieutenant or the lab technician who came in and said, 'He went that way' or 'This happened' or 'Doctor, here are the X-rays' and he'd say, 'Get lost, kid,' I'd go out and that would be the end of it." After 18 months, Universal let Eastwood go.

He persevered, however, supplementing his meager wages as a bit player by serving as a lifeguard. Occasionally he drew unemployment. The lean years might have dragged on indefinitely, but one day in 1959 he was visiting a friend in the CBS studio cafeteria and was spotted by a producer who was casting for a new television Western. The producer offered Eastwood a screen test, and he won the role of Rowdy Yates on the popular series *Rawhide.* The show—centered on a cattle drive to Missouri—ran for seven years, garnering top ratings through 1962. Although Eastwood was never fond of his Rowdy Yates character, he did find the weekly television schedule a good training ground, both in terms of acting experimentation and nuts-and-bolts production.

During the 1964 hiatus in *Rawhide,* Eastwood accepted a $15,000 offer to make a feature film in Spain for Italian director Sergio Leone. Eastwood later said he only took the assignment because it gave him a chance to visit Europe. Whatever his motivation, he found himself involved in a project that would catapult him from a dead-end television career to lifelong stardom in the movies.

The film was called *A Fistful of Dollars.* Eastwood portrayed a hired gun, a nameless man who successfully manipulates—and ruthlessly kills—rival gangs of bandits. The script was wordy. Eastwood slashed pages of dialogue and convinced the director that audiences would root for a terse hero. He was right. While he was back in America filming a new season of *Rawhide, A Fistful of Dollars* was causing a sensation in Europe. Over the next two years, Eastwood returned to Europe to film *For a Few Dollars More* and *The Good, the Bad, and the Ugly,* both also featuring the "Man with No Name."

Even Eastwood thought the Italian trilogy—first of the so-called "spaghetti westerns"—was too violent for American audiences. Nevertheless, United Artists bought the rights to the films and released them in the United States. *Premiere* contributor Peter Biskind wrote of the movies: "The critical reaction was mixed. The films were acclaimed—and disdained—for their hip, surreal cynicism. The trilogy established the formula for the Eastwood western: the Man with

No Name squinting in the fierce midday sun, laconic, cool, and laid-back but remorseless and vengeful at the same time, coming from nowhere, going nowhere, without a past, without a future.... Eastwood's films ushered in a new era of cinematic violence. Some 50 people are killed in *A Fistful of Dollars.* The line between the hero and the heavy was becoming blurred. With the war in Vietnam heating up, there was no time for niceties."

The success of the Leone westerns enabled Eastwood to secure similar roles in American films. By 1970 he had become a top box office draw with leads in movies such as *Hang 'em High, Coogan's Bluff, Kelly's Heroes,* and *Two Mules for Sister Sara.* Eastwood's superstardom was written in stone in 1971, when his own fledgling production company released *Dirty Harry.* An action movie set in San Francisco, *Dirty Harry* introduced Eastwood as Harry Callahan, a dedicated policeman whose search-and-destroy mission against a psychotic killer is frustrated by legal bureaucracy. "The film caused an uproar," wrote Grenier. "Eastwood was called a brute, a fascist, and worse. But he had his defenders, too, and it was curious how those sympathetic with the film in general tended to like Eastwood's acting, while those who hated the film thought he was the worst performer who had ever stepped in front of a movie camera."

No matter what the critics thought, the American public flocked to see *Dirty Harry.* The movie grossed three times more than any other Eastwood vehicle up to that time, and it set the stage for a series of popular sequels, including *Magnum Force, The Enforcer, Sudden Impact,* and *The Dead Pool.* "What *Dirty Harry* did in the 1970s was to outrun an American political phenomenon by close to a decade," claimed Vinocur. "In the series involving the rebellious detective, Eastwood caught a mood of blue-collar discontent with a country portrayed in the films as being run by bureaucrats, sociologists, appeasers and incompetents. American society's deepest incapacity, the Dirty Harry films said, was in failing to protect the normal lives of its normal people, and its most galling trait was rationalizing crime and the intolerable with guidance-counselor jargon .... What's lasted from the Dirty Harry movies, and really gone from them into American folk culture, isn't the [slaughter], but Harry's cool, and with it, the films' sense that submission to violence is as morally reprehensible as creating it. The films say it is possible not to cower."

Eastwood made a career out of standing up to reprehensible violence. He evinced the same kind of cool determination in westerns like *The Outlaw Josey Wales, High Plains Drifter,* and *Pale Rider.* He even offered similar characters in other action movies, such as *The Gauntlet, Firefox,* and *Tightrope.* At the same time, however, Eastwood showed an experimental flair—a willingness to produce, direct, and star in movies that provided an alternative to his ever-cool killer hero. In *Honkytonk Man,* for instance, he portrayed a Depression-era singer in need of a lucky break, and in *Play Misty for Me* he appeared as a disc jockey pursued by an overzealous fan. Biskind contended that Warner Bros., Eastwood's distributor, "is not going to lose much on an Eastwood picture, no matter what it's about."

Only Clint Eastwood could have convinced Warner Bros. to finance and distribute a comedy in which he starred with a sassy orangutan. The studio executives were aghast at the idea, but allowed Eastwood to proceed with *Every Which Way but Loose.* The film was released in 1978 and quickly became one of the year's biggest hits. It cost about $8 million to make and grossed about $85 million, despite the critics' almost unanimous disdain for the picture. A sequel, *Any Which Way You Can,* performed almost as well in 1980.

As early as 1980, the critical community began to reassess Eastwood's contribution to cinema. Open hostility turned to grudging acceptance and then to admiration as the decade progressed. The critical about-face had two main causes. First, more and more people began to appreciate Eastwood's contribution as producer and director of a number of his films, especially the smaller, more personal offerings like *Play Misty for Me* and *Honkytonk Man.* Second, the swing toward conservative politics gave heightened credibility to Eastwood's heroes and their justified vigilantism. While Eastwood told the *New York Times Magazine* that he "never begged for respectability," he nonetheless flew to Paris to accept the honor of Chevalier des Arts et Lettres—a national award—in 1985.

Since then Eastwood has more often opted for the more personal, character-driven projects. Known in the business as a director who brings movies in ahead of schedule and under budget, he is rarely thwarted on a potential project. This freedom to pursue offbeat work has produced *Bird,* a critically-acclaimed feature about a black jazz musician, and *Unforgiven,* a western that significantly alters the perception of violence in that particular genre. Eastwood did not think that *Unforgiven* would find a large audience, because the film seeks to demythologize violence. On the contrary, critics paved the way

with rave reviews, and the grim western earned more than $100 million nationwide by the end of 1992.

In *Unforgiven,* wrote Biskind, Eastwood has come full circle. "*Unforgiven* is *Dirty Harry* turned on its head," the critic noted. "After two decades, Harry, still above the law, has become the sadistic sheriff [played by Gene Hackman] . . . while [the] killer [is] now reformed. By killing [the sheriff], Eastwood purges the identity that has imprisoned him throughout his career." A *Vogue* critic likewise contended: "In this surprising movie there is no superhuman figure and no obvious moral line. It's a western that debunks the western and explodes the myth of the cowboy hero." *Unforgiven* earned Eastwood his first Academy Awards, for best picture of the year and best director, as well as a shelf full of other citations.

For more than 25 years Eastwood has made his home in Carmel, California, a quaint coastal village in the northern part of the state. The town has always been a tourist attraction, but it made national news in 1986 when its most famous citizen ran for mayor and won. Eastwood sought the $200-per-month position because he disapproved of zoning laws in the village. After serving one term—and changing the laws—he stepped down with no regrets. He says he has no interest in running for national office.

Not surprisingly, the popular star is often the target of tabloid journalism, especially since he is very reluctant to talk about his private life. Eastwood was married for 25 years to the former Maggie Johnson. After they separated in the late 1970s, he spent more than a decade living with actress Sondra Locke, his co-star in numerous films. That relationship ended bitterly in 1989; Locke sued for palimony. More recently Eastwood has been linked with another co-star, Frances Fisher. The actor prefers to live outside Hollywood and to spend time with friends who are not involved in the entertainment industry. And he is known as a loyal employer whose production crew includes people who have worked for him for 15 years.

By 1993 Eastwood had made 41 major motion pictures and directed 17 of them himself. The actor told *Premiere:* "I figure that by the time I'm really old, somebody at the Academy Awards will get the bright idea to give me some sort of plaque. I'll be so old, they'll have to carry me up there." Eastwood did not have to wait that long. At a remarkably fit 62 he won his first two golden statuettes for a film that reflects his personal abhorrence for violence. After the 1993 Academy Award ceremony, Eastwood told reporters that the wait for the award had been worth it. "I think it means more to me now," he was quoted as saying in the *Philadelphia Inquirer.* "If you win it when you're 20 or 30 years old you're wondering, 'Where do I go from here?...' You learn to take your work seriously and not yourself seriously, and that comes with time."

Sources

Commentary, April 1984.
McCall's, June 1987.

Newsweek, July 22, 1985; April 7, 1986; April 24, 1986.
New York Times, June 17, 1979; January 11, 1981.
New York Times Magazine, February 24, 1985.
People, December 24-31, 1984; August 7, 1989.
Philadelphia Inquirer, March 31, 1993.
Premiere, April 1993.
Show, February 1970.
Time, January 9, 1978; April 6, 1987.
Vogue, February 1993.

—*Anne Janette Johnson*

Linda Ellerbee

AP/Wide World Photos

Journalist and broadcaster

Born Linda Jane Smith, August 15, 1944, in Bryan, TX; daughter of Lonnie Ray and Hallie Smith; has been married four times; children (first marriage) Vanessa, Joshua. *Education:* Attended Vanderbilt University.

Addresses: *Publisher*—c/o G. P. Putnam's Sons, New York, NY

Career

WVON-Radio, Chicago, IL, newscaster and disc jockey, 1964-67; KSJO-Radio, San Francisco, CA, program director, 1967-68; associated with KJNO-Radio, Juneau, AK, beginning in 1969; worked as a reporter for Associated Press (AP), Dallas, TX; KHOU-TV, Houston, TX, reporter, 1972-73; WCBS-TV, New York City, reporter, 1973-76; National Broadcasting Corp. (NBC-TV), New York City, *NBC Nightly News* correspondent in Washington, DC, 1975-78, co-anchor of weekly series NBC News *Weekend*, 1978-82, co-anchor and general editor of NBC News *Overnight*, 1982-83, co-anchor of weekly series *Summer Sunday USA*, 1984, *Our World* and *Sunday Best*; correspondent for *Today*; also anchor and reporter for a series of news shows for Nickelodeon; anchor and reporter for television news specials including *AIDS in the Heartland, A Conversation with Magic, Plan It for the Planet,* and *Ms. Smith Goes to Washington.* Syndicated journalist and author of books.

Sidelights

"We call them Twinkies," said Linda Ellerbee in her book *And So It Goes: Adventures in Television,* and she went on to describe them: "On television acting the news, modeling and fracturing the news while you wonder if they've read the news—or if they've blow-dried their brains, too." They are the image of television newspeople that Ellerbee has spent a career trying to rectify. And in her own way, she's succeeded.

Individual, outspoken, or just plain brash—Ellerbee has carved a niche in television news that has brought her fame and no small amount of controversy. She's been fired from more prestigious news organizations than most reporters could hope to work for; she's caught flack for doing television commercials that some think exploited her unbiased image; and she's graphically shared episodes from her life—including her treatment for alcoholism, her problems with her children, and her battle with breast cancer—that others might think twice about revealing.

But the essence of Ellerbee is her willingness to put herself into a story. Born in a small Texas town, Linda Jane Smith grew up fascinated by movies, radio and, especially, writing. She entered Vanderbilt University in the early 1960s but, no typical co-ed even in her "madras wraparound skirts, Bass Weejuns loafers, white blouses with Peter Pan collars and . . . circle pin," left at age 19, in 1964: "I moved around some, married some, had two babies, worked for three radio stations, one of whom hired me to read the news because I sounded black—my Texas heritage—and the black woman it had hired did not."

Ellerbee's travels took her as far as Juneau, Alaska, where she worked as a reporter for a radio station—and was fired for what she called a "personality conflict." But it was talent, if not personality, that got Ellerbee her next job, with the Associated Press in Houston. Hired to write wire reports for member newspapers and television stations, Ellerbee fell victim to the electronic age. In 1972, the AP had just installed some sophisticated word processors. Ellerbee used one terminal to write a letter to a friend—a letter that disparaged the state of Texas, the AP, and the Vietnam War, among other topics. "I was no fool; I hit the keys on the word processor that would give me a printed copy of the letter—and would *not* send the letter out on the AP wire," as she related in her book. "The letter was mailed and I went home, unaware I had also hit the key that put the letter on hold in the computer." The next day, the AP hosted some members at NASA to demonstrate the new equipment. Someone hit a button, and Ellerbee's damning letter was sent by wire to four states. "I was fired only because the AP's legal department told them it absolutely was against the law to shoot me, no matter how good an idea it might be," she concluded.

But even that episode turned out fortunate. Ellerbee's letter amused as many as it offended, and she was offered a job, sight unseen, at Houston's CBS television affiliate. A dedicated print journalist, Ellerbee hadn't considered television as a career. The money they offered—twice what Ellerbee had been earning at Associated Press—proved the final temptation, and she first went on the air in January of 1973. The woman Ellerbee replaced was Jessica Savitch, who would precede Linda into network news.

Ever the nonconformist, Ellerbee showed up for work in her usual uniform of jeans and t-shirts, still convinced that what she had to say was more important than what she was wearing while saying it.

For the next several years, Ellerbee moved from local news to a big-city affiliate—WCBS in New York—

and then to a network, NBC. She interviewed world leaders and ordinary people, always trying to stay a step ahead of others' perceptions of what a "woman reporter" should be like. (According to the accepted wisdom of that time, women lacked the guts to cover a hard news beat. "Certainly, they were too frail to carry those big cameras," Ellerbee notes in *And So It Goes.* "They would faint at the sight of a little blood. They would blush at the language of your average camera crew . . . . They would trip over their high heels.")

Even when she was covering the House of Representatives for NBC, Ellerbee was offended by what she saw as a double standard. "In 1982," she noted, as an example, "Barbara Walters pointed out that she was generally considered to be the 'Grand Dame' or the old broad—depending on your bias—of television news. She was fifty. Dan Rather was considered the brash young kid who had replaced Walter Cronkite. He was also fifty. It raises a question."

As a brash young kid herself, Ellerbee advanced into the echelon of the anchor. She sat at the desk for NBC News's *Weekend* beginning in 1978. The magazine show, which aired Saturday nights once a month, was designed to give a new perspective of current issues. Ellerbee and co-anchor Lloyd Dobyns (who, the former admits, coined the phrase "and so it goes," which Ellerbee then co-opted as her signature line) brought what *People* reporter Kristin McMurran called a "refreshing blend of stylish poetry and wry delivery" to the news.

Perhaps too stylish. *Weekend,* though it picked up a cult following, died an ignoble death after being shifted around the NBC schedule by then-programming head Fred Silverman (who didn't much care for the show, Ellerbee revealed in a *Contemporary Authors* [CA] interview), finally ending up on a weeknight—which brought unintended irony to the show's name. Rebounding, Ellerbee won another anchor spot, this time on NBC News's *Overnight.* This weekday show, which aired in the wee hours following *Tonight* and *Late Night,* represented a departure for its anchor. "On *Overnight,* women made coffee *and* policy," she wrote, referring to the mostly female production and executive staff.

Though acclaimed for its insightful feature stories and offbeat points of view, *Overnight*'s life was even briefer than *Weekend*'s—just one season. Its quick demise puzzled Ellerbee, who told *CA:* "The show did succeed . . . . Even NBC, when it canceled it, said, 'The show is wonderful. The show is a success.' The problem was that their studies showed that there never would be enough people awake at 1:30 a.m.

for them to make a profit on the show. It didn't matter how much audience we had. Had we had it all it wouldn't have been enough."

Ellerbee had another go at anchoring an NBC show in 1984. *Summer Sunday USA* was another in the network's ongoing attempts to produce a hit news-magazine. (NBC's track record since the 1970s has stood at more than a dozen failed magazine shows.) Ellerbee hosted the show with reporter Andrea Mitchell ("Two women anchoring a network news-cast? Yes, and wasn't it time?" she noted). Like so many newsmagazines, *Summer Sunday* was a mix of breaking news, features, and interviews. Unfortunately for the show, it was scheduled opposite the reigning powerhouse of the format, CBS's *60 Minutes*. Ellerbee recounted her network's rationale: Her producer "said it would be experimental and we shouldn't worry about the ratings because he wasn't worried. . . . He said nobody would compare it to *60 Minutes*. Later, of course, everyone did, and it's amazing the number of NBC executives who seemed shocked when *60 Minutes* ran through *Summer Sunday* like Sherman through Georgia."

Ellerbee's next network stop was on ABC, where she enjoyed working on a prime-time series called *Our World*, which took detailed looks at specific periods of recent history. "Each program was like a video scrapbook of a particular time, *The Summer of 1969*, *The Autumn of 1949*, *Two Weeks in May, 1960*, etc.," as she explained in her book *Move On: Adventures in the Real World*. That show lasted a season. "I decided to quit ABC, to quit network news," recalled Ellerbee. The reason, she says, "is everything."

But Ellerbee was back—this time on CNN—by 1988, reporting on the presidential campaigns. Shortly after that, the reporter found herself the subject of news. In May of 1989, a new commercial for Maxwell House coffee aired. The spot featured Ellerbee. "Some people said I was wrong to do [the commercial] because I was a journalist. However, I hadn't worked as a daily reporter since 1985. I wrote true stories about real events and people, but I did it as a columnist for newspapers, a commentator for television and an author of books." The choice to promote Maxwell House "was all mine. Nobody twisted my arm."

The response to the commercial was mixed, to put it mildly: "Within two weeks I'd been derided and defrocked by any number of serious folks. The *New York Times* ran an editorial saying it would be just fine if [the retired] Walter Cronkite wanted to do a commercial for Hathaway shirts but it wasn't okay for Linda Ellerbee to drink coffee and *say so*, not that

I did say so. The same editorial suggested I had attempted to fool people by passing a commercial off as a news program. Sure. The commercial was thirty seconds long, just like every news program I've ever done. I sat in a big easy chair next to a five-pound can of coffee, just the way I always did on NBC News." What especially galled her, as Ellerbee continued, was the editorial's implication that "the people who watch television are so dumb . . . they wouldn't know it was a commercial. Gimmee a break."

Never one to shrink from disclosure, Ellerbee reveal-ed her fight with alcoholism—and her stint in the Betty Ford Clinic—in the pages of *Move On*. She completed the program and joined the ranks of recovering alcoholics—but another medical setback would arise. In the early 1990s Ellerbee was diag-nosed with breast cancer. At the time, she was hosting a series of young-adult news shows for Nickelodeon; even so, she kept working on the show

---

"I have a good man, my kids are doing well, I'm enjoying my work and I don't have to worry about money."

---

and her column, even after a double mastectomy and chemotherapy treatment.

In March, 1993, Ellerbee told Ginny Stolicker of the *Oakland Press* that she's never been happier: "I have a good man, my kids are doing well, I'm enjoying my work and I don't have to worry about money" (Ellerbee, since leaving the networks, had become a successful author and a much-in-demand speaker).

For a *McCall's* article that same year, Ellerbee related her "five best things I know." Number one: *Do what you believe is right*. And right up next to that is *A good time to laugh is anytime you can*. "Cancer is serious," she elaborated. "I *could* die from it. But there are funny things about it too. For example, before I went to the Caribbean on vacation . . . I bought some breast protheses for swimming. They're supposed to Velcro onto your skin, but I didn't like the thought of that. So I simply inserted them into my bathing suit. They looked beautiful when I went into the water, but when I came out, one had migrated around to my back!... Now, how can you not laugh at such a thing? You either laugh or cry your eyes out."

A few years ago, Ellerbee had been in negotiations for a screen adaptation of one of her books. To date, that hasn't happened, but the urge to perform remains. She did a cameo role on the sitcom *Murphy Brown*, and told *CA* as far back as 1984 that one ambition in the long run "is to be out of [the news] business and living happily on a beach somewhere. If I have to work, I'd like to direct movies... Good ones. Movies with a story and nice pictures."

Selected writings

And So It Goes: Adventures in Television, Putnam, 1986.

Move On: Adventures in the Real World, Putnam, 1991.

Sources

Books

Contemporary Authors, Volume 115, Gale, 1984.

Periodicals

McCall's, January 1993.
Oakland Press, March 1, 1993.
People, June 27, 1983.

—*Susan Salter*

Nick Faldo

Professional golfer

B orn in July, 1957 in England; married, with children.

Addresses: *Agent*—John Simpson, International Management Group, One Erieview Plaza, Suite 1300, Cleveland OH 44114.

Career

P rofessional golfer playing in tournaments since the early 1980s; winner of the British Open in 1987, 1990, and 1992, the Masters Tournament in 1990, and the Johnnie Walker World Championship in 1992.

Sidelights

I f British golf pro Nick Faldo could name the secret of his success, he would call it "the circle," which he visualizes as a personal continuum that begins with total dedication to his sport and leads to improvement. He believes that such an approach fosters a renewed enthusiasm for his ultimate goal: to be the best golfer in the world. "If you are constantly working on things, trying to get better, it's a great pressure release," he told Jaime Diaz of the *New York Times.* "You see improvement, you stay focused on small goals, and you keep ticking along. It's all part of the circle." Since the late 1980s, Faldo has shown that such commitment has its rewards; he has accumulated an impressive list of golf victories, attained the level of such golf masters as Jack Nicklaus and Arnold Palmer, and proven himself a

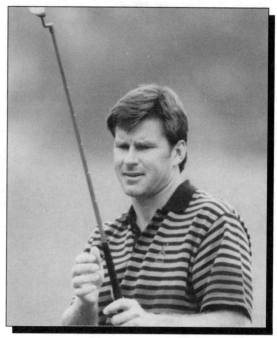

AP/Wide World Photos

contender for the position of honor on which he has set his sights.

While Faldo fantasized about achieving a Grand Slam—that is, winning the four major tournaments of golf, including the United States Open, the British Open, the Masters, and the Professional Golfers Association (PGA) Championship—he knew that his game needed work. So, in 1985, he sought the advice of golf teacher David Leadbetter, who agreed that Faldo was a strong but incomplete golfer. As he had failed the previous year in the final rounds of the British Open, Masters, and PGA Championship, he wanted a swing that would hold up in the major tournaments. Rating Faldo's swing, which then used a lot of wrist, as a six on a scale of ten, Leadbetter estimated that it would take two years of constant practice to get results. Faldo agreed to work as hard as he could, and, after two mediocre seasons, won the 1987 British Open at Muirfield.

This marked a pivotal turn in Faldo's career, starting him on a series of tournament victories. He won three majors in two years, and four majors in four years. This first statistic has elevated him to a level shared by only seven others, each a legendary name in golf history: Jack Nicklaus, Arnold Palmer, Tom Watson, Ben Hogan, Bobby Jones, Walter Hagen, and

Gene Sarazen. Even the usually unflappable Faldo, whose swing had become masterful under the guidance of Leadbetter, felt somewhat dazed by his success. "It seems unbelievable that I went through all that searching so recently," he said to Diaz. It seems moons ago."

The fourth triumph of Faldo's career came when he won, by five shots, the 1990 British Open, which took place in St. Andrew, Scotland. According to his agent John Simpson, of the International Management Group, this victory was worth more than $10 million in income. A few weeks after the British Open win, Faldo started a golf-course design company that charged about $1 million per project. To concentrate further on the four major championships, he reduced his schedule from 30 tournaments in 1990 to 25 tournaments in 1991. While Faldo acknowledges that he could still learn much more about the game, he assesses his achievements with a quiet confidence. "The way I've progressed in the last three years has nothing to do with age," he remarked to Diaz, a week after he turned 33. "Really, I think I can compete at the top level for the rest of this decade."

Faldo has continued his winning streak well into the 1990s. On the day he turned 35, in July of 1992, he again won the British Open, tying the 54-hole scoring record for the golf championship, which he himself had set in 1990. Yet this tournament was nerve-wracking for its entire duration, and hard-won for Faldo, who was almost edged out by opponent John Cook. In his speech after his victory, he not only shed tears but gave the press a verbal tromping. What angered him was their open musings about his performance as the tournament progressed; such comments, he felt, fed into his self-doubts and counteracted the focus and concentration that remain paramount to winning. When Faldo, whose steely resolve has earned him a comparison to golf legend Ben Hogan, was asked why he had cried after winning the British Open for the third time, he replied, according to *Sports Illustrated*, "I'm just an emotional little old petal."

The composure and stoicism with which Faldo tends to handle his victories does not diminish his desire to complete "the circle"—to make improvements and achieve the high expectations he sets for himself. He also hopes that others will not forget his contributions to golf: "I don't like to think about whether I'm the best player in the game," he explained to Diaz. "But when it's over, I'd most like to be remembered as someone who could really play the game. I want people to say in years to come: 'Did you see Nick Faldo play in his heyday? I did, and it was quite something.'" It is unlikely that he will be forgotten soon. He recently won the 1992 Johnnie Walker World Championship in Montego Bay, Jamaica, and has a new round of master's tournaments slated for the summer of 1993. As the *New York Times* observed: "Nick Faldo deserves the title of golf's heavyweight champion." He wears the title well.

Sources

New York Times, July 24, 1990; July 19, 1992.
Sports Illustrated, July 27, 1992.
Wall Street Journal, July 24, 1990.

—*Carolyn C. March*

Dianne Feinstein

AP/Wide World Photos

U.S. Senator

Full name, Dianne Goldman Feinstein; born June 22, 1933, in San Francisco, CA; daughter of Leon (a surgeon) and Betty Goldman (a model); married Jack Berman (an attorney), c. 1957 (divorced, 1960); married Bert Feinstein (a neurosurgeon), 1962 (deceased, 1978); married Richard C. Blum (an investment banker), January 20, 1980; children: (first marriage) Kathy. *Education:* Bachelor's degree in history from Stanford University, 1955. *Religion:* Jewish.

Addresses: *Home*—San Francisco, CA. *Office*—331 Hart Senate Office Building, Washington, DC 20510.

Career

Member of California Women's Board of Terms and Parole, 1960-66; member of San Francisco Board of Supervisors, 1970-78; president of board of supervisors, 1970-71, 1974-75, 1978; mayor of San Francisco, 1978-88; U.S. senator from California, 1992–.

Sidelights

On November 27, 1978, Dianne Feinstein told reporters she was retiring from politics. After eight years, the president of the San Francisco Board of Supervisors had seen enough. Just two hours later, down the hall from Feinstein's city hall office, San Francisco Mayor George Moscone and Supervisor Harvey Milk were assassinated by a fellow supervisor. As Feinstein cradled the dying Milk in her arms,

her plans were suddenly altered. Instead of retiring, she was elevated to the post of mayor.

What followed was, many believe, Feinstein's defining moment. In the ensuing weeks, Feinstein helped heal the emotionally devastated city. She went on to serve a decade as mayor, establishing a national reputation for strong leadership, savvy back-room politicking and unwavering commitment on issues she felt strongly about. In 1992, Feinstein used those abilities to get elected to the U.S. Senate. In the so-called "Year of the Woman," she was one of four (including fellow Californian Barbara Boxer) elected to the Senate. She quickly used her political finesse to gain an appointment to the powerful Appropriations Committee. "Everything I know about politics I learned from my Uncle Morris," she told the *Los Angeles Times*. "He's the one who taught me that people will talk to you if you will listen."

Uncle Morris Goldman, a Democrat, was a San Francisco businessman who liked to walk the streets and talk to people, often taking his niece with him. Likewise, Leon Goldman, Feinstein's father, was a respected surgeon who used to take his daughter with him during patient rounds. Leon Goldman hoped that Dianne would grow up to be a doctor, but she found the sights and smells of the ward intimidating. Dianne Goldman and her two younger sisters were raised in San Francisco's affluent Marina area and, from the outside, their life looked golden. But the girls' mother, Betty, suffered from a rare degenerative brain disease that remained undiagnosed for years. It impaired her judgment and caused her to be unpredictable and volatile. "There was alcoholism," Feinstein told the *San Jose Mercury News.* "I would pour out some of the bottles and fill them half with water. There was violence. There were suicide attempts."

Feinstein recalled that her mother once chased her around the dining room table with a carving knife. And on the night before her college boards, Dianne was kicked out of the house and slept in the garage in the family car. Still, she told the *Mercury News,* "I did not have a terrible childhood. Some terrible things happened, but I did not have a terrible childhood." She went to Stanford University, initial-

> "I don't go to pieces in a crisis...I'm strong...I have the staying power, the motivation, the drive and the ability to do what has to be done."

ly planning to follow her father's plans and become a doctor. But poor grades in science classes—coupled with an A+ in American political thought—changed her course. She helped found the campus's first Democratic Club. As a junior, she was elected student body vice-president. Actually, she had wanted to run for president but, in an unscientific poll, realized she could not win. "I stood on the Quad, talking to people, and I found out that they would rather elect a monkey, a giraffe or an ant before they would elect a woman," she told the *Mercury News.*

While a senior, she won an internship with the Coro Foundation on Criminal Justice. A term paper she wrote during the internship later caught the eye of Governor Edmund G. "Pat" Brown when he was hunting for someone to appoint to the Women's Parole Board in 1960. During Feinstein's six years on the board, she sat in on more than 5,000 parole hearings. She later said the position made concern about crime a driving force in her career, forging her

opinions in favor of the death penalty and tough criminal sentencing.

In the mid-1960s she married Bert Feinstein, a neurosurgeon who was 19 years her senior. Actually, this was her second marriage. In her early twenties, she had married Jack Berman, an attorney and later a judge. They later divorced. The Feinsteins had a baby daughter in 1966, and Dianne stayed home to work full-time for her family for a few years. In 1969, she jumped back into politics, becoming the first woman ever elected to the San Francisco Board of Supervisors. By virtue of receiving more votes than any other candidate, Feinstein served as board president for five of her eight years as a supervisor. She made crime issues her specialty, developing a strong relationship with the city's police department. And she worked hard to understand the problems of other classes and other cultures. She began making regular trips to low-income, high-crime neighborhoods of the city to read to children and counsel them. "She is genuine in her talk, and she is my friend," The Reverend Cecil Williams, pastor of San Francisco's Glide Memorial Church, told the *Mercury News.* "What I like about her is that she works with kids nobody else will touch."

Feinstein established a reputation for being tough and savvy, but a centrist when liberalism was popular. She ran twice for mayor and lost. In the mid-1970s, her husband, Bert, contracted cancer, and she spent a considerable amount of time nursing him. Soon after he died in 1978, she decided to leave office.

The very day she announced her decision, Mayor George Moscone and fellow supervisor Harvey Milk were assassinated. As president of the supervisors, she immediately became acting mayor. Her first task was announcing the killings to the press and public. A decade later, looking back at film clips of the event, she told the *Los Angeles Times,* "It shows that I don't go to pieces in a crisis, that I'm strong...that I have the staying power, the motivation, the drive and the ability to do what has to be done."

When she took over San Francisco, in the wake of the City Hall murders, the Jonestown, Guyana mass suicides, and racial rioting, the city was in shock, with nearly everyone seeking calm, forceful leadership. "I feel a very great need to heal and bind," she told the *New York Times.* She was later credited with doing so.

In 1979 Feinstein won her first mayoral election. She served two terms and, wrote *Time*'s Jordan Bonfante, "was given high marks overall for having developed an envied transit system, a strong police force that reduced certain categories of crime and, later on, an elaborate anti-AIDS program. Again and again, she showed a talent for bringing warring factions together. At the time, however, she was almost constantly beset by controversy. Liberals assailed her for allowing an overblown 'Manhattanization' of the downtown business district and overemphasizing tough law enforcement. Conservatives criticized her for leaving a shortfall of $140 million in the 1988-89 budget and for catering to minorities, especially the increasingly powerful gay community." "As a supervisor, all she could think of was tax, tax, tax," former GOP rival John Barbagelata told *Time.* "And as mayor, she was ambitious, selfish, expedient and hypocritical."

She also clashed with the Bay Area feminists, vetoing a comparable worth bill and drawing heat for failing to appoint enough women to positions of authority at City Hall. Feinstein told the *Mercury News,* "I had to deal with the nitty-gritty, potholes in the streets, graffiti on the buses, flowers in the parks, books in the schools, and I was the first mayor to deal with AIDS. In those roles it was management, not advocacy that was needed." Above all, she was a hands-on mayor with an obsession for detail. She regularly monitored the police radio and kept watch on the streets to make sure they were kept clean. She ordered staff members to wear suits and ties, installing a dress code after Moscone allowed blue jeans.

In 1984, Democratic presidential nominee Walter Mondale considered naming Feinstein as his running mate. He interviewed her—among eight others—for the job before settling on U.S. Representative Geraldine Ferraro of New York. Feinstein later said she was invigorated by the process, and her name has since been mentioned as a possible vice-presidential candidate for future Democratic presidential races.

Feinstein spent a decade in office as mayor. She decided to step down at the end of 1987 to spend more time with her third husband, Richard Blum, whom she married in 1980. And she was hospitalized in 1989 after complications from a hysterectomy. In 1990, however, she decided to re-enter politics, running for governor of California. She got a late start in the campaign, but won an easy primary victory over Attorney General John Van de Kamp. In the general election against Republican Senator Pete Wilson, however, Feinstein was surprisingly hurt by a lack of enthusiasm among women voters. "Being a woman is not enough. You've got to be a feminist, too," author Celia Morris wrote in *Newsday.* Morris, who authored a book on Feinstein's 1990 campaign,

called *Storming the Statehouse,* wrote, "You need women's groups not only to endorse you, but also to care passionately that you win . . . . For the most part women weren't invested in (Feinstein's) campaign. As mayor of San Francisco, she'd made some 280 appointments but increased the percentage of women in those offices by only 1 percent. She'd not only failed to fight for issues women cared about, but also had repeatedly refused invitations from women's groups to take part in their annual conferences."

Feinstein was also criticized for running a colorless, uninspired campaign. Wilson slammed her as a soft-on-crime tax-and-spender whose husband's far-flung investment portfolio was chock-full of potential conflicts of interest. The strategy staggered Feinstein. Only in the final week of the campaign did she right herself and make a populist counterattack. But it was too late, and she lost the race by three percentage points.

She didn't stay away long. Almost immediately after losing her first bid for statewide office, Feinstein began her next, targeting the U.S. Senate seat held by Republican John Seymour. "In the months after her 1990 defeat, Feinstein chose not to leave the campaign trail, and she spent weeks traveling the state's hinterlands to bolster her base," wrote Esther Shrader of the San Jose *Mercury News.* "And Feinstein—who was forced to lend her own campaign $3 million in 1990—quickly showed a new fund-raising prowess to back up her bold words."

This time, Feinstein emphasized gender. Her billboards, posters, and buttons read, "Two percent is not enough," referring to the fact that just two of the 100 senators were women. She made frequent mention of the all-male Senate Judiciary Committee and its controversial handling of allegations made by Anita Hill against Supreme Court nominee Clarence Thomas. "Look at that committee," she told the *Los Angeles Times.* "Look at George Bush's Cabinet. That's not what the country looks like. That's not what our children look like. Then you ask yourself the next question—who is at the table when the decisions that affect my life are being made?"

Feinstein's campaign was well funded and well directed. She won the seat by 14 percentage points. Three other women were elected to the Senate in 1992, including fellow Californian Barbara Boxer. Feinstein immediately won a seat on the coveted Appropriations Committee, filling an opening that was specially created to give the newly elected women immediate impact. Appropriations is the committee that controls money for all federal programs and is considered the most important in the

Senate. "We've needed a woman there for a long time," U.S. Representative Don Edwards, D-California, told the San Jose *Mercury News*. "This is the committee that controls the purse strings."

Because Seymour was filling out the Senate term abandoned by Wilson, Feinstein will have to stand for reelection again in 1994. Given her statewide races in 1990 and 1992, she said she has lots of practice for the task. And, perhaps, she said, she could help get more women elected to the Senate. "Six out of 100 isn't all that much," she told the *Mercury News*. "It's a beachhead. But as a beachhead, if we do well, we will be able to bring in more troops behind us."

Sources

Books

Morris, Celia, *Storming the Statehouse: Running for Governor with Ann Richards and Dianne Feinstein*, Macmillan, 1992.

Periodicals

Dallas Morning News, October 18, 1992.

Detroit Free Press, April 17, 1990

Los Angeles Times, January 13, 1992; May 24, 1992; May 31, 1992; June 4, 1992; July 1, 1992.

New York Times, March 18, 1990; June 10, 1990; July 1, 1990; September 30, 1990.

Newsday, June 9, 1992.

Newsweek, June 18, 1990.

Philadelphia Inquirer, June 6, 1992.

Time, June 18, 1990.

San Jose Mercury News, January 14, 1990; November 4, 1990; March 5, 1992; May 13, 1992; May 24, 1992; May 31, 1992; June 3, 1992; October 8, 1992; November 4, 1992; November 11, 1992; January 5, 1993; January 7, 1993; January 10, 1993.

—Glen Macnow

Bill Gates

Reuters/Bettmann

Chairman of Microsoft Corporation

Born William Henry Gates III, October 28, 1955, in Seattle, WA; son of William (an attorney) and Mary (a corporate director and university regent) Gates. *Education:* attended Harvard University, 1973-1975.

Addresses: *Office*—16011 NE 36th Way, Redmond, WA 98052-6399.

Career

Began developing and marketing computer software as a teenager; co-founded Traf-O-Data (computer traffic analysis company) while in high school; co-founded Microsoft Corporation, 1975, chairman and CEO, 1982—.

Sidelights

In the late 1960s, when the computer industry was struggling to modify its cumbersome and costly machines for personal, everyday use, a teen-age Bill Gates designed a class scheduling program so that he could take courses with the prettiest girls in his high school. Fewer than 25 years later, Gates's Microsoft Corporation is a multibillion-dollar colossus whose industry dominance inspires in its competitors a predictable mixture of awe, envy, and bitterness.

Observers point to the two sides of Bill Gates to explain how this whiz kid could have come so far. His technical acuity distinguishes him, perhaps more than any other CEO in America, as a corporate leader who understands every subtlety of his company's products. And his business savvy has brought him an immense advantage over other techno-mavericks of his generation—geniuses who were at home with computers, but at a loss with balance sheets and payrolls. "There are so many early guys who did so much good stuff in this industry, but who just didn't have the drive or the commitment to either building a company or leading one," Gates was quoted as saying in the *New York Times.* Gates's unmatched success in the mercurial computer industry has delivered fortunes to stockholders and, not surprisingly, to the chairman himself. Routinely compared to John D. Rockefeller, Gates is, by many accounts, the richest person in the United States, with an estimated net worth of $7 billion.

William Henry Gates III was born October 28, 1955, to a prominent, well-to-do Seattle, Washington, family. As a child, he was a gifted math student and a sucker for technological gadgets, but it was in high school where his wizardry found its most rewarding outlet. In addition to designing the class-scheduling program, Gates, with friend Paul Allen, who would also co-found Microsoft, started Traf-O-Data, whose computer program transcribed and analyzed data on traffic patterns of towns outside of Seattle. At age 19, after completing his sophomore year of pre-law at Harvard University, Gates, bitten by the entrepreneurial bug, quit academia. The impetus had come from Allen, who, like other computer wonks, was excited by the invention of the first microcomputer kit, the Altair 8800. Now computers, however primitive, were affordable and could be set up in a living room rather than in a high-tech lab. The problem was that the operating system language, written for larger, mainframe computers, took up all of the machine's tiny memory, leaving no room for it to do anything. Allen enlisted Gates, and the two of them wrote a condensed operating-system language, which they licensed to the manufacturer of the Altair 8800.

Microsoft Corporation, established in 1975, stumbled initially, as its first five customers went bankrupt. But the company was buoyed by its founders' youthful energy and their confidence that the computer industry was on the verge of a dramatic sea change. Importantly, Gates saw that production costs in the

> *"Our success is based on only one thing: good products. It's not very complicated. We're not powerful enough to cause products that are not excellent to sell well."*

fast-changing market of the future would fall more heavily on hardware—that is, the machines themselves. The biggest money-makers were going to be operating-system languages and application software, programs that could be modified and improved at relatively low cost.

Microsoft broke into the big leagues in 1980, when IBM, the industry leader, asked Gates to provide an operating system for its new personal computer. At first, Gates declined the offer, but then he remembered having seen an operating system that he believed would work with the IBM. He bought the system from a small Washington company for $50,000, revamped it, and licensed it to IBM for $125,000 as MS-DOS, for Microsoft Disk Operating System. Because the enterprising Gates had retained ownership of MS-DOS, Microsoft was masterfully positioned for the boom to come. When IBM unveiled its PC in 1981, sparking the personal computer craze, MS-DOS became the dominant operating

system in the market. And when IBM made its hardware technology available to other companies, spawning the clone boom, Microsoft, free to sell its wares to whomever it pleased, fanned out as the ubiquitous supplier of operating systems. The one rising hardware company that provided its own operating system was Apple, whose user-friendly system of icons manipulated by a mouse was the cornerstone of the success of its Macintosh PCs. Unabashedly wanting the best of both worlds, Gates positioned Microsoft as the key provider of Macintosh software, such as Microsoft Word, a word processing program. "Microsoft has soared because Gates is wise in the ways of technology and tough and tenacious when it comes to business," William J. Cook wrote in *U.S. News & World Report.*

Microsoft went public in 1986, in what some analysts described as the deal of the year. When the per share rate, which was supposed to have been between $16 and $19, started at $21 and then stabilized at $31.50, Gates, who owned 45 percent of the company, became a millionaire several hundred times over. Although his millions would turn into billions, money-making was not Gates's alone. A hundred shares bought for $2100 in March 1986 was worth, in February of 1993, $77,850.

Much of Microsoft's success in spotting and filling market niches stems from Gates's unusual ability to speak expertly on the mathematical complexity of computer languages and, at the same time, to appreciate the average user's prayer for computer operations to be simple and approachable. An outgrowth of this harmony was the unveiling, in 1987, of Windows, an operating program featuring simplified commands and eye-catching graphics. At first IBM, whom Gates had targeted to adopt the system, was hopeful of creating an operating program in-house, but Gates convinced IBM management that his product fit the time needs of the industry giant and the computer needs of its customers. A wrinkle in the success of Windows was a suit brought by Apple claiming that the program had illicitly copied the "look and feel" of Macintosh's operating system. But in 1992, the core of the suit was dismissed, as the judge declared that this "look and feel" was too vaguely defined to find protection in law. By early 1993, Windows was selling at the rate of one million copies a month. The second part of Microsoft's one-two punch was the company's manufacturing of application software to take advantage of its hugely successful operating system. Microsoft's Excel program claims 73 percent of the $756 million Windows spreadsheet market, and the company's Microsoft

Word commands 53 percent of the Windows word-processing market.

Gates's management style is often cited as one reason why Microsoft can be a $3-billion, 12,000-employee behemoth and still behave, in terms of agility and market-reaction speed, like a small company. Rather than saddling his employees, most of whom are programmers, with a bloated bureaucracy that stifles creativity, and a dress code that forces conformity, Gates has fashioned a work environment of flexibility, openness, and unfettered intellectual rigor. The result is that new recruits often accept a salary cut and 60- to 80-hour work weeks. Employee turnover at Microsoft is less than six percent, well below industry standards. While Microsoft puts a premium on individual ingenuity, the egalitarian spirit has a limit, and the limit is named Gates. Kathy Rebello wrote in *Business Week*, "Employees speak knowingly of 'Bill meetings,' which sound only slightly better than the Spanish Inquisition. Gates peppers his workers with technical questions. He challenges, he makes judgments, he finds flaws—whether it's a faulty algorithm or a poorly targeted marketing plan. Employees have been known to crib for weeks, even holding practice meetings, for one 60-minute session with Gates."

In 1991 and 1992, as other computer companies scaled back their work forces in response to a nationwide recession, Microsoft, outselling its three largest competitors combined, hired ambitiously. A host of ironies accompanied this success. Gates, whose products enabled other companies' computers to be used, had grown bigger than those other companies. Also, for decades young mavericks had decried the stranglehold that conservative IBM had on the computer industry. Now, as IBM began to fracture, arguably as a result of such conservatism, the mavericks at the helm of their own companies bemoaned the dominance of Microsoft and fellow-maverick Gates. Pointing out that Microsoft operating systems run nearly 90 percent of the world's PCs, and that the company commands 44 percent of the world software market, critics fear that Gates's baby is killing competition and stifling the same innovation it claims to champion. Answering this charge, Gates was quoted in *Business Week* as saying, "Our success is based on only one thing: good products. It's not very complicated. We're not powerful enough to cause products that are not excellent to sell well."

But much of the criticism, rather than questioning the quality of Microsoft products, suggests that the high-quality software of other companies is being locked out of the market because of Gate's predatory business practices. Rivals say that Microsoft, by sometimes announcing the development of its products years before they actually exist, preempts the sale of extant, competitive products because customers are willing to wait for the Microsoft products. In a twist of fate, IBM, which had effectively used "preannouncing" against competitors in the 1960s, became the victim of this technique in 1991, when Microsoft revealed that in 18 months it was going to release its new, high-power operating system, Windows NT. As a result, orders for IBM's new system, OS/2 Version 2.0, were put on hold. Gates answers these allegations by saying that customers and outside software developers are entitled to know the company's product direction.

Rivals also claim that Microsoft's application designers have advanced knowledge of the company's continually evolving operating systems, and can, therefore, sooner bring to market software programs that take advantage of the operating systems' subtleties. The fact that Microsoft enjoys near-monopoly domination of the operating systems market and an overwhelming share of the software market led the Federal Trade Commission to launch an investigation into Microsoft's business. Gates argues that the charges against his company stem from a predictable resentment of an industry leader. "In its heyday, IBM was never loved," he was quoted as telling *Fortune*.

Some analysts say Microsoft's dominance is far from destructive—customers appreciate a stable provider of quality products—and most concede that the company in the future will not be able to match the staggering growth and success of the past. As Microsoft's staple MS-DOS becomes obsolete, the company will compete with other companies, most notably an Apple-IBM alliance called Taligent, to deliver the next generation of operating systems. Moreover, Microsoft faces huge challenges as it enters computer areas whose potential it had not anticipated, such as work stations, and as it plots the ambitious incorporation of software in common, consumer electronic products, such as fax machines and televisions. In the eyes of many observers, Gates's phenomenal success at riding the information wave of the 1980s does not guarantee a repeat performance in the 1990s. Nor is it the case that other aggressive entrepreneurs will necessarily crash into the sea if they attempt to surf side-by-side with Gates on the next information wave. Joe Guglielmi, CEO of Taligent, was quoted as telling *Business Week*, "Today, everyone is in fear of Microsoft. But in the end, everyone will compete. There are thousands of Bill Gateses out there who will find pieces of this market and win them."

Sources

Business Week, February 24, 1992; March 1, 1993.
Forbes, December 7, 1992.
Fortune, December 28, 1992.
Newsweek, November 30, 1992.
New York Times, August 25, 1991.
U.S. News & World Report, February 15, 1993.

—Isaac Rosen

Whoopi Goldberg

Archive Photos/Darlene Hammond

Actress

Name originally Caryn Johnson; born November 13, 1955, in New York, NY; daughter of Robert and Emma (a nurse and Head Start teacher; maiden name, Harris) Johnson; married c. 1973 (divorced); married David Claessen (a cameraman), 1986 (divorced); children: (first marriage) Alexandrea Martin.

Addresses: *Home*—Connecticut. *Agent*—Creative Artists Agency, Inc., 9830 Wilshire Blvd., Beverly Hills, CA 90212.

Career

Chorus member in Broadway productions of *Pippin, Hair,* and *Jesus Christ Superstar* in the early 1970s; member and co-founder of the San Diego Repertory Theater, 1975-80, and of improvisational troupe Spontaneous Combustion; member of Blake Street Hawkeyes, Berkeley, CA, 1980-84; appeared in one-woman show *The Spook Show,* in Berkeley and on tour across the United States and Europe, 1983-84; appeared in one-woman show *Whoopi Goldberg* on Broadway, 1984-85; actress in films, including *The Color Purple,* 1985, *Jumpin' Jack Flash,* 1986, *Burglar,* 1986, *The Telephone,* 1987, *Fatal Beauty,* 1987, *The Long Walk Home,* 1990, *Ghost,* 1990, *The Player,* 1992, *Sister Act,* 1992, *Sarafina!,* 1992, and *Made in America,* 1993. Actress in television series, including *Baghdad Cafe,* 1990, and *Star Trek: The Next Generation,* 1988—. Television specials include *Tales from the Whoop, Hot Rod Brown, Class Clown,* and *Whoopi Goldberg Direct from Broadway.* Organizer of and performer in Comic Relief benefits.

Awards: Bay Area Theater Award, 1983, for *Moms;* Grammy Award for Best Comedy Album, 1985; Academy Award nomination for best actress, NAACP Image Award, and Golden Globe Award for best actress, all 1985, all for *The Color Purple;* Emmy nomination, 1985, for guest appearance on television series *Moonlighting;* Academy Award for best supporting actress, 1990, for *Ghost.*

Sidelights

I don't believe there's anything I can't do out there," declared actress-comedienne Whoopi Goldberg to *New York Times* writer Isabel Wilkerson. A quick look at her resume confirms the star's belief in herself. She has won acclaim for her comedy, her dramatic abilities, and her writing; she has proven herself capable of handling the very different demands of the movie screen, stage work, and television. She can captivate an audience all by herself or blend smoothly into an all-star film cast. Perhaps most importantly, she knows how to survive. In both her personal life and her professional career, Whoopi Goldberg has repeatedly turned negative situations into positives, to emerge as a winner.

Goldberg's fertile imagination first manifested itself when she was growing up in a public housing project in the Chelsea section of Manhattan, where she became known as a flawless mimic. She loved to imitate old movies she saw on the family's television, particularly the romantic comedies of the 1930s and the horror films of the 1950s. Goldberg's mother encouraged the child's creative bent. "She would say, 'Get on the bus, go hear the Leonard Bernstein concert, go see the children's ballet, go to the museum,'" John Skow quoted the actress as saying in *Time*. Goldberg's mother also allowed her daughter to participate in the Helena Rubinstein Children's Theater at the Hudson Guild. From the age of eight until she was ten, Goldberg performed in that venue. "I could be a princess, a teapot...a rabbit, anything," she remembered to Skow. "And in a way, it's been children's theater ever since. I've only recently

---

"I don't want them to say, 'Oh, she's a Black actor, we can't use her.' I want them to say, 'Oh, here's a great role. Call [Meryl] Streep. Call Diane Keaton. Call Whoopi Goldberg.'"

---

begun believing that I've grown up, and acting is what I do."

Although the stage seemed a natural environment to Goldberg, school did not. "I couldn't understand what they were doing," she told *Ebony* reporter Laura B. Randolph. Years later, she would be diagnosed with the learning disability dyslexia, but at the time, she was simply labeled as retarded. "You don't want to be *retarded* all your life," she observed. "I was *retarded* for a good part of mine, according to all the paperwork, and I just couldn't handle it." Her discouragement led her to drop out of school in her late teens and drift into drug abuse. At first it was casual, but in time, she became addicted to heroin. "Junkies never know they have to stop and I don't know now how I did," she told Randolph. "It took many tries....You fall a lot because it's *hard*." The experience left her with a strong message for young people: "There ain't no joy in a high—*none*....You *think* there's a joy in a high because it feels good

temporarily. But it feels good less and less often, so you've got to do it more and more often. It ain't your friend....I tell kids, 'Save the money and just kill yourself because [if you're using drugs] that's what you're doing.'"

After kicking heroin, Goldberg married her drug counselor and became more politically active, participating in civil rights marches and student demonstrations. She also returned to the acting she'd found so satisfying as a young child, working in the choruses of Broadway productions such as *Hair, Jesus Christ Superstar,* and *Pippin.* Her life was definitely on a more positive track, but she faced another setback when, shortly after she gave birth to a daughter, her marriage crumbled. She had no real means of supporting herself and no real prospects. When a friend in California sent her a one-way ticket to Los Angeles, Goldberg snapped it up, happy to escape her situation in New York even if she had no idea what life on the West Coast would hold for her.

Settling with her daughter in San Diego, Goldberg found that things weren't much easier than they had been in New York. For six years she struggled to support herself financially and to establish herself as an actress. She worked odd jobs as a bricklayer, a hairdresser, a bank teller, and a makeup artist for a funeral parlor, but it was never enough to pay the bills; she ended up on welfare, an experience she remembers as terribly demeaning. "The welfare workers used to make these surprise visits because you weren't allowed to have friends—especially not friends to whom you might want to be polite and *feed* something," she recalled to Randolph. "If a welfare worker did surprise you and you happened to have a friend in the house with a plate of food in front of them, it would be deducted from your money the next month."

Despite such indignities, Goldberg at least had the satisfaction of knowing that she was developing as an actress. She had joined the improvisational troupe Spontaneous Combustion and had also became a founding member of the San Diego Repertory Theater, where she played the lead in *Mother Courage* and significant roles in *Don't Drink the Water, Getting Out,* and *The Grass is Greener.* In Spontaneous Combustion, she began to work up her unique collection of offbeat characters, partly in response to her frustration with the lack of good roles for black character actors. Her stage name originated at this time when friends, teasing her about her personal habits, tagged her "Whoopi Cushion." "I was very flatulent," she explained to Skow. Trying to add some class to the name, she gave it a French twist—

"Whoopi Couchant." That was still less than digni-fied, according to her mother, so she adopted the title Whoopi Goldberg, claiming that there were Gold-bergs in her ancestry somewhere.

Her first work as Whoopi Goldberg was a series of two-character performances with standup comic Don Victor. The act was a hit around San Diego and they were soon booked for a performance in San Francis-co, but Victor walked out on the eve of that engagement. Goldberg showed up alone and apolo-getic, but at the encouragement of writer-comedian David Schein, who was to share billing with Gold-berg and Victor, she went onstage alone. She thought she could carry at least 20 minutes by herself; she was onstage for an hour, and the audience loved her. Goldberg returned to San Diego just long enough to pack her bags, then moved to the Bay area for a romantic and professional liaison with Schein.

The duo wrote and performed *The Last Word,* a satire on the relationship between the sexes, and collabo-rated in various other productions through the Blake Street Hawkeyes, an experimental theater group cofounded by Schein. On her own time, Goldberg continued to develop her cast of inner characters, showcasing four of them in an improvisational act she called *The Spook Show,* which debuted in Berkeley in 1983. During the one-hour course of *The Spook Show,* Goldberg became by turns a cynical but well-educated junkie named Fontaine, a severely handi-capped young woman who dreams she can walk, a white "Valley girl" who has given herself a coat-hanger abortion, and a nine-year-old black girl who wears a yellow skirt on her head to fulfill her wish for long blonde hair. Each part of the performance was a perceptive blend of entertainment and social commentary, and the show was a hit. Before long *The Spook Show* was touring the United States and Europe.

In 1983, Goldberg was invited to perform her show as part of a workshop series in New York City. Many who saw her were impressed with her range and talent, and none more so than noted director-produc-er Mike Nichols. Arranging a meeting with Goldberg, he told her that he wanted to develop and expand her act and bring it to Broadway. Retitled *Whoopi Goldberg,* the show opened at the Lyceum Theater on October 24, 1984. While a few critics felt that Goldberg's talent needed further development, most agreed that her expressive face and chameleon-like ability to transform from one character to another were truly remarkable. Before the show closed in the spring of 1985, it was taped and later broadcast on HBO as *Whoopi Goldberg Direct from Broadway.*

Goldberg's run of good fortune was not over. Film director Steven Spielberg saw her Broadway show and was so impressed that he signed her for the lead in his adaptation of Alice Walker's Pulitzer Prize-winning novel, *The Color Purple.* The part was a complex one, requiring Goldberg to progress from teenaged innocence through repeated abuse and trauma to fulfillment through an intimate affair with a woman blues singer. "Her performance was the best part of a good film," noted Skow, and it won her an Academy Award nomination. The attendant publicity transformed Goldberg into a major celebri-ty, and she was the subject of profiles and gossip in numerous national publications.

"I'm fighting the label of 'Black' actress," she told a writer for *Ebony* during that period, "simply because it's very limiting in people's eyes, especially people who are making movies. I don't want them to say, 'Oh, she's a Black actor, we can't use her.' I want them to say, 'Oh, here's a great role. Call [Meryl] Streep. Call Diane Keaton. Call Whoopi Goldberg.'" But Goldberg found that breaking Hollywood's color barrier was more difficult than she had anticipated. Despite her phenomenal success in *The Color Purple,* few really good roles came her way. According to Skow, "in the next few years, in role after role, her acting was the best part of a succession of bad, mediocre and upper-mediocre films," including *Jum-pin' Jack Flash, Burglar, The Telephone,* and *Fatal Beauty.* Rumors spread around Hollywood that her career was in serious trouble, and she came under fire for her poor judgement in selecting scripts. Skow quoted her response to that criticism: "I did the pictures I was offered.... Do you think I would sit around and say, 'Here's great scripts, here's crappy scripts; I'll do the crappy ones?'"

Goldberg also found herself censured by certain elements of the black community because of the types of roles in which she appeared. That was "really... tough," she told Randolph. "Reading stuff that... Black folks have said. They talk about the kind of roles that I do and then turn around and say how tough it is to find work. I'm working my ass off and they're kicking it... for working.... I don't change my skin every day. Every day I'm out there, every movie I make, I'm Black." Meanwhile, movie executives continued to confine Goldberg to asexual roles, believing that white audiences would be disturbed by any romantic coupling between her and a white male lead.

After limping through the late 1980s, Goldberg's career took an upturn with her Academy Award-winning performance in the 1990 picture *Ghost.* With her deft, trademark blend of humor and sensitivity, she played a fraudulent psychic who reunites lovers separated by death. The film, a box-office smash, did much to restore the luster to her tarnished reputation, as did the follow-up projects *The Player* and *Sister Act*. The financial success of these films allowed her to take a chance in the more artistic *Sarafina!*, a musical about a schoolteacher in South Africa; predictably, it failed at the box office, but both the film and Goldberg were praised by critics. She also received good marks for her appearance as host of the Grammy awards, for her contributions to the Comic Relief benefits for the homeless, and for her recurring guest role as bartender Guinon in the syndicated television series *Star Trek: The Next Generation*. In the 1993 film *Made in America*, she finally succeeded in breaking the racial taboos that have angered her throughout her career; she and her white male lead, Ted Danson, were portrayed as romantically involved and even shared an onscreen kiss.

Goldberg took on a new challenge in 1992—a syndicated talk show, designed to provide "an eclectic, slightly off-kilter alternative to...David Letterman, Jay Leno and Arsenio Hall," according to *New York Times* writer Isabel Wilkerson. Conceived by Goldberg herself, the show has none of the standard talk-show trappings such as a band, an announcer, a live audience, or an opening monologue. Instead, the half-hour offering features Goldberg in intimate conversation with one other person—always someone who interests her personally. Among the first guests to appear were rapper Ice-T, Vice President Al Gore, and white supremacist Tom Metzger. Goldberg told Wilkerson that she began the show in part because she felt she was being forced into a "zany comedian" pigeonhole. "I always seem to get caught up in other people's minds in one specific way," she complained. "And I guess it's because they want me one specific way. But how boring is that? I'm much happier to try all kinds of things. No, I'm not going to be great at everything, but that's O.K.... I don't think in terms of failure....I think of things as not the right time or something that's outside of my capabilities. I don't feel like anyone outside of me should be setting limitations. People should be encouraging people to shoot for the moon."

Sources

Books

Blacks in American Films and on Television, Garland, 1988.

Periodicals

Ebony, March 1985; March 1991.
Entertainment Weekly, January 7, 1993.
Esquire, February 1985.
Essence, March 1985.
Harper's, January 1987.
Nation, December 21, 1992.
Newsday, November 4, 1984.
Newsweek, March 5, 1984.
New York Daily News, October 21, 1984.
New York Times, October 21, 1984; April 5, 1991; September 18, 1992; November 29, 1992.
People, May 28, 1984; August 13, 1984; December 23, 1985.
Rolling Stone, May 8, 1986.
Time, June 1, 1992; September 21, 1992.
Village Voice, October 30, 1984.
Vogue, January 1991.
Washington Post, December 25, 1984.

—Joan Goldsworthy

Tommy Hilfiger

Courtesy of Tommy Hilfiger Corp.

Fashion designer

Born Thomas J. Hilfiger, March 24, 1952, in Elmira, NY; son of Richard (a jeweler) and Virginia (a nurse); married in 1980; wife's name, Susan; children: Alexandria, Richard.

Addresses: *Office*—Tommy Hilfiger USA Inc., 25 West 39th St., New York, NY 10018.

Career

Began retailing and design career while in high school; operated retail chain, People's Place, Elmira, NY, 1971-79; sold his interest in People's Place, 1979; designer for Jordache Co., New York City, 1980; founded sportswear company, Twentieth Century Survival, 1981 (folded, 1983); free-lance fashion designer, 1983-84; designed Coca-Cola Clothes collection for Murjani International Ltd., 1984; established Tommy Hilfiger Corp., 1986.

Sidelights

Tommy Hilfiger burst onto the fashion scene in 1985 with verve and not a little moxie. The boyish-looking designer, now 41, proclaimed his arrival on New York's Seventh Avenue with a fill-in-the-blanks billboard puzzle. "The 4 great American designers for men are: R____ L____, P____ E____, C____ K____, and T____ H____." The billboard also displayed the logo of the least-known of the four—a red-white-and-blue nautical flag—and told consumers to get ready to add another name to their lexicon of household words. Months later, a blitz of television commercials and magazine ads proclaimed: "First there was Geoffrey Beene, Bill Blass and Stanley Blacker. Then Calvin Klein, Perry Ellis and Ralph Lauren. Today, it's Tommy...." The small print of the introductory magazine ads read: "Tommy's clothes are easy-going without being too casual, classic without being predictable. He calls them classics with a twist. The other three designers call them competition." Placing himself among the cream of fashion's top designers may have stretched the truth just a bit, and it clearly ruffled the feathers of many in the fashion industry. Its mavens were offended by what *New York* magazine called "a relative nobody trying to be somebody by comparing himself to the incomparables." "It's like when [actress and entertainer] Pia Zadora puts herself in the same league as Barbra Streisand and Liza Minelli," Jack Hyde, consulting head of the menswear design and marketing department at the Fashion Institute of Technology, told *New York*. "Tommy Hilfiger is not a designer, he's a creation. In my 40 years in this business, I have never seen an advertising campaign so arrogant and tasteless." In the same interview, Hyde noted that there is nothing wrong with Hilfiger's clothing designs, which are stylish updates of nautical looks and preppy, Ivy League fashions. "Everyone else has done well with those looks, so why shouldn't he? But why not just come out and say we're marketing a successful line? Why all this song and dance about a new great designer? In the fashion world, it's not you or your publicity agent saying you're great that makes you great. It's *Women's Wear Daily*, *GQ*, the *Daily News Record*, and merchants.''

Hilfiger, now considered an overnight success, was backed by Mohan Murjani, a managing director of Murjani International Ltd., which is credited with making Gloria Vanderbilt the designer jeans queen in the late 1970s. Murjani noted in *Newsweek* that the entire introductory marketing campaign was designed to ''accelerate the success of Tommy Hilfiger. It would have happened anyway, it just would have taken longer.'' In *New York* magazine, Murjani further defended Hilfiger: ''If you're a talented, hardworking designer, you'll get discovered, although admittedly, for most designers, it's a long

> *It's been a long climb from the basement—literally—to being the darling of Wall Street. Hilfiger has been involved with the fashion business since he was 17.*

road. All we did was condense the time frame, help develop Tommy's success by adding marketing to the mix. Without marketing support, it's a slow build— maybe it would have taken Tommy ten years instead of two. We are a company that believes in marketing.'' Murjani invested approximately $20 million in advertising and promotion into Hilfiger's splashy 1985 debut, according to *Newsweek*.

Indeed, Hilfiger, who never attended design school, may have the last laugh. The sportswear designer, who concentrates on ''nouveau prep'' fashions for men, took his company public in September of 1992, with the initial listing on the New York Stock Exchange at $15 a share. By February 1993, the stock climbed to $25 a share, 22 times 1993's anticipated earnings. Hilfiger's own 13 percent stake in the company alone is worth at least $50 million, according to *Forbes*, which also noted that the designer draws an annual salary of $900,000, plus 1.5 percent of all sales above $48 million. In 1992, the company's revenues reached $107 million.

It's been a long climb from the basement—literally— to being the darling of Wall Street. Hilfiger has been involved with the fashion business since he was 17. The second of nine children, he grew up in Elmira, New York, where his father, Richard, was a jeweler, and his mother, Virginia, worked as a nurse. In 1970, while still in high school, Hilfiger, Larry Stemerman, and another friend raised $150 and bought about 20 pairs of bell-bottom jeans, then resold them from a local basement. This launched the nascent retailing team into the buy-and-sell business, which evolved into a retail store called People's Place. By 1972, the single store had blossomed into a chain of seven jeans boutiques located on Upstate New York college campuses. The pals made ''a lot of money,'' Hilfiger recalled in an interview with *People* in 1986, and couldn't spend it fast enough. ''I was wild. I used to go to London for weekends...I had a Porsche, a Mercedes, a Jaguar and a Jeep.''

However, Hilfiger soon realized that operating retail stores was not what he truly wanted to do for the rest of his life. While buying merchandise to stock the stores, Hilfiger began sketching ideas for jeans and jackets for some of his suppliers. ''Being able to make money just for giving ideas to a company seemed incredible,'' he told *Forbes*. By the late 1970s, Hilfiger and his partners were running into financial difficulties with the People's Place chain. Hilfiger and partner Stemerman filed for bankruptcy under Chapter 11. It's a part of his life that Hilfiger has told several publications that he prefers not to discuss. As he told *People*, ''It's embarrassing.'' In 1979 Hilfiger sold his remaining interest in the People's Place stores, moved to New York City, and became a designer for Jordache jeans. After a year he was fired by Jordache for reasons that *People* said ''neither side will discuss.'' Hilfiger then pooled $50,000 with friends and started a sportswear company called Twentieth Century Survival. That company survived for approximately one year before it folded. Hilfiger was designing women's sportswear on a project-by-project, free-lance basis when he met apparel mogul Mohan Murjani. ''He was exactly what I had envisioned a designer to be,'' Murjani told *People* magazine.

This fortuitous meeting in the early 1980s was the basis for a long-lasting business relationship. The two immediately found they had much in common. ''I found him great, warm and egoless, a rare trait in the world of designers,'' Murjani told *New York* magazine. Murjani invited Hilfiger to develop his own label collection of sportswear while overseeing the design team for Murjani's Coca-Cola Clothes line, which sold more than $100 million (wholesale) in clothing items in 1984, the first year the Coca-Cola collection was available in retail outlets. According to *New York* magazine, Hilfiger's initial collections sold $5 million wholesale in 1985, the line's first year, jumping to $16 million (wholesale) in 1986.

The success of the Coca-Cola clothing line, and the acceptance by fashion-forward consumers of his early collections, helped feed the publicity engine behind Hilfiger. The designer, who described his collections in *New York* magazine as looking like they "walked out of the Harvard yearbook," was initially nervous about his collections and the marketing push behind them, although Murjani conducted a market research study that showed there was a niche in the marketplace for a traditional, Ralph Lauren-type look for younger men. "I learned to trust Mohan's instincts," Hilfiger told *New York* magazine.

Still, Hilfiger was reluctant to push his designs, *New York* magazine reported. "We literally had to force Tommy into this kind of outrageous ... ad," said George Lois, chairman of Lois Pitts Gershon Pon/ GGK, the New York ad agency that created Hilfiger's campaign. "He wasn't bowled over by tooting his own horn; he worried about what this made him look like. We had to convince him that the bottom line in this business is to sell product, and that this would wake Seventh Avenue up to Tommy Hilfiger and sell product."

Since the Tommy Hilfiger Corp. was founded in 1986, the company, under Hilfiger's personal supervision, has specialized in "sportswear that is designed to combine classic American styling with unique details and fit to give time-honored basics a fresh and updated look," the stock prospectus reads. The collection is targeted to men, 18 years and older, who "desire high quality, designer image clothes at competitive prices."

The Hilfiger collection itself is organized into three primary product lines: Core, Core Plus, and Fashion. The core line is comprised of the company's seasonless products, or "basics," such as pleated chino pants, shorts, five-pocket denim jeans, solid-knit polo shirts, button-down oxford shirts, and crew neck cotton sweaters. The Core Plus line is comprised of a broad selection of seasonal "basics," which are spun-off from the Core collections, but offer a greater variety of fabrics, colors, and patterns, such as stripes or plaids. There are four different Core Plus product offerings annually, timed to correspond with the seasons. The Fashion line represents the company's most updated component. Fashion items consist of a group of clothing coordinated around a seasonal theme selected by Hilfiger. Fashion items generally are priced higher than comparable Core Plus items. Most Hilfiger designs include the designer's signature green-stitched buttonholes.

The concept behind Hilfiger's collections are clothing "that will appeal to a young preppy with a Brooks Brothers state of mind"—a customer profile that might fit Hilfiger himself, who was described by the *Philadelphia Inquirer* as a preppy with a "Jerry Lewis set of teeth [who] looks so young, so clean, so spunky that he could pass as a member of the U.S. gymnastic team," said *New York* magazine.

Hilfiger, who describes his collections in several published reports as having a "nautical look and Gatsby feeling," is the company's principal designer and provides leadership and direction for all aspects of the design process, overseeing a design staff of 17 people, the stock prospectus said. Tommy Hilfiger collections are sold in more than 1,100 department and specialty retail stores. The company, in its prospectus, noted that its strategy is to continue to grow by expanding its in-department-store shop program, whereby retailers set aside specific floor space for Hilfiger's designs. The in-store shop program totaled 63 shops by early 1992, with 37 additional shops completed by year's end.

"Tommy Hilfiger is doing a phenomenal business because he gives the customer something he can understand—tradition with a twist," Joe Iacono, a retail executive at Bloomingdale's, told *New York* magazine. "He fills a major void. He uses basic fabrics and attracts a broad selection of customers— anyone from 18 to 65 can wear his clothes. A lot of jazzier things from other designers might look good on the selling floor, but would you wear them? Men aren't as daring as women; they won't take as many fashion risks."

Despite the ongoing popularity of Hilfiger's collections, and the success of Hilfiger's stock offering on Wall Street, Fashion Avenue gossips have kept up their sour grapes campaign. Hilfiger's critics, *Newsweek* reported, contend that Hilfiger's publicity drives display "far more creativity than his clothes." Yet none of that behind-his-back talk bothers Hilfiger. The youthful designer told *Forbes* that it doesn't matter what the gossips say, since "We know how to ring the [cash] register."

Sources

Forbes, February 1, 1993.
Newsweek, October 6, 1986.
New York, September 22, 1986.
People, July 7, 1986.

Additional material obtained from publicity packet and stock prospectus supplied by Tommy Hilfiger USA, New York, NY.

—*Laurie Freeman*

Jimmy Johnson

AP/Wide World Photos

Football coach

Born James William Johnson, July 16, 1943, in Port Arthur, TX; son of C. W. (a plant superintendent) and Allene Johnson; married Linda Kay Cooper, 1963 (divorced, 1989); children: Brent, Chad. *Education:* University of Arkansas, B.A., 1965.

Addresses: *Office*—c/o Dallas Cowboys, 2401 E. Airport Freeway, Irving, TX 75062.

Career

Football coach, 1965—. Louisiana Tech University, defensive line coach, 1965-66; Wichita State University, assistant coach, 1967; Iowa State University, defensive coordinator, 1968-69; University of Oklahoma, defensive line coach, 1970-72; University of Arkansas, defensive coordinator, 1973-76; University of Pittsburgh, assistant head coach/defensive coordinator, 1977-78; Oklahoma State University, head coach, 1979-83; University of Miami, head coach, 1984-88; named head coach of Dallas Cowboys, February 25, 1989.

Selected awards: Named Big Eight Coach of the Year, 1979; Coach of the Year citations from Pigskin Club (Washington, DC) and Walter Camp Foundation, both 1986; NFL Coach of the Year citations from Associated Press and United Press International, 1990; NFL Coach of the Year citation from *Football Digest*, 1991.

Sidelights

Jimmy Johnson has spent a lifetime in pursuit of victory on the football field. The single-minded Johnson worked his way through the college coaching ranks and wound up, in 1989, at the head of the Dallas Cowboys. In only four seasons he turned the franchise around and led a talented pool of young players to a stunning upset of the favored Buffalo Bills in Super Bowl XXVII. He is, in many respects, the consummate football coach—focused, determined, ruthless, and highly effective. Football is not a game to him. It is a job, one that he means to perform to the very best of his ability.

NFL coaches are notorious for their work habits. The various demands of the position keep them busy up to 16 hours a day. Many have been known to sleep in their offices during particularly hectic game weeks. Jimmy Johnson has brought this goal-oriented work style to full fruition. A relative newcomer to the NFL, he is already a legend for his devotion to the Cowboys. He spends 14 hours a day, seven days a week in his office at Cowboy Center, and even his family and closest friends know not to disturb him. By his own admission, he has never celebrated Thanksgiving or Christmas, and does not know his parents' birthdays. Anything other than football is a distraction. "For all his seraphic good looks, Jimmy Johnson doesn't really care what you think," wrote Jim Murray in the *Los Angeles Times.* "His world is 100 yards long by 160 feet wide and has hash marks."

The rewards for being such a driven perfectionist are obvious. Johnson inherited a 3-13 Dallas team and, after two rebuilding years, took the Cowboys to the playoffs in 1991 and 1992. His spotless clothes and carefully coiffed hair have become trademarks on the Dallas sidelines, indications of the iron control he seeks to impose on everything around him. Nor does Johnson make apologies for his workaholic ways or the fact that he has stripped his life bare of everything but football. "I used to think it would be great to be a CEO of some major company, work 40 hours a week and make all this money and be the best at my business," Johnson told the *Philadelphia Inquirer.* "Then I started meeting some of those CEOs

---

"We're looking for smart football players who can run and make good plays. You've got to look at a player and say, 'Does he perform?' I want performers. I want playmakers."

---

and they were working Saturdays and Sundays, they were working 12 hours a day. I saw the people that are truly at the top and want to stay at the top, they don't put a token effort into it. So as long as I want to stay at the top, I'm going to work this schedule."

James William Johnson was born in 1943 in the Texas Gulf Coast town of Port Arthur. His parents, C.W. and Allene Johnson, had moved to Texas from Arkansas in search of employment. At first Johnson's father worked as a mechanic in an oil refinery, but he soon chose to be a plant superintendent at a large area dairy. One of the conditions of the dairy job was that the superintendent live in a company house on the dairy property and be on call 24 hours a day, seven days a week. "Jimmy saw sometimes you had to put your job first," his father said in the *Chicago Tribune.* "It probably stuck with him."

Johnson was not particularly big or strong, but he had a zealous desire to win and be the best at whatever he tried. Even a simple Monopoly game would become, for him, a test of wits and determination. He liked any sort of contest in which a person of lesser strength could win by outsmarting an opponent. Football seemed a logical choice for him, and he earned all-state football honors at Thomas Jefferson High School as a two-way lineman.

Today a bust of Johnson rests in the library at Jefferson High next to one of his classmate, Janis Joplin. "What a seemingly odd couple," notes Jere Longman in the *Philadelphia Inquirer.* "For one, an existence used up all at once, like a pack of firecrackers. For the other, a career entering its prime . . . on no less a commanding stage than the Super Bowl." In fact, Johnson and Joplin rarely crossed paths in Port Arthur, but they did share a singular determination to forge a path into the limelight.

Many Port Arthur teenagers look forward to careers in the area oil refineries or other local businesses. Johnson was different. He parlayed his high school football fame into a scholarship to the University of Arkansas. There, despite his relatively small size, he became an All-Southwest Conference defensive lineman. In his senior season the Razorbacks won the national championship. Johnson, who married after his sophomore year, earned substantial income by playing bridge for money in his spare time. "Bridge is a game of strategy," he told the *Chicago Tribune.* "You have to be analytical, figure out what cards other people have. Even if you have worse cards, you can win. That was part of the attraction for me." On Razorback road trips, Johnson roomed with teammate Jerry Jones. The two young men got along well, but they rarely socialized away from football. Still, Johnson's passion for the game was not lost on Jones, who left the University of Arkansas to become a multimillionaire with business holdings in oil and gas exploration, banking, real estate, crude oil production, shipping, and refining, and even poultry processing.

Johnson majored in psychology. After earning his degree in 1965 he planned to pursue graduate study and possibly work as an industrial psychologist for a corporation. Instead, he accepted a position as a defensive line coach at Louisiana Tech University and became absolutely absorbed by football strategy. Coaching also offered him an immediate way to support a wife and two sons. Johnson told the *Chicago Tribune* that coaching "was like bridge, only better. There was X's and O's strategy, but it wasn't only that. The challenge was to get players emotionally into practice and games. It was rewarding to me to take players and challenge them mentally. We could use strategy and psychology and take players who weren't as good as the other team's and win. Winning like that was fun."

In 1966 Johnson spent the year in Picayune, Mississippi, as a high school football coach. The following year he returned to the college ranks. He served as an assistant coach at Wichita State University, a defensive coordinator at Iowa State University, at the University of Oklahoma, and at his alma mater, Arkansas. By 1977 he was an assistant head coach and defensive coordinator for the University of Pittsburgh. He was so successful with the Pittsburgh team that after only two seasons he was offered a head coaching job. It was just the sort of challenge he relished—Oklahoma State University, a perennial underdog to the more powerful, vastly more successful University of Oklahoma. Johnson assumed head coaching responsibilities at Oklahoma State in 1979.

The Oklahoma State program was not highly regarded before Johnson arrived, but he soon changed that. After his first season he was named Big Eight Coach of the Year, and during his four-season tenure he guided Oklahoma State to two bowl games and won one. In 1984 he received an even more promising position. He was named head coach of the University of Miami Hurricanes, a veritable collegiate football powerhouse. Johnson spent four years in Miami and guided the Hurricanes to a phenomenal 52-9 record. The teams captured two Orange Bowl titles and the 1987 national championship. Two other times they finished as runner-ups to the national championship.

The high-profile Miami job included recruiting, devising game strategies and training players, gladhanding wealthy alumni, and a host of administrative tasks. Johnson devoted himself wholeheartedly to the challenge, just as he had at all his other colleges. He literally had no time for his wife and sons. Holidays passed without him and birthdays too. Sometimes he would not see his children for weeks at a time. "It's different from how I hear a normal family works," son Chad told the *Chicago Tribune*. Likewise, Brent Johnson remembered: "Growing up, my mother was always there for us. In order to accomplish what he has, [Johnson] put everything else aside, including his family . . . . My dad and I know each other now, but we didn't know each other for a very long time . . . . That's him. You accept him as he is or lose him."

As his Hurricanes held the national spotlight, Johnson knew that he would soon be offered a chance to coach in the NFL. He never dreamed he would begin his NFL career as a head coach, though. Usually college coaches begin as offensive or defensive coordinators, or even as special squad coaches. Not

Johnson. His college friendship with Jerry Jones led to a unique opportunity.

In 1989 Jones bought the ailing Dallas Cowboys for $135 million. Throughout the franchise's 30 years of existence, it had been coached by one man—the legendary Tom Landry. Although they fell on hard times in the mid-1980s, Landry's Cowboys had earned the nickname "America's Team" by playing in five Super Bowls. Landry, a spokesman for the Christian faith, was "ranked with the Alamo as a [Texas] state shrine," to quote Murray. Jones drew the scorn of Cowboys fans everywhere by firing Landry and announcing that Johnson—a college coach without a minute's experience in the NFL— would be the new Cowboys leader. The citizens of Dallas sneered. They nicknamed Jones and Johnson "Jed and Jethro," referring to their Arkansas roots. The two men drew boos wherever they went, especially during football season.

"Never have two men began a career in such a profusion of community hostility as Jerry Jones and Jimmy Johnson," Murray remarked. "There is no evidence it bothered Jimmy Johnson at all. The man with the altar-boy looks went about his work oblivious to the reaction of the community. Not his table. He had a football team to build, not a community to woo. He ignored them . . . . He was in a cocoon."

"Maybe the criticism that I incurred when I first got here helped me," Johnson said in the *Washington Post*. "If you've already got your nose bloodied, you might as well just step on out there and get in the fray." Johnson found himself in charge of a barely functional franchise with only one star player, Herschel Walker. During their first seasons running the Cowboys, Jones and Johnson dismantled the team and shopped voraciously for promising draft picks and free agents. They made more than 50 personnel changes in four years, including a trade that sent Walker to the Minnesota Vikings for a wealth of early round draft choices.

"We've realized probably half-a-dozen players from that trade," Johnson told the *Washington Post*. "You get the picks, but you still have to do something with them. The Walker trade wouldn't look nearly as good had we not used one of those picks to draft Emmitt Smith. If you don't get the right people, it's not going to be a good trade."

Jones and Johnson approached the business of running a football team like two corporate raiders on the scent of a company takeover. Jones took a hiatus from his vast business empire and joined Johnson in the single-minded pursuit of a Super Bowl contender. The duo rebuilt their team around young talent like quarterback Troy Aikman, defensive end Tony Tolbert, running back Emmitt Smith, and receiver Michael Irvin. The Cowboys went 1-15 in 1989 but improved to 7-9 in 1990 and made the playoffs in 1991.

By 1992 Johnson had proven himself to the Landry faithful. The 1992 Cowboys posted a 13-3 regular season record, then trounced the Philadelphia Eagles 34-10 in one playoff game and the San Francisco 49ers 30-20 in another. The San Francisco victory served notice that the Cowboys had arrived as a new dynasty under their determined coach.

The Cowboys landed in Super Bowl XXVII against the favored Buffalo Bills. For the Bills it was a third Super Bowl appearance in as many years, and the previous two losses made the Buffalo players hungrier than ever for a victory. The game, held at the Rose Bowl in Pasadena, California, featured a war-torn but solid veteran team versus a youthful, exuberant squad just ripening for top-level competition. And the game turned out to be one of the most lopsided Super Bowls ever. The Cowboys won 52-17, forcing a Super Bowl record of nine turnovers.

At game's end Johnson smiled and cavorted with his players, even responding with humor when they doused him with water and mussed his hair. Asked the secret of his success—other than the obvious total devotion to his work—Johnson told the *Philadelphia Inquirer:* "We're looking for smart football players who can run and make good plays. You've got to look at a player and say, 'Does he perform?' I want performers. I want playmakers." He added that anyone who *didn't* perform for him could find another job.

Johnson admits he likes to be in control of every situation. In 1989 he divorced his wife of 25 years, claiming he could brook no more distractions from football. He lives alone in a spotless house near the Cowboys' corporate headquarters. He can drive to work in five minutes. The coach's philosophy of life is mirrored in his always-perfect hairstyle. "I just don't like for my hair to hang in my eyes," he told the *Chicago Tribune.* "It bothers me and I like to be neat. I like for things to be in order, whether it's my home, or my sons, or my clothes, or my hair or my football team. I don't like penalties on my football team. I don't like foolish mistakes. I like things to be right. It just so happens that's the way I like my hair. So I have to have a little touch of spray. I'm being honest with you. You want me to tell you something not true and all of a sudden sneak out a can of spray? I'm not a closet sprayer."

A Super Bowl victory has not diminished Johnson's love for football. He relishes new challenges and takes great satisfaction in the prospect of further seasons in the NFL. His contract with the Cowboys runs through 1999. "I can tell you this," he concluded in the *Chicago Tribune*, "I'm very, very happy with Jimmy Johnson. I really like him a lot. And not in a way of being boastful and arrogant, but in a way I'm happy with my situation in life. I enjoy winning football games."

Sources

Chicago Tribune, September 20, 1992; January 26, 1993.
Los Angeles Times, January 27, 1993.
New York Times, January 17, 1993.
Philadelphia Inquirer, January 18, 1993; January 28, 1993; January 31, 1993; February 1, 1993; February 2, 1992.
Washington Post, January 24, 1993.

—Mark Kram

Larry Johnson

Professional basketball player

Full name, Larry Demetric Johnson; born March 14, 1969, in Tyler, TX; son of Dortha Johnson; single. *Education:* Graduated from Skyline High School in Dallas; attended Odessa (TX) Junior College, 1987-89, and University of Nevada at Las Vegas, 1989-91.

Addresses: *Home*—Charlotte, NC, and Dallas, TX. *Office*—c/o Charlotte Hornets, One Hive Drive, Charlotte, NC 20217. *Agent*—Steve Endicott, Athletic Associates Inc., 15303 Dallas Parkway, No. 970, Dallas, TX 75248.

Career

Professional basketball player (plays forward) with the Charlotte Hornets, 1991—.

Awards: Named U.S. high school basketball player of the year by *Parade* magazine, 1987; named junior college player of the year, 1988, 1989; NCAA Division I player of the year, 1990, 1991; John R. Wooden Award and James A. Naismith Award as top collegiate player, 1991; named NBA rookie of the year, 1992; named to the NBA All-Star team, 1992-93.

Sidelights

Basketball transformed Larry Johnson from high school outcast to hero. It has rewarded him with national player-of-the-year honors and a multimillion-dollar contract to play for the NBA's Charlotte Hornets. Johnson is a body-banging, rim-rattling all-star power forward. His story is one of rising from abject poverty to success. Today he is considered one of the NBA's brightest young talents, a charismatic star. His story is also one of decisions, both timely and wise: to join the Police Athletic League; to leave the neighborhood for high school; to leave Dallas for college; to stay in school rather than jump to the NBA before graduating.

Basketball plucked Larry Johnson from the projects of South Dallas. He grew up in a neighborhood known as Dixon Circle, where he was, by his own admission, a childhood troublemaker—he threw rocks at cars, he stole, he broke windows. As a 10-year-old he was picked up by the police for fighting so often that he was on the verge of being sent to a detention home. Because the facility was full, however, officers would just pick him up each weekend and drop him off at the Police Athletic League (PAL) gym for enforced recreation. "It took me off the streets," Johnson told the *Philadelphia Inquirer*. "If the Police Athletic League helped anybody, it helped me. No telling what would have happened to old Larry otherwise."

At the gym, he spent hour after hour playing football, baseball, and basketball. His first love was boxing. "Boxing was, guy hits me, the fight is on," he told the *St. Paul Pioneer Press*. "I hit him, he's going, 'Bell, what bell, do you hear a bell?' No judges were needed."

By the seventh grade, Johnson already stood six-foot-two. He began to dominate PAL League basketball games, averaging 45 points per contest. Still, despite his athletic interests, Larry continued to get into trouble. His mother, raising him on her own, blamed the neighborhood. "Everything [in the neighborhood] was drugs, fighting and killing," Dortha Johnson told the *Charlotte Observer*. "Larry is a pretty average kid when you consider where he came from."

When it came time to go to high school, Johnson's mother and his junior high school coach decided he should leave the district to go to Skyline High, the city's biggest school. Skyline was known for tough basketball and tough discipline. Larry rode the bus 45 minutes each way every day. "I was somewhat of an outcast," he told the *Charlotte Observer*. "I didn't have any real friends. Everyone knew I was from Dixon, which is like a 'hood. I was never Larry. I was the kid from Dixon, or the kid from South Dallas."

The coach at Skyline was J.D. Mayo, a disciplinarian who made his players lift weights and pledge not to smoke, drink, take drugs, or gamble. Johnson, who had never met his father, embraced Mayo as a role model and flourished under his coaching. Larry started for the varsity team as a ninth grader, and during his four years there, the Skyline Raiders never lost a home game. Mayo first nicknamed Johnson "The Baby," but eventually changed the monicker — first to "Baby-Man," then just to "The Man."

By his senior season, Johnson was named the national high school player of the year. Chicago Bulls star Michael Jordan, in Dallas for a game, stopped by to see him play, which Johnson still considers the thrill of his life. College recruiters also came by. Dave Bliss, the coach at Southern Methodist University, told the *Observer* that the first time he went to see Johnson, "I walked into the weight room and he was doing thrusts—and the weight machine was coming off the ground. But the first thing that sticks out about him is his character. He has an amazing capacity to make a situation better by his mere presence."

Larry had planned to go to Southern Methodist, hut he failed to meet the minimum NCAA standards in his first Scholastic Aptitude Test. When he took the SATs again, his score improved so dramatically that SMU officials, already reeling from a football scandal, asked him to take it a third time. He refused and

instead attended Odessa Junior College in Texas for two seasons. "Junior college was good for me," he later told the *Peninsula Times Tribune*. "I had a coach who kept me into things and thinking positive. It was good basketball, but more than that, it prepared me for the academic scene at a university."

Johnson averaged 22 points per game as a freshman and 30 as a sophomore at Odessa. He was named national junior-college player of the year after both seasons. He then accepted a scholarship to the University of Nevada at Las Vegas, a school famous for its excellent basketball program and infamous for its athletic scandals.

Johnson arrived at the UNLV campus in September 1989, shortly after six of the school's players were suspended for failing to pay incidental charges from trips. Soon after, two players were suspended for fighting with Utah State players and coaches after a game. The Running Rebels, fairly or not, was cast as a team of misfits and thugs who'd as soon fight as play basketball, coached by a rogue who has spent most of his career sparring with NCAA investigators.

Larry Johnson in the SlamDunk competition at the NBA All-Star game in February, 1992. AP/Wide World Photos.

"We were always characterized as hoodlums," Johnson later told the South Carolina's *Columbia State*. "Both times we played Duke, we'd read in the newspaper how it was a case of evil against good, and I think that made us mentally tough. It was always us against the world. We didn't let what other people said bother us. We just made it our business to do whatever it took to win."

UNLV knew how to win. With Johnson leading the way, the Rebels won the NCAA championship in 1990, annihilating Duke by 30 points in the title game. "Larry's strength is astonishing," Duke coach Mike Krzyzewski (also in *Newsmakers 93*) told the *Washington Post* after that game. "He's got to be the strongest guy in college basketball. Plus, he's got agility and a soft touch. He's a special player now and he will be a special player for 10 years."

Johnson, a power forward, averaged 21 points and 11 rebounds per game as a junior and was named to the All-American team. He considered leaving school to enter the NBA draft, where he would have certainly been among the first three players picked. But he decided to stay, both to improve his game and help UNLV toward a second straight national title. "I need to stay in school, it's the right thing to do," he told the *San Jose Mercury News*. "I'm having a hard enough time just adjusting to the Division I level. I don't think I'm ready for the NBA."

UNLV's 1990-91 team was regarded by many as one of the greatest in college basketball history. The team rattled off 34 straight victories and was on the verge of winning another title when Duke won a rematch in the NCAA semifinals. It was a disappointing finish, but Johnson, again, was an All-American and won several honors as the best player in college basketball. In 35 games, he averaged 23 points and 11 rebounds.

Wrote Gene Wojciechowski of the *Los Angeles Times*: "He weighs 250 pounds. Body fat? Not unless you're measuring with tweezer-sized calipers. Once planted under the basket, opposing centers and forwards need a forklift to budge him. Lesser-built players smack up against him as if Johnson were a manhole cover. They stagger away in a daze." At 6-foot-7 and 250 pounds, Johnson was most often compared with NBA star Charles Barkley (see *Newsmakers 88*) in terms of his hammer-on-anvil inside play. He also resembles Barkley in that he runs the floor and handles the ball like a point guard. Others said he possessed a combination of Karl Malone's body and Magic Johnson's verve for the game.

On June 26, 1991, the Charlotte Hornets made Johnson the first pick of the NBA draft. Many pro scouts rated Syracuse's Billy Owens as a more talented player, but the Hornets viewed Johnson as a leader and Owens as a follower. "I think I can do for Charlotte what I did for Las Vegas, what I did for Odessa J.C. and what I did in high school," Johnson told the *Charlotte Observer*, "and that is play hard and play the best and I can and hopefully bring us some victories."

Johnson held out for all of training camp and the eight-game pre-season of 1991 before signing a massive six-year, $20 million contract to play in Charlotte. His impact was immediate. In his second game he pulled down 10 rebounds. By mid-season, he was the runaway choice for rookie of the year honors. "He's strong, quick and very aggressive," Boston Celtics great Larry Bird (see *Newsmakers 90*) told the *Columbia State* after their first meeting. "He is powerful and when he does get the ball he can jump over anybody." Likewise, Chicago Bulls forward Horace Grant told the *Miami Herald*: "Larry Johnson is a rock. It's very hard to get around him. I think he'll be an all-star very soon."

Even as a rookie, Johnson was emerging as the Hornets' best player and on-court leader. He took the role reluctantly, telling the *Charlotte Observer*: "As far as being the man, you can't do those things until you earn the confidence of your teammates. When that happens, you feel free to go out and make mistakes. Once you feel they have the confidence in you to take the shot, then you know you can make it."

Johnson's style in the pros—as in college—was to bang bodies under the backboard, to pound his opponents into submission. Wrote the basketball writer Al Hamnik of the *Gary Post-Tribune*: "Scary. That's what he is. Larry Johnson, hunched over and palming the ball as if ready to dunk on Godzilla, is coming at you like a killer tornado—swirling, snarling, seething." Johnson himself told the *Post-Tribune*: "I never try to hurt anybody, you understand. But I play to win. And I do play rough. Real rough. If I let anyone beat me without a fight, I don't think I could live with myself."

Johnson finished the season 11th in the league in rebounding (11.0 per game) and 24th in scoring (19.7 per game). He was the consensus choice for NBA Rookie of the Year. The team improved to 31 wins, up from 26 the year before. Overall, there was optimism in Charlotte. "Larry's a guy we know we can build our franchise around," Hornets coach Allan Bristow told the *State*. "He's our building block, our foundation; he's our untouchable . . . . A leader is tough to get. It's an intangible that a lot of teams don't have. Look at the Lakers without Magic [Johnson], and the Celtics without Bird. We have a leader, not a loud leader, but a mature leader who leads by example."

Following Johnson's great rookie season, he became a favorite not just of fans and coaches, but also from commercial sponsors. Converse sneakers, which was in Chapter 11 bankruptcy protection in early 1992, signed Johnson to become its lead endorser. "We told him, 'You have the opportunity to be THE GUY for us,'" Converse vice president Roger Morningstar told the *Charlotte Observer*. "Larry looks like he was chiseled out of granite. We knew he would be very popular with our target audience [12- to 24-year-olds]. We just didn't know Grandmama would be nearly this popular."

Grandmama was the character created for Johnson, a slam-dunking senior citizen in pillbox hat, floral dress and Converse sneakers. The point of the ad campaign was that even Johnson's alleged grandmother could beat you in basketball if she wore the right sneakers. Johnson was initially reluctant about dressing in drag, but the ad campaign proved funny and made Johnson a hit on Madison Avenue. He was soon signed as the sole endorser of NBA Authentics sportswear. His No. 2 Hornets jersey became the second-leading seller nationwide behind only the No. 23 of Michael Jordan.

The aggressive style of the Converse commercial was reflective of Johnson's on-court approach. "I love the dunk," he told the *Gary Post-Tribune*. "I love to jump right into somebody's face and jam it so hard that your elbows go flying, your legs kick out and folks just kind of scatter beneath you. The faster you do it, the more intimidating. You gotta go up tough and come down hard, which is pretty much my game." On the flip side, Johnson was considered one of pro basketball's nicest men off the court. He was popular with fans and reporters. In 1992 his $180,000 contribution to the United Way was the largest given by an American athlete.

Johnson began the 1992-93 season with two goals: he wanted to play in the NBA All-Star game and he wanted the Hornets to make the playoffs for the first time in franchise history. Both aims were accomplished. In February he was voted a starter on the Eastern Division All-Star team, the first Hornet ever

to get that honor. And, in April, the Hornets finished the season with a winning record and made the playoffs. They beat the Boston Celtics in the first round before running up against the world champion Chicago Bulls. Johnson averaged 22.1 points per game and 10.5 rebounds in his second season.

During the season, Johnson spends much of his off-time working out. "I practice hard," he told the *Gary Post-Tribune*. "Three or four times a day, I do quick drills and squats until my legs burn. Sometimes, I'm out taking shots at 2 in the morning." Otherwise, he savors his privacy, and prefers hanging out at home to haunting nightclubs and bars. His idea of a good time is making some popcorn and renting a video tape.

Johnson's long-term goal is to play his entire career in Charlotte. He wants to be linked with the city the way Magic Johnson is with Los Angeles and Larry Bird is with Boston. "I want to play 11, 12 years right here and then retire—and win us some national championships, and be the Michael Jordan of Charlotte," he told the *Charlotte Observer*. Then, he hopes to go back to South Dallas and Dixon Circle. His housing project has been razed, but the basketball court is still there. Johnson is considering buying the land the court sits on and building a recreation center. "I want to do something helpful," he told the *Observer*. "Ain't no telling how many little Larrys can come out of Dixon."

Sources

Charlotte Observer, January 10, 1990; June 27, 1991; October 31, 1991; October 13, 1992; November 6, 1992; February 20, 1993; February 21, 1993.
Columbia State (SC), June 30, 1991; January 11, 1992.
Gary Post-Tribune (IN), April 2, 1992.
Los Angeles Times, March 31, 1991.
Miami Herald, December 13, 1991.
Peninsula Times Tribune (CA), January 10, 1990.
Philadelphia Inquirer, March 20, 1991.
St. Paul Pioneer Press, March 31, 1991; January 19, 1992.
San Jose Mercury News, March 22, 1990.
Sporting News Official NBA Register, 1992-93.
Street & Smith's Basketball, 1992.
Washington Post, April 5, 1990.
Wichita Eagle, January 13, 1993.

—Glen Macnow

Neil Jordan

Writer and director

Born c. 1950 in Sligo, Ireland; married (separated as of early 1993); children: two daughters by marriage and two sons by partner Brenda Rawn. *Education:* Attended University College, Dublin.

Career

Writer-director. Worked as playwright, musician, and writer; made documentary film on John Boorman, 1981; additional films include *Angel* (also known as *Danny Boy*), 1982; *The Company of Wolves*, 1984; *Mona Lisa*, 1986; *High Spirits*, 1988; *We're No Angels*, 1989; *The Miracle*, 1991; *The Crying Game*, 1992; *Interview With a Vampire* (tentative), c. 1993; *Jonathan Wild* (tentative), c. 1993.

Awards: *Guardian* Prize for fiction, 1979; Academy Award for best original screenplay, Academy Award nomination for best director and director's guild of America nomination, all 1993, all for *The Crying Game*.

Sidelights

I like nonsense in films," declared Irish moviemaker Neil Jordan in an article he prepared on his favorite cinematic "guilty pleasures" for *Film Comment* magazine. While Jordan's most celebrated works have hardly been nonsensical—especially tensely romantic sleeper hits like *Mona Lisa* and *The Crying Game*—they reflect his avowed impatience with realism and his predisposition toward faith and wonder. "The stories that I tell," he told Marlaine

Glicksman of *Film Comment,* "start from realistic beginnings and proceed to very unrealistic, mythological territories." Labeled "a quiet subversive" by *American Film*'s John Powers, Jordan has followed an unorthodox path, starting out as a novelist and moving into film through British television. After the surprise success of *Mona Lisa* in 1986, he came to Hollywood, made two expensive flops and nearly gave up on the movie business; he then returned to Ireland and his own methods. 1992 saw the release of *The Crying Game*, which became a smash, received a slew of Academy Award nominations—Jordan took home the statue for best original screenplay— among other laurels, and won this "subversive" another shot at Tinseltown. "I think people are starved for good films," he told Bernard Weinraub of the *New York Times.* "And when something comes along that tells a story in an intelligent way, they embrace it."

Born in Sligo, Ireland, in 1950, Jordan grew up in Dublin. "My childhood was like every other Irish kid of my generation," he recalled to Weinraub. "I was taught by priests who beat the hell out of you. Our family was kind of eccentric. The house was always full of books. It was a very strict household in a way, extremely religious. It was also very enlightened." Dublin's profound literary tradition—particularly the work of the legendary writer James Joyce—influenced his decision to write fiction and eventually to study English at University College. "I started writing when I was about fourteen," he told *Interview*. "Stories, poetry, plays. Approximations of the people I was reading at the time—Graham Greene, Dostoyevski, Yeats, Joyce. One has an urge to write at certain times." He later worked as a writer with a Dublin "fringe" theater group: "We used to write plays about social issues that affected people in Dublin at the time. We used to write children's plays, street theater, musicals." Jordan also made money as a musician in traveling bands, going up to Northern Ireland even during times of violent confrontation there; this experience informed the story of his first film, *Angel*. He married while quite young, and his marriage produced two daughters, but he and his wife ended up separating; divorce is illegal in Ireland. Jordan later had two sons with his assistant and partner Brenda Rawn.

> *"The thing I'd love most to make would be a backstage musical set in outer space."*

As a fiction writer, Jordan produced a short story collection, *A Night in Tunisia*, and the novels *The Past* and *Dream of the Beast*. In 1979 he won the *Guardian* newspaper's fiction prize. "I became quite a literary young lion," he reflected to *Interview*. Despite the acclaim and approval he received from the Dublin literary elite, however, he found the experience of "sitting alone writing" an unpleasant one. "Basically everything that I've done in a more public milieu has been to get myself away from writing fiction—an alternative and an escape from it. It just happens that movies have been the most engrossing and the most fulfilling."

He made his way into film through television. Having written some scripts, he sent one to celebrated director John Boorman, who invited Jordan to visit the set of his 1981 medieval fantasy *Excalibur*. Not wanting to be idle on the set, Jordan made a documentary about the making of Boorman's film, which was shown on TV. He also had the opportunity to share ideas with the veteran filmmaker. "John allowed me to see that films could be accessible to personal vision," he told *Interview*. Jordan showed

his script for *Angel* to Britain's Channel 4; they expressed interest and agreed to let this untested writer direct his own screenplay. Boorman acted as the film's executive producer. The story of an Irish musician who becomes embroiled in sectarian violence, the 1982 film starred Stephen Rea and was titled *Danny Boy* in the United States. Jordan told Ray Sawhill of *Interview* that the film offended almost every political and artistic constituency in Ireland.

Jordan's next project was *The Company of Wolves*, an adaptation of an Angela Carter story he co-scripted with Carter prior to her 1992 death. According to Ty Burr of *Entertainment Weekly*, the film is a "psychosexual fairy tale, a cult lulu that throws 'Little Red Riding Hood,' Freud's *Interpretation of Dreams* and one of those old Universal werewolf movies into a blender." An exploration of a young girl's feelings about her emerging sexuality, the film was, Jordan noted in his discussion with Sawhill, an attempt "to make something that would illuminate what my daughters were going into." Released in 1984, it was the first film to gain Jordan international attention; it actually made money in the United Kingdom.

Mona Lisa was Jordan's breakthrough. Co-written with David Leland, it tells the story of a petty London crook (played by Bob Hoskins, who would go on to fame in Hollywood) who falls in love with an elegant black prostitute (Cathy Tyson) in thrall to a vicious mobster (Michael Caine). Its gritty realism gives way to a deeply romantic sensibility. "What I hoped to do," Jordan explained to *American Film*, "was set up the expectation that one is watching a film noir or gangster movie and then turn it into something different: a love story. I wanted to see something on the screen with real passion in it—a man and a woman facing the dilemmas of the heart." He declared in a *Film Comment* interview that "If I have a point of view, it probably emerges more in that film than in anything else I have done." Burr of *Entertainment Weekly* noted that the writer-director's "obsession with love among the damned fits neatly within the thriller format."

Because of *Mona Lisa*—an art-house smash in the U.S.—Jordan got the opportunity to direct a big-budget Hollywood film. Setting out to make a whimsical ghost story in the tradition of such lighthearted films as *Topper*, he wrote *High Spirits*, a supernatural-romantic romp set in an Irish castle. With a cast that included Peter O'Toole, Liam Neeson, Beverly D'Angelo, and Steve Guttenberg, the project no doubt looked very good on paper. Unfortunately, Jordan was unprepared for movie-making-by-committee; having worked unhampered on his first three films, he was soon undone by studio meddling. The final cut was not his and the Tri-Star release bombed. "The people I worked with were at the grosser end of Hollywood and the independents," he told *Film Comment*. "They wanted something totally different than I did and the thing got mangled in-between. After *High Spirits*, I was almost gonna retire."

Once bitten but not sufficiently shy, Jordan made another Hollywood film, 1989's *We're No Angels*. It was the first movie he directed without having a hand in the writing; noted playwright David Mamet provided the script, a remake of a once-filmed comic fable about escaped convicts disguised as priests. Assured of cooperation from Paramount, Jordan pursued his vision—assisted by stars Robert De Niro, Sean Penn, and Demi Moore—but the film fizzled upon release. "The director's second misfire is pretty awful," Burr reflected, "but it keeps jerking intriguingly toward something funky and real." It seemed Jordan and Hollywood were mismatched, despite the filmmaker's obsession with American film of even the most disreputable sort: "The thing I'd love most to make," he told *Interview*'s Sawhill, "would be a backstage musical set in outer space."

Jordan was again tempted to give up moviemaking. "The movies were getting worse and worse, the business seemed more difficult to get anything through," he told the *New York Times* in 1993. "You looked at what was coming out: such paucity of invention. I kept thinking, 'Why not take up something more rewarding?'" His 1991 release, *The Miracle*, was funded independently, and took place in Dublin. Starring Beverly D'Angelo—whom Jordan had been dating for some time—as a Hollywood actress, the film follows two starstruck Irish teenagers who become obsessed with her true identity, among other things. *The Miracle* touches on many of Jordan's filmic obsessions, as recounted in interviews and his "guilty pleasures" article: the backstage drama, musical numbers, religious fantasy, a circus and, of course, the mystery of America. Also, its young male protagonist is a musician with a literary frame of mind.

Jordan had been tossing around a story called "Soldier's Wife" since 1983 and finally realized it could work well as a film. He rapidly transformed the tale into a screenplay and, as he told Weinraub of the *New York Times*, "the more I wrote it as a film, the more I wanted to make it." Getting financing for the picture—titled *The Crying Game* after a Dave Berry song—turned out to be difficult. The script's portrayal of IRA terrorists and transvestites didn't exactly thrill prospective financiers; producer Stephen Woolley went out on the furthest limb to secure the $5 million the film required. Stephen Rea agreed to star in the film but had to turn down other work while the precarious project faced shutdown on a regular basis. Finally, in late 1991, principal shooting took place. Investors pressured Jordan to shoot a different ending and, as he told *Entertainment Weekly*, he filmed it "just in order to show them it didn't work, so I could get permission to go back and shoot my original ending."

The Crying Game follows a reluctant and kindhearted IRA operative named Fergus (Rea) from Ireland—where he guards and then befriends Jody (Forest Whitaker), the black British soldier his group has kidnapped—to London where, as promised, he looks up Jody's beloved, Dil (Jaye Davidson), with whom he becomes infatuated. Soon his IRA comrades (Miranda Richardson and Adrian Dunbar) press him into action and he faces a choice between their cause and Dil's love. The story's primary secret—kept by critics and audiences alike with a fierce loyalty—fueled mainstream success for the film and a number of honors. Jordan was nominated for best director by the Director's Guild of America and the Academy of Motion Picture Arts and Sciences; the Academy handed Jordan the best original screenplay Oscar while the film was nominated for best picture and Rea, Richardson, and Davidson were nominated in the best actor, best supporting actress and best supporting actor categories. Critics heaped praise on the film: *People* called it an "exhilarating whirlwind of a drama," while David Ansen of *Newsweek* declared that "It leaves one giddy." *New York Times* critic Vincent Canby voiced some criticism but ultimately admired *The Crying Game*: "At times the film comes close to trash, or at least camp, but it's saved by the rare sensibility of Mr. Jordan, who isn't frivolous."

In the wake of *The Crying Game*'s success, Jordan was reportedly slated to direct the film version of Anne Rice's *Interview With a Vampire* and to be working on, among other things, *Jonathan Wild*, which he described to *Entertainment Weekly* as an "18th-Century gangster film." Whether his fortunes in Hollywood would be better this time out remained to be seen, but his faith in filmmaking appeared to have been restored for the time being. "It's such a wonderful medium," he remarked to the *New York Times*. "It's only denigrated by its practitioners."

Selected writings

A Night in Tunisia, 1979.

The Past, 1980.
Dream of the Beast, 1983.
"Neil Jordan's Guilty Pleasures," *Film Comment,* November 1992.

Sources

American Film, July 1986.
Entertainment Weekly, February 12, 1993.

Film Comment, January 1990; November 1992.
Interview, December 1989.
New York Times, September 26, 1992; January 9, 1993.
Newsweek, November 30, 1992.
People, December 14, 1992.
Time, January 25, 1993.

—Simon Glickman

Wendy Kopp

©*Mesopotamia/Bill Kelly, courtesy of Teach for America*

Education activist-entrepreneur

Born in Dallas, Texas. *Education:* Bachelor's degree from Princeton University, 1989 (majored in public policy).

Addresses: *Office*—Post office box 5114, New York, NY 10185.

Career

Founded and directs Teach for America, 1989—, an organization devoted to alleviating the teacher shortage in the United States.

Sidelights

Wendy Kopp seized on the idea when she was a senior at Princeton, during an education conference: Create a national teaching corps modeled after the Peace Corps. Recruit some of America's best and brightest college seniors and, after they graduate, send them out to teach in the nation's neediest public schools. Their enthusiasm, idealism, devotion, and brains will bolster and invigorate those schools, Kopp believed, and elevate the status of teaching as a career choice. "Back when I was in college," she told *Working Woman,* "students were incredibly active and involved in causes on their campuses. But after graduation, they went off to work on Wall Street. They never considered teaching—in part because of its downwardly mobile image."

A public-policy major, Kopp expounded on the idea in her senior thesis. Unlike most dissertations, however, this one was not tossed into a trunk to be forgotten. Kopp moved quickly. "She wandered in one day and announced she was going to organize a teachers corps, would do it in a year, and raise several million dollars," Marvin Bressler, chairman of Princeton's sociology department and Kopp's thesis adviser, told the *New York Times.* "I said, 'Listen, kid, this is obviously deranged.' But she has a kind of really compelling gentle stubbornness."

Upon graduating in the spring of 1989, Kopp founded Teach for America and set out to follow the game plan detailed in her thesis: Recruit top graduates who did not major in education and help them sidestep state licensing laws and teacher certification requirements. Run them through an eight-week crash summer course and arrange for them to teach two years in poor rural and urban schools suffering from teacher shortages. Kopp's recruits would receive the standard salary for beginning teachers, to be paid by the host school systems. By signing up, they also could delay repaying federal student loans for the two years they were in the corps.

Kopp, a Dallas native, told the *New York Times* she was unconcerned that her idealistic recruits might be unable to meet the challenges of the nation's most disadvantaged public schools. "Luckily, I don't worry all that much," she said. "I really have this attitude that things will work out. All those little obstacles that people think will stop everything—you can get around anything."

The timing of her venture was fortuitous, *U.S. News & World Report* wrote, because "a severe shortage of talented teachers is threatening to undercut attempts to improve the performance of public schools....Between now and 1997, rising enrollments combined with a wave of teacher retirements are expected to produce a need for 1.5 million new teachers—many more than the education schools are turning out." The climate was right, too: When she started Teach for America, many states were experimenting with reform programs that put unaccredited teachers in the classroom—new graduates who didn't have teaching degrees as well as professionals from other fields.

Critics have said such alternative routes to the classroom don't provide adequate training or super-

> "I really have this attitude that things will work out. All those little obstacles that people think will stop everything—you can get around anything."

vision. Some teachers' unions called them scab programs, according to *Newsweek*. As John Palmer, dean of the education school at the University of Wisconsin was quoted as saying, "We would never say because there's a shortage of doctors or engineers, 'Take a bright person, give them a few weeks of preparation and let them build bridges or perform surgery.'" In the same article Keith Geiger, president of the National Education Association, the nation's largest teachers' union, said: "I am not interested in people who go into teaching for three or four years until they grow up and see what they want to do in life."

Teach for America found far more supporters than detractors, however. Around January of 1990, Kopp's crew started recruiting at 100 leading colleges and universities. They appealed to students' idealism and strived for an aura of selectivity which, Kopp believed, would help reverse the teaching profession's reputation as a low-prestige career. "Part of the reason people apply to the Peace Corps is

because they know it's selective," she told *U.S. News & World Report*. "In order to attract people with the most career opportunities, we have to compete with graduate schools, investment banking and management consulting, which offer prestige and a high profile."

Students responded immediately. In the first few months, Teach for America received 2,500 applications. The applicants endured a rigorous interview process and were required to conduct 15-minute teaching demonstrations. Meanwhile, Kopp persuaded schools to hire her recruits for the 1990-91 academic year. Five hundred seniors were chosen, trained, and sent to schools in Los Angeles, New York City, New Orleans and Baton Rouge, Louisiana, and rural Georgia and North Carolina.

Getting Teach for America off the ground, however, required more than good timing, the right social climate, and adventurous, public-spirited college grads. It also required money. And fund-raising has been Kopp's most phenomenal success. Soon after completing her senior thesis at Princeton, Kopp distilled it into a 30-page prospectus which she sent to 30 CEOs at randomly selected leading companies. When writing to corporations and foundations, "my age was impossible to ignore, [so I] mentioned it in the very first sentence," Kopp told *Working Woman*. "Some people thought I was crazy, but it was an eye stopper, and in a few cases it opened doors. If I had one thing going for me, it was that I understood the mindset of the people we were trying to attract: college seniors. I'm sure several companies invited me to make a presentation simply because they were curious."

The day after she graduated, the Mobil Foundation came through with $26,000 in seed money which allowed Kopp to visit school districts, corporations and foundations. About the same time, Union Carbide donated Manhattan office space for Teach for America's headquarters. "So that summer I moved to New York and talked to everyone who would listen," Kopp told *Working Woman*. "I set up appointments with corporate executives, foundation heads, and educators....Back at the office I wrote 100 letters a week—some just to update companies that had turned us down."

Soon, Chrysler, the Merck Company, and the Starr Foundation each donated $100,000. Xerox also signed on during Teach for America's early months. In September, a few months after she graduated, Kopp began assembling a staff of other recent grads. In just over a year, she raised more than $1 million for Teach for America's administrative costs and summer training institute. Robin Hogen, vice president of the Merck Company Foundation, told *U.S. News & World Report* that Kopp was "disarmingly effective" at eliciting corporate support and her idea deserved funding. "It's the kind of radical high-risk, high-reward thinking that's needed to begin to turn around the crisis in public education," Hogen said. Kopp also recruited an advisory board made up of business leaders, politicians and prominent educators. Another panel developed the training institute for the corps' teaching prospects.

Once Teach for America was operating—not existing merely as an idea—it was easier to solicit money. "With big names on her masthead and confidence that school officials would hire the people she proposed to send them," wrote the *New York Times*, "Kopp was able to secure larger grants. As more companies gave money, she returned to those who had earlier rejected her because of her lack of a track record."

By 1992 Teach for America had 1,200 teachers working in seven states and had raised more than $12 million from about 200 corporations—including $3 million from Philip Morris, according to *Working Woman*. "I think what sold Philip Morris was the same thing that has won over a lot of other companies: We have a clear vision of what we are trying to accomplish, and we have a track record," Kopp told *Working Woman*. "It also pays to write letters. I was reminded of that one day when the program was almost two years old. The phone rang in my office and the secretary said the call was from Ross Perot.... Apparently, he had taken an interest in one of the many letters I had sent him and was calling to invite me to meet with him in Dallas the following week to talk about what he could do to help us. The result was a $500,000 check."

Kopp told the *New York Times* that her abilities in the business world developed during four years with the Foundation for Student Communication at Princeton. The organization publishes *Business Today* magazine and conducts a yearly conference between students and business leaders. In Kopp's four years at the foundation—she was president during her senior year—its budget grew fivefold to $1.5 million, and she met dozens of corporate executives. "Everything I do is based on that experience," she told the *New York Times*. "It taught me a lot about how to strategize and how to manage people. I realized there's an incredible amount of money in the world and people are looking for good things to support, and if you can just get in the door you can have a good chance of making it fly."

There have been snags along the way, however. "Corps members sent to New Orleans arrived in the middle of a teachers' strike. Those in New York nearly lost their jobs in January because of a city-wide budget crunch," wrote the *Economist*. "Some Los Angeles recruits had trouble getting paid."

School administrators cited deficiencies in some recruits' teaching methods but gave them high marks for enthusiasm and energy, the *New York Times* related. Some Teach for America teachers said the training they received did not prepare them for the harsh realities of the classroom. Overall, however, "organizers can point to many successes," according to the *Economist*. "The corps has been well-received in schools, and members have filled newsletters with stories of their 'tough-but-worthwhile' experiences. The program's attrition rate of 11 percent is slightly higher than average for first-year teachers, but is still impressive because the posts were unusually tough."

Wendy Kopp, it seems, has made Teach for America fly.

Sources

Forbes, October 14, 1991.
Fortune, Spring 1990 (education issue).
New Republic, December 16, 1991.
Newsweek, July 16, 1990; October 1, 1990.
New York Times, December 5, 1990; June 20, 1990.
People, December 31, 1990.
U.S. News & World Report, January 29, 1990.
Working Woman, June 1992.
World Monitor, November 1992.

—David Wilkins

Denis Leary

Comedian

Born in 1958; grew up in Worcester, MA; father worked as an auto mechanic, mother as a homemaker; married Ann Lembeck; children: Jack, Devin (daughter). *Education:* Emerson College, B.A., 1979.

Career

Worked as a comic in local clubs in Boston and New York since 1979; featured in comedy show *Paramount City,* produced in London in 1990; writer and actor in one-man comedy show *No Cure for Cancer,* opening in Edinburgh, Scotland, in 1991 (show was also produced as a book, cable television special, and album); has made commercials for MTV and Nike on NBC since 1992; appeared in three movies since 1993: *National Lampoon's Loaded Weapon 1, The Sandlot,* and *Gunmen.*

Sidelights

As part of his stand-up routine, comedian Denis Leary tells his audience, "I think you hear me knockin'. And I think I'm comin' in." For this comic of the '90s, whose slicked blonde hair, scuffed leather jacket, and voice like gravel have become trademarks, the door to success has recently been flung wide open. His searing humor and vulgar language push the boundaries of irreverence, often cutting through politically sensitive issues. John Leland of *Newsweek* called him "topical but twisted, like Lenny Bruce in the way-fast lane." Though Leary has earned the nickname "Denis the Menace,"

with his chain smoking and "speed ranting" on stage, he claims to be, in real life, a milder version of the persona he presents to his audience. "[My act] is really just an exaggeration of what I think and how I say it," he told Leland. "The anger is real."

Leary's rough edges and tough stage persona came, in part, from growing up in Worcester, Massachusetts, which he described to Hilary Sterne of *GQ* as a "dank, polluted, angst-ridden city filled with factories and friction." He grew up in an Irish-Catholic family, and in his youth, Leary was first an altar boy and then a Catholic-school renegade. "By the time I was thirteen, I knew I didn't believe the stuff they were telling us," he recalled to Christopher Farley in *Time.* "That was part of the fun of it, getting caught doing stuff you weren't supposed to be doing." At St. Peale's High School in Worcester, Leary played hockey and tried out his off-beat humor on his classmates.

At Emerson College in Boston, Leary majored in English and helped found the Emerson Comedy Workshop. After graduation in 1979, he played in local clubs and taught classes at Emerson in comedy, acting, and scriptwriting. He also took odd jobs—as a delivery-truck driver and a mixer at a sulfuric-acid plant—which he thought would make for good stories. "Leary really inspired me," comic Anthony Clark, who graduated from Emerson in 1986, told Farley. "You'd see comics doing all the safe stuff—stewardesses, Gilligan's Island, socks in the drawer—that's all *garbage!* Leary was always up front, on the edge, even when the club managers wanted to limit his time 'cause he was so raw."

More than anything after college, Leary wanted work as an actor. But acting jobs were scarce in Boston, and since comedy was familiar to him, he figured that if he developed a five-minute act, he would get some stage time. Comedian Colin Quinn, who played the Paper Moon Club with him, joked in *GQ* that Leary's early material "wasn't as insightful as the stuff he does now . . . . He had this one Bill Buckner joke he'd stretch out for about an hour and twenty minutes." Eddie Brill, who graduated from Emerson in 1980, agreed that his friend's start in comedy was not as auspicious as it might have been. "When Leary first started doing stand-up," he told Farley, "like all of us—he sucked." Life began to change for Leary when his father died of a sudden heart attack on his sixtieth birthday in 1985. In response to such an event, noted Brill in the same source, "you can either go into a fetal position or do what Leary did—just lash out. He became really deep and funny."

Leary's decision to move to New York in 1987 showed a new seriousness about his chosen profession. He acknowledged that both his father's death and the loss of other friends to drug overdoses added a new dimension to his outlook on life and presentation of it to an audience. "That's when the whole mortality thing hit me in the head," he told *New York.* "AIDS, the ozone—it's a funny world, right?" In 1990, Leary and his wife, Ann, who was six months pregnant at the time, flew to England to tape an episode of a comedy show called *Paramount City.* On the day of the taping, Ann went into premature labor, and, with the complications that followed, Leary found himself in London for five additional months. When it was suggested that he get involved in the Edinburgh International Arts Festival, which comics Eric Bogosian and John Cleese had both played, Leary fine-tuned his own style: "Somewhere between Eric Bogosian's on-the-edge character monologues and Spalding Gray's finely detailed reminiscence," he explained to *GQ,* "I thought there was room for something that combined elements of both. A first-person piece that went over the edge."

His efforts resulted in a one-man comedy show called *No Cure for Cancer,* which opened in Edinburgh and was sold out by its second day. Leary took

it back to New York, where it had a sold-out run at the Actor's Playhouse. *GQ* described the show—which came out as a book in November of 1992 and as a Showtime cable special in January of 1993—as "a kind of speaker-blowing anthem to politically and socially incorrect behavior." In *No Cure for Cancer,* Leary uses dark humor to poke fun at the pretensions of 1990s society and pop culture, professing his own love of smoking cigarettes and eating red meat. He satirizes what he calls our "self-help escalator" and claims to "want it all," even a Patriot missile launcher and Michael Jackson's original nose mounted on a plaque and hung in his living room. While *Publishers Weekly* observed that *No Cure for Cancer* allows Leary's "energy and wit shine through," it also noted that he sometimes goes too far—for example, when he muses in regard to Teddy Kennedy that "we always shoot all the wrong guys" and suggests that the family pet can make a great meal when one is stranded.

It was this kind of raw humor, however, that caught the attention of MTV director Ted Demme, who told Farley that "Leary's the kind of guy that's saying all the things you're afraid to talk about and think." Demme approached him to do commercials for MTV in 1992, and in his sixty seconds of air time, Leary not only manages to plug the network but insult its stars and audience at the same time. It was also around this time that he was approached to do commercials for Nike, maker of pricey athletic shoes and clothing. Such appearances have earned Leary instant fame and new opportunities. Joe Pytka, who directed the Nike spots, told Sterne that Leary is "like early Richard Pryor in that his humor is just so apt and perceptive. It's not stuff about his wife and all that; he's really talking about the human experience. A lot of in-your-face comics just use technique alone. Denis's stuff has the content to go with it."

Riding on the wave of his stage and television success, Leary now wants to focus on making movies. He has gotten roles in three new movies: playing a lounge singer in *National Lampoon's Loaded Weapon 1,* a father in the baseball comedy *The Sandlot,* and a street tough in the action drama *Gunmen.* His comic routine on the show *MTV Unplugged* aired recently, and he is also working on a more personal off-Broadway show called *Birth, School Work, Death* and a pilot for an MTV series called *Hellhole.* But Leary takes his fame and numerous career prospects with typical stoicism, and could not stop himself from imagining the worst scenario for his future in the business. "Hey, who knows?" he exclaimed to Sterne. "Maybe I'll be doing Taco Bell commercials in three years."

Sources

GQ, November 1992.
Newsweek, October 5, 1992.
New York, September 28, 1992.
Publishers Weekly, September 28, 1992.
Time, March 1, 1993.

—Carolyn C. March

Living Colour

Rock band

Members are Vernon Reid (guitar), born c. 1958 in London, England; Corey Glover (vocals); Muzz Skillings (bass), born c. 1964; and William Calhoun (drums); Skillings replaced by Doug Wimbish, 1992.

Addresses: *Record company*—Epic Records, 666 Fifth Ave., P.O. Box 4455, New York, NY 10101. *Other*—Black Rock Coalition, P.O. Box 1054, Cooper Station, New York, NY 10276.

Career

Reid played guitar with bands the Decoding Society and Defunkt; Glover did acting work in films and commercials; Skillings and Calhoun worked as session musicians; band played on New York City club and college circuit, signed with Epic Records, 1987, released first album, 1988.

Awards: Grammy for best hard-rock performance for "Cult of Personality," 1989; MTV Video Music Award for best new artist, 1989.

Sidelights

The New York rock and roll band Living Colour, with its hard-hitting songs and expert musicianship, had all the ingredients for success when it first approached the music industry. Yet record labels didn't know what to do with the band, for the simple reason that all four of its members were black. Despite music-business stereotyping, Living Colour proceeded to banish all doubt with their 1988 debut

album *Vivid*, which went gold, and their 1990 follow-up *Time's Up*, spearheading a wave of eclectic and critically acclaimed bands who challenged racial conventions.

Guitarist Vernon Reid, who started the band in 1985, struggled for years to realize his dream of an all-black, all-rock band. An early inspiration was rock guitar giant Jimi Hendrix, whose trailblazing songs remain some of the most popular music of the late sixties. For Reid, Hendrix provided an example of a black musician fusing traditionally black forms like the blues with psychedelia and other new styles. Yet the popular tendency to deemphasize Hendrix's blackness frustrated Reid. When he was in high school, Reid told Charles Shaar Murray, author of the book *Crosstown Traffic: Jimi Hendrix and the Rock 'n' Roll Revolution*, that he heard a white Florida deejay say "that Hendrix was black, but the music didn't sound very black to him [the DJ].... and I flipped out. At the time I was very culturally aware of the race issues because of [black activists] Martin Luther King [Jr.] and Malcolm X and all the ferment that was happening in the Black Power movement. I didn't really connect it all so much with *music*, but that really threw it in my face. It was a phone-in show, and I spent all night trying to call in. I fell asleep with the phone in my hand." This early incident focused Reid's attention on the attitudes he would eventually change.

Reid was born in London, England, to West Indian parents and raised in Brooklyn, New York. He assembled the first version of his band in 1983, while still playing with drummer Ronald Shannon Jackson's jazz-fusion band The Decoding Society. Several different musicians played with early incarnations of the band, which would be named Living Colour in 1986, including jazz pianist Geri Allen. Reid met vocalist Corey Glover at a party during this period, and their common interests led them to collaborate. Reid left The Decoding Society in 1985 with the determination to form what *Rolling Stone*'s David Fricke termed "a full-tilt *rock* band celebrating the continuing vitality and enduring promise of Robert Johnson, Billie Holiday, Bo Diddley, Sly Stone, Ornette Coleman, and Bad Brains (to name but a few), with the muscle and volume of Led Zeppelin."

That same year Reid co-founded the Black Rock Coalition (BRC), an organization designed to support African-American musicians hoping to break out of the straitjacket of "black" and "white" music categories. By 1990 the organization had a membership of 175 individuals and 30 bands, though Living Colour was the first to achieve mainstream success.

At a BRC meeting Reid met bassist Muzz Skillings, and soon thereafter ran into drummer Will Calhoun, who was playing for Harry Belafonte at the time. Glover left the band briefly to act in the film *Platoon*,

and singer Mark Ledford fronted the band for its appearance at the Moers Jazz Festival in Europe in 1986. When Glover returned, the band played club dates in the New York area in 1987 and 1988.

Mick Jagger, lead singer of the pioneering British rock band The Rolling Stones, heard Living Colour at a club date and was sufficiently impressed to produce two songs for the band, "Glamour Boys" and "Which Way to America." The songs served as demos that helped them secure a record deal with the Epic label and were remixed for the LP *Vivid*, which was released in 1988. The album was slow to take off, and the first video, "Middle Man," aired only scantily on MTV. The second video, for the song "Cult of Personality," marked a breakthrough for the band, inspiring heavy radio airplay and increased record sales.

The video for "Cult," a metallic rock tune with lyrics about blind obedience to leaders, featured film clips of politicians as diverse as Italian fascist Benito Mussolini and U.S. president John F. Kennedy, interspersed with energetic footage of the band onstage. Other songs from *Vivid* that fared well on radio and MTV were "Glamour Boys," which, like

"Cult," became a Top 40 hit, "Open Letter (to a Landlord)," and "Funny Vibe," a song about racism which included a guest appearance by the rap group Public Enemy (see *Newsmakers 92*). The LP went gold, then double platinum. Living Colour won a 1989 Grammy for "Cult," and numerous trophies at the MTV Video Music Awards, among them best new artist. *Rolling Stone*'s Alan Light referred to *Vivid* as 'one of the most promising—and with over one and a half million copies sold, one of the most successful—rookie efforts in years." Reid's band had answered industry concern that, in Fricke's words, "black rock was a contradiction in terms."

Shortly thereafter, Jagger invited the band to join the Rolling Stones on their 1989 *Steel Wheels* tour. Backstage after one of these shows, Living Colour was approached by Little Richard, one of the first black rock and roll artists to gain mainstream success in the fifties. "Hi!" Richard greeted the band. "I'm one of those glamour boys you been singin' about!" For the band, Richard's encouragement was stunning and uplifting. "That was *the* moment," Reid told Fricke. "Having Little Richard say 'You guys are doing the right thing'—if I needed validation, that's it."

Little Richard subsequently contributed a rap to the song "Elvis is Dead" on the band's next album, *Time's Up*. This song both ridiculed the host of "Elvis sightings" publicized in tabloid newspapers and reminded listeners that Elvis was a white singer making use of a black musical tradition. The song also featured a saxophone solo by former James Brown sideman Maceo Parker. A host of other noted musicians contributed to the LP, including rappers Queen Latifah (see *Newsmakers 92*) and Doug E. Fresh. The album's first single, "Type," made the Top Ten with radio airplay, and its video fared well on MTV. Epic shipped 400,000 copies of the album to stores initially, and within a week the company was taking reorders. *Time's Up* entered *Billboard*'s album chart at Number 82, and reached the Top 20 the next week.

The second LP was, as Reid remarked to *Interview*'s Charlie Ahearn, "a few steps removed from where we were when we did *Vivid*." Indeed, *Time's Up* explored a wide range of musical styles, including rap, soul, and African "High Life" music, and also included spoken-word passages about black experience on "History Lesson" by noted actors Ossie Davis, Ruby Dee, and James Earl Jones. Among the subjects treated in the lyrics were sexuality in the age of AIDS, information technology, and the motivations of drug dealers. According to *Rolling Stone*'s

Light, the album "represents the fulfillment of the band's promise.... The challenge of a second record is to avoid formula, and this spectacular album is a tribute to Living Colour's bravery." *Time's Up* was voted one of the best albums of the year in a *Rolling Stone* readers' poll, and Living Colour was voted among the best bands.

In 1991 Living Colour joined the massive Lollapalooza concert tour, along with such diverse performers as hard rockers Jane's Addiction (now defunct; see *Newsmakers 92* for sketch on frontman Perry Farrell), rapper Ice-T (also in *Newsmakers 92*), and punk mischief-makers The Butthole Surfers. At the outset of the tour, the band released and EP, *Biscuits*, which included covers of Hendrix's "Burning of the Midnight Lamp," soul great Al Green's "Love and Happiness," and James Brown's "Talkin' Loud and Saying Nothing," as well as an outtake from *Time's Up*, "Money Talks," and two live tracks. Yet *Entertainment Weekly*'s David Brown called the record "overambitious...Living Colour may indeed be the successors to Hendrix and [James] Brown, but they need to make their biscuits with a simpler recipe." (The tunes, however—"Talkin' Loud and Saying Nothing" in particular—became immensely popular.)

Such criticisms still acknowledge Living Colour as the fulfillment of Vernon Reid's ambitions: a successful modern black rock group with a solid connection to a black rock tradition. After years of frustration, the band Living Colour has become a rock heavyweight.

Selected discography

Vivid (includes "The Cult of Personality," "Glamour Boys," "Open Letter (to a Landlord)," "Middle Man," "Funny Vibe," and "Which Way to America"), Epic, 1988.
Time's Up (includes "Type" and "Elvis is Dead"), Epic, 1990.
Biscuits (EP; includes "Burning of the Midnight Lamp," "Love and Happiness," "Talkin' Loud and Saying Nothing," and "Money Talks"), Epic, 1991.
Stain, Epic, 1993.

Sources

Books

Murray, Charles Shaar, *Crosstown Traffic: Jimi Hendrix and the Rock 'n' Roll Revolution*, St. Martin's Press, 1989.

Periodicals

Down Beat, October 1990.
Entertainment Weekly, July 19, 1991.
Interview, September 1990.
Rolling Stone, September 6, 1990; November 1, 1990;
    December 13-27, 1990; March 7, 1991.

                          —Simon Glickman

Marky Mark

AP/Wide World Photos

Rap performer

Born Mark Wahlberg, June 5, 1971; youngest of nine children of Alma and Donald Wahlberg (now divorced); raised in Dorchester, a suburb of Boston, MA.

Addresses: *Home*—Near Boston, MA.

Career

Leader of Marky Mark & The Funky Bunch rap music group, 1990—; has released two albums, *Music for the People* and *You Gotta Believe*. Has also modeled for designer Calvin Klein's underwear ads.

Sidelights

Rap star Marky Mark Wahlberg's baby-face and bulging muscles are showing up everywhere. Fans can catch his musical routine on MTV, his peek-a-boo underwear in moody magazine ads, and his highly publicized appearances in Boston courtrooms on assault charges. He may travel by limousine to concerts and engagements, but he hasn't lost the tough edge honed on the rough streets of his hometown, Dorchester.

Mark's rise began on the shirttail of big brother, Donnie Wahlberg, one of the celebrated songsters of the teen heartthrob pop group, New Kids On The Block (see *Newsmakers 91*). After a brief stint with the New Kids, he quit, but made his comeback in 1990 as Marky Mark and the Funky Bunch to concentrate on issue-oriented rap music. New Kid Donnie still keeps tabs on his youngest brother by offering advice,

helping to produce Mark's albums, and even writing much of his younger brother's music. "Everything that I do, I always talk to my brother about, and the same with him," Mark told *YM*. "With him and me, it's cool."

While the New Kids On The Block's style and product were mostly wholesome, squeaky-clean, boy-next-door stuff, the younger Wahlberg's image reflects the mean streets of his youth. His raps touch on a life scratched out around the perils of gang violence, the drug scene, and day-to-day survival of the fittest. His first album, *Music for the People*, went platinum, with three dance tune rap singles hitting *Billboard*'s Top 10: "Good Vibrations," "Wildside," and "I Need Money." "I'm a positive person," Marky Mark told *TV Guide*, "and if I can give a positive outlook to people who, like me, grew up without many opportunities, then that's a great accomplishment."

Album number two, *You Gotta Believe*, offered more message and less dance music. It hasn't been quite as successful as its predecessor, but Mark considers it a necessary next step in his self-expression. "[*You Gotta Believe*] just deals with all of the accusations and the misconceptions of Marky Mark, you know," he told *Teen Machine*. "A lot of people kind of say, 'Well, the single's not doing that well,' but it's a hit to me because it's out there and people who normally wouldn't have heard a 'Good Vibrations' type of record are hearing Marky Mark and they're hearing where I'm coming from. And, you know, if I have to slow things down for a few months to make my point, then I will."

Slowing down, he's not. In a two-month period his Funky Bunch hit stages in Japan, France, New York, London and San Francisco. Teen magazine covers aren't complete without Mark's mug, and paparazzi dog his every step. Hordes of fans lined up for autographed copies of his photo-biography, *Marky Mark*, by Lynn Goldsmith. The marketing machine that made big business out of New Kids On The Block is hard at work on the next Wahlberg.

Mark gives a good concert, if the hordes of screaming teenagers who scrap for tickets are any indication. The highlight of his high-energy performance comes when he rips off his shirt and drops his pants to reveal boxer shorts and his pumped-up body. Mark started bodybuilding when he quit smoking, around 1991. He makes a point of scheduling workouts even while touring. "If I don't go to the gym, I'll be crazy all day," he told *People*. "Weight lifting is the only time to let my frustrations out. And the cuties love it!" The "cuties" include preteen girls, older women, and gay men. This may seem a tough line to walk without offending someone, but Mark is trying. He's made his own heterosexual preference plain, but has begun to accept engagements in gay clubs. In his trademark fashion statement, Mark wears oversized, beltless jeans which dip strategically to reveal the designer label on his Calvin Klein briefs. Never one to miss a marketing maneuver, Klein promptly signed the young rapper to model in the designer's tony magazine and television ads. The *Wall Street Journal* reported that sales of Klein's underwear line promptly rose 34 percent.

Mark views modeling as a method to reach another audience with his music, rather than a new career move. "I'm not a Calvin Klein model. I didn't model for Calvin Klein," Mark told *Super Stars*. "They shot me, you know, we did a photo shoot with [photographer] Herb Ritts [see *Newsmakers 92*] the way I would normally wear my jeans and my underwear. That's the way the whole deal was set. It was like, I'm not gonna go and put on tight jeans and do all this stuff, because that's not me and that's not gonna tie in with my rapper image. But if you want to show the way I've been wearing his underwear and jeans and stuff like that, then fine, as long as I have full approval of the photos and the video footage!" Mark's public

presence has turned controversial on occasion, and detractors point out his "positive outlook" has been somewhat selective.

In 1986 he was in trouble for taunting and throwing rocks at black elementary school children, and in 1988 he spent 45 days in jail for assaulting two Vietnamese men while attempting to steal their case of beer. In 1992 he broke the jaw of a security guard in a fight at a public tennis court near his old Dorchester neighborhood, and in February of 1993 he appeared on a British television show in which reggae singer Shabba Ranks made anti-gay statements. The rapper was deluged with criticism from the Committee Against Anti-Asian Violence, and the Gay & Lesbian Alliance Against Defamation. Mark responded by agreeing to appear in public service advertisements against bias crimes and issued a public statement, "I denounce racial violence of all kinds."

Mark quit school at age 16, and admits that hanging out on street corners led to his legal troubles. Now he is working for his high school equivalency diploma with typical intensity. "I've learned a lot in the past year, but school is still a priority for me," he told *YM*, "and that's why I'm going back to get my GED [General Equivalency Diploma]. I got all my tests done except science. Science, boy, I'm terrified of science but I will pass, because I want it, and I'll work hard for it, you know what I'm saying? I'm gonna have my diploma. Then, when I need to learn more about business and the real world, I can go and take a course."

This may be good planning, since the future of rap music is questionable. "I hope maybe that I'll be able to do other things. Maybe do educational films," he told Lisa Schwarzbaum in an *Entertainment Weekly* interview. "I'm lookin' at possibly doin' somethin' that can be helpful. Somethin' that would suit me. Somethin' that fits or that deals with somethin' I can really relate to. I think that would be cool."

Selected discography

Music for the People (contains "Good Vibrations," "Wildside," and "I Need Money"), 1991.
You Gotta Believe, 1992.

Sources

Entertainment Weekly, January 15, 1993.
New York Times, February 18, 1993.
People, July 27, 1992; March 1, 1993.
Super Stars, May 1993.

Teen Machine, May 1993.
TV Guide, March 28, 1992.
Wall Street Journal, January 15, 1993.
YM, February 1993.

—Sharon Rose

Terence McKenna

Photograph by Kathleen T. Carr

New Age lecturer and author

Grew up in Colorado; married wife, Kat, in 1977 (divorced). children: Finn. *Education*: University of California at Berkeley, B.S., c. 1968.

Career

Has written several books and given numerous lectures on the psychedelics movement since the late 1970s; created Timewave workshop at Esalen Institute in Big Sur, CA; collaborated with brother Dennis on *True Hallucinations*, 1971, and with brother Brian on Canadian documentary *The Killing Ground*, 1988.

Sidelights

For Terence McKenna, it is no small claim to be the prophet of the coming psychedelic revolution. He believes that much of the discontent in our current society can be traced to a loss of contact with plants and other natural products, called psychedelics, that are capable of producing hallucinations in users. In recent years, McKenna has written several books detailing his theories, the title of one indicating his expansive but connected interests: *The Archaic Revival: Speculations on Psychedelic Mushrooms, the Amazon, Virtual Reality, UFOs, Evolution, Shamanism, the Rebirth of the Goddess, and the End of History*. A regular on the spiritualist/new-age lecture circuit, he has gathered a substantial following, catching, as Mark Jacobson of *Esquire* put it, "a tiny but unmistakable culture wrinkle and . . . riding with it."

In another of his books, *Food of the Gods: The Search for the Original Tree of Knowledge—A Radical History of Plants, Drugs, and Human Evolution*, McKenna asserts that psilocybin, the psychoactive component in the *stropharia cubensis* mushroom, is the missing link in the evolution of human consciousness, at one time enhancing brain development when eaten by humans. He suggests, according to Richard Restak of the *Washington Post*, that the use of natural psychedelic compounds originated in partnership societies where "social relations are primarily based on the principle of linking rather than ranking." Eventually, these cooperative societies were replaced by "dominator" societies such as our present one, where "male dominance and a social economy based on rape and plunder" emerged. With this shift from a partnership culture to a hierarchical dominator culture, psychedelic plants could no longer be tolerated: "In short, encounters with psychedelic plants throw into question the entire world view of the dominator culture."

But even with his own extensive experiments with mushrooms and other hallucinogenic plants, McKenna maintains that the psychedelic position does not condone recreational drug use and would like to reconsider the term "drug" to describe psychedelics. "The . . . behavior of the dope fiend . . . plays into the hands of the power structure, which, as we all know, is behind the coke-and-smack trafficking to begin with," he told Jacobson. "To combat this manipulation, synthetic drugs of all types must be banished from the pharmacopoeia." With this distinction between synthetic drugs and hallucinogenic plants, McKenna's attitude toward LSD and its derivatives is more complex. While he recognizes the role of LSD in opening perceptual doors during the 1960s, he criticizes the "better living through chemistry" ethic that he attributes to LSD users who participate in the current science cult. For him, psychedelics, such as psilocybin mushrooms, DMT (Dimethyltryptamine), and the South American brew ayahuasca, should be the focus. He described them, according to Jacobson, as "Gaian information centers capable of imparting the most necessary global news."

McKenna grew up in the 1950s in a remote Colorado town, with brothers Brian and Dennis. "I've always gravitated to the patently weird," he told Jacobson, recalling his love of the Book of Knowledge, *Weird Tales*, and creature features. As a teenager, he read Carl Jung's *Psychology and Alchemy* and memorized large passages from the novels of James Joyce. He might have pursued an academic career if his life and interests hadn't shifted dramatically in college in Berkeley, California, during the 1960s. It was there that he first encountered LSD, which, he told Jacobson, "would set my course." He figures that he took LSD at least 150 times while in college, qualifying this assertion to Jacobson with "not a lot."

While McKenna has been dubbed the Timothy Leary of the '90s, both by his followers and by Leary himself, he asserts that he never sought this distinction—it just evolved that way. After graduation from Berkeley, he and his wife, Kat, whom he met during his "opium-and-cabalist" phase in Jerusalem, moved with their two children to Occidental, a small town north of San Francisco. McKenna and Kat had secured a parcel of land on the big island of Hawaii, where they established Botanical Dimensions, a garden/farm dedicated to the collection of tropical medicinal plants, most of which were endangered by habitat destruction. There was little profit in this prospect, however, so McKenna decided to see if he could earn a living from his interest in psilocybin mushrooms. His consumption of these mushrooms, he joked to Jacobson, "turbo-charged [my] innate Irish ability to rave and turned [me] into a mouthpiece for the incarnate Logos."

It was in the late 1970s that McKenna gave his first talks on mushrooms at Berkeley. With Kat, he later formed a company called Lux Natura, which circulat-

ed tapes of his lectures and disseminated spores guaranteed to grow magic mushrooms. Joining such seasoned practitioners as Robert Anton Wilson and John Lilly, he gained popularity, and his lectures were broadcast on underground radio stations. McKenna eventually made it to what Jacobson referred to as "the new-age equivalent of a Catskill comic's big room" and now runs a week-long workshop called Timewave at the Esalen Institute in California's Big Sur, for which people pay over $700 to attend. It is common for him to receive messages of love and encouragement on his answering machine from unknown supporters, and for strangers to approach him with long narratives of their drug experiences.

His numerous other projects have enabled McKenna to collaborate with each of his brothers. With his brother Dennis, for instance, he wrote *True Hallucinations*, an epic account of their journey to the Amazon in 1971 to search for the mythical shamanistic drug of the Witoto tribe, called oo-koo-he. In 1988 McKenna teamed up with his brother Brian to produce *The Killing Ground*, a two-hour documentary that looks at World War I from a Canadian perspective. Directed by Brian McKenna, and including on-site interviews conducted by Terence, *The Killing Ground* highlights the fact that more than 60,000 Canadian soldiers were killed in the war, about 14,000 more than the United States lost in Vietnam. As *Maclean's* writer John Bemrose noted, "What gives the film its emotional impact is the dramatized sections in which actors, dressed in army uniforms, speak the thoughts of individual soldiers.... Their testimonies bring the Great War down to the poignant and comprehensible level of individuals who knew their chances of surviving were slim."

But McKenna is not without his critics, people who doubt his legitimacy and believe that the legalization of psychedelics, which is his ultimate goal, would only worsen the problems of society. Restak wondered if McKenna would "like to be on a plane piloted by a captain convinced that peyote enhances his visual acuity" and Jacobson asked himself, "[Is] he a sweet-throated trickster, a reckless thrill seeker? Or an honest Magellan of the mind, a trustworthy, if slightly gone, visionary?" McKenna seems sincere, however, not wanting to incite fear and disgust in people, only action. His divorce from Kat after 16 years of marriage, and watching his children grow up, have underscored for him the importance of human relationships. As Restak put it, "Perhaps what is needed . . . is a society more tolerant of people like McKenna who possess the skills and the stability to travel to the chemical outbacks of the psyche and return to speak about their marvelous encounters and the wisdom they have gained." Terence McKenna, with characteristic humbleness, would have to agree.

Selected writings

Food of the Gods: The Search for the Original Tree of Knowledge—A Radical History of Plants, Drugs, and Human Evolution, Bantam, 1992.
The Archaic Revival: Speculations on Psychedelic Mushrooms, the Amazon, Virtual Reality, UFOs, Evolution, Shamanism, the Rebirth of the Goddess, and the End of History, Harper, 1992.

Sources

Esquire, June 1992.
Library Journal, February 15, 1992.
Maclean's, November 7, 1988.
Publishers Weekly, April 20, 1992.
Washington Post, March 22, 1992.

—*Carolyn C. March*

LeRoy Neiman

AP/Wide World Photos

Painter and printmaker

Born June 8, 1927, in St. Paul, MN; son of Charles and Lydia (Serline) Runquist; married Janet Byrne, June 22, 1957. *Education:* Attended School of Art Institute of Chicago, 1946-50; University of Illinois, 1951; DePaul University, 1951.

Addresses: *Office*—c/o Hammer Galleries, 1 West 67th St., New York, NY 10023.

Career

Instructor at School of Art Institute of Chicago, 1950-60; associated with Saugatuck (MI) Summer School, 1957-58, 1963, and School of Arts and Crafts, Winston-Salem, NC, 1963; instructor of painting, Atlanta Youth Council, 1968-69; printmaker-graphic artist, 1971—; artist at the 1972 Olympics for ABC-TV, Munich, Germany; official artist of the 1976 Olympics for ABC-TV, Montreal, Canada; also artist for the 1980 and 1984 Olympics; computer artist for CBS-TV (Super Bowl), New Orleans, LA, 1978; official artist for the Goodwill Games, CNN-TV, Moscow, USSR (now Russia), 1986.

Exhibited at one-man shows at Oehlshlaeger Gallery, Chicago, IL, 1959, 1961; O'Hana Gallery, London, England, 1962; Gallerie O. Bosc, Paris, France, 1962; Hammer Gallery, New York, NY, throughout the 1960s, 70s, and 80s; Huntington-Hartford Gallery of Modern Art, New York, NY, 1967; Heath Gallery, Atlanta, GA, 1969; Abbey Theatre, Dublin, Ireland, 1970; Museo de Bellas Artes, Caracas, Venezuela, 1972; Indianapolis Institute of Arts, IN, 1972; Hermitage Museum, Leningrad, USSR (now Russia),

1974; Tobu Gallery, Tokyo, Japan, 1974; Springfield (MA) Museum of Fine Arts, 1974, 1984; Minnesota Museum of Art, St. Paul, MN (retrospective), 1975; Knoedler Gallery, London, England, 1976; Casa gratica, Helsinki, Finland, 1977; Renee Victor, Stockholm, Sweden, 1977; Meredith Long Galleries, Houston, TX (retrospective), 1978; Oklahoma Art Center, Oklahoma City, OK, 1981; Harrod's, London, England, 1982; Hanae Mori Gallery, Tokyo, Japan (retrospective), 1988; New State Tretyakov Museum (retrospective), 1988; Butler Institute, Youngstown, OH, 1990.

Work represented in the permanent collections of Minneapolis Institute of Arts; Illinois State Museum, Springfield; Joslyn Museum, Omaha, NE; Wodham Collection, Oxford, England; National Art Museum of Sport, New York, NY; Museo De Ballas Artes, Caracas, Venezuela; Hermitage Museum, Leningrad, USSR (now Russia); Indianapolis (IN) Institute of Arts; University of Illinois; Baltimore (MD) Museum of Fine Art; The Armand Hammer Collection, Los Angeles, CA.

Executed murals at Mercantile National Bank, Hammond, IN; Continental Hotel, Chicago; Swedish Lloyd Ship S.S. *Patricia*, Stockholm, Sweden; ceramic tile mural, Sportsman Park, Chicago.

Awards: First prize, Twin City Show, 1953; second prize, Minnesota State Show, 1954; Clark Memorial Prize, Chicago Show, 1957; Hamilton-Graham Prize, Ball State College, 1958; municipal prize, Chicago Show, 1958; Purchase Prize, Mississippi Valley Show, 1959; Gold Medal, Salon d'Art Moderne, Paris, 1961; Award of Merit as nation's outstanding sports artist, Amateur Athletic Union, 1976; Olympic Artist of the Century Award, 1979; Gold Medal Award, St. John's University, 1985; honorary doctorates from St. John's University, 1980, and Iona College, 1985.

Sidelights

LeRoy Neiman's vividly colored depictions of sports and leisure activities have attracted an extremely large audience worldwide, making Neiman one of the best-known artists of his time. While most twentieth-century artists have eschewed the figure in favor of the abstract, Neiman celebrates the story-telling quality of people in his large body of work. Whether paintings, prints, or illustrations, Neiman's art exudes a sense of immediacy and accessibility that have made it phenomenally popular. Neiman's work was at first not taken seriously by the art establishment, but has since been included in the permanent collections of such institutions as the Baltimore Museum of Fine Art, the Art Institute of Chicago, the Indianapolis Museum of Art, the Minneapolis Institute of Arts, the Minnesota Museum of Art, and the Hermitage in Leningrad, Russia.

Born and raised in St. Paul, Minnesota, Neiman paid little attention to fine art. In grade school, he was more interested in the art of self-defense—gang fighting and boxing. Sandlot team sports, ice skating, and hockey competed for his leisure time with amateur football, minor league baseball, ski jumping, motorcycle hill climbing, and harness racing. His natural artistic talent became evident when Neiman tattooed schoolmates' arms with pen during recess at a local Catholic school. From age 12 to 14, he painted prices on grocery store windows, which he enlivened with renderings of Thanksgiving turkeys, produce, and bottled items. He later retouched canvases of Ripley's "Believe-it-or-Not" Side Show and designed posters for high school football games and dances. On his own, Neiman studied portraits of governors in the State Capital Building.

In 1942 Neiman dropped out of high school and enlisted in the U.S. Army. He trained as an Army cook and served in Europe. He often painted murals on the walls of mess halls and kitchens. During the occupation of Germany, he worked with Army Special Services painting stage sets for Red Cross shows. Neiman's experiences during his military service confirmed his decision to pursue an artistic career.

Upon his discharge, Neiman earned high school credits and studied at the St. Paul Art Center (now the Minnesota Museum of Art) with colorist Clements Haupers. Neiman studied and painted landscapes, figures, still lifes, and anatomy. Because Haupers was an enthusiast of French painter Paul Cezanne's work, he taught Neiman to use color, space, and rhythmic action in the style of Cezanne.

Under the GI Bill, Neiman then studied with Russian emigre painter Boris Anisfeld at the School of the Art Institute of Chicago. "In the beginning I was totally undisciplined," Neiman recounted in *LeRoy Neiman Retrospective Exhibition: Paintings, Drawings, Watercolors, Prints, 1949-1975 (Retrospective, 1949-1975).* "Haupers and Anisfeld were important because they acted like artists, looked like artists, and felt like artists. They taught me the craft of painting, and also the notion of being totally involved with and dedicated to art; you need to know that the artist really exists and is something beyond the picture itself." Anisfeld exposed Neiman to the dramatic and psychological use of color, and the work of other instructors at the institute ran the gamut of styles, from figurative to abstract.

Neiman the student found himself drawn to the varied works of many artists. Among them were the Action Painters, such as Jackson Pollock, Franz Kline, and Willem de Kooning, who used fields of pure color as the arena for their work. In subject matter, Neiman was attracted by the works of painters who depicted the American urban scene, such as Everett Shinn, Reginald Marsh, and Jack Levine. At this time Neiman also became interested in Oriental brushwork and fashion illustration. His mission, as he gradually became aware of it, was to combine the opposing styles of naturalistic figurative painting with symbolic color. At the same time, Neiman investigated life's social strata from the working man to the millionaire, striving to capture not only what he saw, but the entire reality of a certain experience.

In 1949 Neiman joined the faculty of the Chicago Art Institute and taught figure drawing and fashion illustration, a position that he would hold for 10 years. Treating fashion illustration like drawing and watercolor painting, he depicted women's high fashion for prestigious stores and magazines. At this time he began sketching the leisure activities and sports of Chicagoans. He also started a regular association with *Playboy* magazine owner, Hugh Hefner, who would finance Neiman's explorations of nightlife throughout the world, commission paintings and murals for 18 Playboy clubs, and publish Neiman's work monthly for more than 25 years.

Neiman struggled with the problem of effectively portraying action with thick oil or acrylic paint. In 1953 he found the solution when the superintendent of a neighboring New York City apartment building, who was cleaning the basement, offered Neiman the remnants of his latex house paints. To his delight, Neiman found that when he used the latex paints on what became his *Idle Boats* painting, they flowed smoothly from his brush. The latex allowed Neiman to vigorously apply paint and in the process create the effects of motion for which he has since become famous.

Another hallmark of Neiman's work is its color—a palette that after the 1950s arrived at its now-famous brilliance. Neiman explained his use of color in *Retrospective, 1949-1975:* "I do not depart from the colors borrowed from life. But I use color to emphasize the scent, the spirit, and the feeling of the thing I've experienced. The behavior and interplay of these colors determine the psychological impact of the painting." In his works for books, magazines, television and computer graphics, paintings, and prints, Neiman uses the brilliant colors that so intrigued him as a student.

Sports of all kinds figure prominently in Neiman's work. He has illustrated sports—including the Olympic Games—for television stations, major magazines, and newspapers, and even worked as an artist-in-residence with the New York Jets football team, the only time a sports team has had an artist on the payroll. "Professional sports I regard as entertainment and amusement, where spectators and business are equally important," Neiman wrote in *Art and Life Style.* "For the athlete, what was fun as a kid becomes business as a pro. But still, deep down, the paying spectator never has the fun of involvement the paid athlete has. It is more fun to do something well than to watch something well done. If painting wasn't fun for me I wouldn't do it. This is at the heart of what my work is about."

Another main subject of Neiman's work is the figure. He always keeps a sketchbook and pens on hand to catch the superficial likeness of the person, whether a celebrity or colorful bystander. "When I paint, I seriously weigh the public presence of a person—the surface facade. I am less concerned with how people look when they wake up or how they act at home. A person's public presence reflects his own efforts at

image development," Neiman wrote in *Art and Life Style.* Neiman has sketched and painted many of the twentieth century's "beautiful people"—athletes, musicians, and movie stars—including President Jimmy Carter, Robert Kennedy, Frank Sinatra, Mae West, Leonard Bernstein, Beverly Sills, Martin Luther King, Sr., Diana Ross, The Beatles, Muhammad Ali, James Brown, Jack Nicklaus, and Roberto Clementi, to name only a few. While he often portrays notables, Neiman is just as likely to pick a remarkable but anonymous figure out of a crowd and sketch him or her on the spot.

By the 1960s Neiman had hit his stride. Although his work was generally ignored by the art establishment, it attracted the attention of the public, who either loved it or loathed it. Neiman's paintings, and especially his prints, were snapped up. When television appearances brought his work to the attention of millions of viewers, Neiman became an artistic superstar, whose works commanded six-figure sums.

> *"You need to know that the artist really exists and is something beyond the picture itself."*

Neiman has been the subject of hundreds of magazine and newspaper articles, which are listed in the catalogs that accompany his exhibitions. He even receives fan mail, just like the stars he portrays. The notoriety does not distract Neiman from his work, however.

He works long hours at his studio, often from eight in the morning to late at night. Neiman works quickly but intermittently on five or six paintings at a time. Instead of canvas, he paints on large panels of specially prepared Masonite of Upson board, many of which measure four feet by six feet. He uses commercial enamels in dull or glossy finishes, and oil glazes. "At first the entire surface of a painting is covered with color, then shaped into forms and values," he wrote in a letter, later published in *American Artist.* "The key and temperature of the painting is generally established at this stage. My preliminary drawings are used as reference, but these are not necessarily followed religiously unless an attitude or gesture is indispensable. More often than not, a color psychologically employed does the better job than a calculated rendering." Neiman needs only five minutes to make a sketch but spends two or three months on a complicated portrayal of events, such as his annual Superbowl painting.

During a career that has already spanned 40 years, the prolific Neiman has created thousands of paintings and many thousands of drawings. In the process, he has won the admiration of the populace and the grudging notice of art critics. As the season of one sport blends into that of the next in an endless parade of athletes, America's premier sports artist can be found sketching faithfully on the sidelines.

Sources

Books

Lein, Malcolm, *LeRoy Neiman Retrospective Exhibition: Paintings, Drawings, Watercolors, Prints, 1949-1975*, Minnesota Museum of Art, 1975.

LeRoy Neiman - Andy Warhol: An Exhibition of Sports Painting, Los Angeles Institute of Contemporary Art, 1981.

Neiman, LeRoy, *Art and Life Style*, Felicie Publishers, 1974.

Neiman, LeRoy, *Horses*, Abrams, 1979.

The Prints of LeRoy Neiman: A Catalogue Raisonne of Serigraphs, Lithographs, and Etchings, Knoedler Publishing, 1980.

Periodicals

American Artist, April 1961.
People, September 19, 1988.
Road and Track, February 1989.
Sporting News, January 2, 1989.

—*Jeanne M. Lesinski*

Delia and Mark Owens

Photograph by Bob Ivey

Conservationist biologists

Delia (Dykes), 44, and Mark Owens, 49, married in 1972; Delia grew up in Georgia, daughter of a trucking company executive; Mark was raised on an Ohio farm, was married and divorced previously, and has one son from his previous marriage. *Education:* Both studied biology at University of Georgia.

Addresses: *Home and office*—Marula Puku Research Center, North Luangwa National Park, Zambia, Africa.

Career

Delia and Mark Owens were biology students at the University of Georgia when they met in 1971. Inspired by the plight of endangered animals of Africa, they moved to Botswana, Africa to launch a research project on the habits of desert animals. They wrote a 1984 bestseller, *Cry of the Kalahari,* chronicling their work, then were rudely ousted from Botswana for their politically unpopular recommendations to protect the environment. They returned to the United States to muster support for another African project, the rehabilitation of Zambia's North Luangwa Park. Their second book, *The Eye of the Elephant: An Epic Adventure in the African Wilderness,* describes their attempts to eliminate poaching of endangered species, improve the Zambian economy, and publicize the benefits of wildlife conservation. The pair also serve as roving contributing editors for *International Wildlife.*

Sidelights

Against all odds, fearless and photogenic, Delia and Mark Owens are a conservationist couple who have teamed up to save endangered wildlife in Africa. They've traded comfortable careers as American academics for the dangers and inconveniences of scientific activism in primitive, remote locations. In spite of the many personal and professional sacrifices their lifestyles demand, the Owenses consider their occasional and gradual successes ample reward.

When Delia met Mark in a protozoology class, she was an undergraduate zoology student, and he was working on a graduate degree in science education. Both loved the outdoors (they spent their summer vacation on a crosscountry motorcycle tour) and dreamed of studying African animals. When they attended a campus lecture on Africa's endangered, disappearing wildlife, they decided that they'd miss the animals entirely if they tarried too long in the classroom. The couple married on New Year's Eve, 1972, and started planning for the adventure of a lifetime. They dropped out of school and took odd jobs to save money—Mark labored in a stone quarry and Delia worked in a department store. After a year, they auctioned off their possessions, purchased a pup tent, and boarded a plane for Africa.

Looking for an untouched wilderness where animals had never been studied, the Owenses chose the Kalahari Desert in landlocked Botswana. They set out through the sand dunes in a third-hand Land Rover, and pitched their tent in Deception Valley, 100 miles from the nearest human settlement. Then they began their study of desert carnivores: lions, hyenas, cheetahs, leopards, wild dogs, and jackals. For seven years they endured illness, isolation, and weather extremes: in the dry seasons temperatures would soar to 120 degrees; during rainy seasons storm winds flattened their camp. Their meager savings stretched beyond thin, and once they almost died of thirst when a rusty water drum sprang a leak.

The payoff came in ground-breaking behavioral discoveries gained by close tracking of the mostly nocturnal predators. The results are detailed in their book, *Cry of the Kalahari,* which became a bestseller and earned the attention and funding (from the National Geographic Society and the Frankfurt Zoological Society) they needed to continue their work. The disappointment came when Botswana officials took offense at their suggestions to avoid ecological disaster. In 1985 they were detained by immigration authorities and summarily ousted from the country. "They fingerprinted us, threatened us, treated us like criminals," Mark told *People.* "We weren't allowed to call the embassy or get a lawyer. It was the low point of our life. The Kalahari was our family, our profession, our identity, our home. We lost everything. It took a lot of healing to get over it."

The Owenses overcame the obstacles and humiliation, and in 1986 they returned to Africa to tackle another project—this time in Zambia's North Luangwa Park. The Luangwa Valley boasts a wide variety of habitats bordered by mountains on the west descending to plains and a winding river on its eastern boundary. It was home to herds of antelope, wildebeest, zebra, buffalo, impala, lions, leopards, elephants, rhinoceros, and cheetahs. Unfortunately, Zambia suffered from severe economic depression and was ill-equipped to support the 2,400-square-mile park. Local villagers who formerly farmed now supported themselves by poaching elephants and rhinos for their valuable ivory.

The Owenses arrived with a complex plan for the survival of animals and renewal of the economy. The plan has required years to launch and only recently seems to be working. The pair strive with the National Parks and Wildlife Service (NPWS) to apprehend poachers, often at great personal risk. Using funds from the Frankfurt Zoological Society and their nonprofit Owens Foundation for Wildlife

Conservation, they've teamed up with the Zambian government and local people to develop the park for international tourism which should direct money back into the neighborhoods that need it. The Owenses call the project "A Park for the People" and hope that if the Zambians view their natural resources as valuable, the animals will be worth more alive than dead.

The plan required courage in the face of obstinate poachers (both Owenses now pack loaded pistols), and some intense conservation education of locals. Delia and Mark have handed out T-shirts to school children, volunteered first aid to villagers, distributed soccer balls stamped with the admonition, "Don't poach, play soccer!" They've loaned out farming equipment and trained ex-poachers to be game rangers. Mark flies daily daring scouting missions in his tiny, single-engined Cessna to discourage poachers, much to Delia's fear and chagrin.

Where Botswana expelled the pair, Zambia almost embraces them. In 1990, President Kaunda publicly thanked them and issued a luncheon invitation. In an article by Delia Owens for *International Wildlife,* for which she and Mark are roving editors, she wrote, "Since our project began, the number of elephants poached each year in the park has dropped from 1,000 to 12, according to our aerial censuses. The North Luangwa Conservation Project, as our program is called, now seasonally employs about 200 local villagers—people who otherwise would poach for a living. Our educational programs reach more than 12,000 students in 30 rural area schools. Only when revenue from tourism begins flowing into local communities can we truly call our project a success. But slowly, the illegal economy is giving way to a legal one . . . . It is a good beginning."

Conditions continue to be difficult, however. Their grass-roofed stone hut research center, Marula Puku, sports solar battery-powered lights and computers, but drinking water must be filtered and boiled for 20 minutes. Baths are taken in the river, and one person washes while the other keeps a sharp eye out for crocodiles. Delia still cooks creative bean dinners over a campfire or wood-burning stove, and gears up for a bumpy, seven-hour drive to shop for supplies. The couple and their work were the subject of a colorful National Geographic television special, *An African Odyssey,* which aired on PBS in 1988. In 1992 the Owens' second book, *The Eye of the Elephant: An Epic Adventure in the African Wilderness,* was published to favorable reviews. Future plans involve a return to America, which the Owenses still consider their home. They hope to find some land in the northwest to build a log cabin and a start up a private nature reserve. Until then, they'll continue their work in Africa. "Now is the time for biologists to become activists," Mark told *People*. "For years, they've been coming to Africa to study animals, and the animals have been disappearing under their noses . . . . It's time for scientists to say, 'We are responsible for the animals we are studying.' It's time to say to those people who would tell us to keep our noses out of Africa's business that this is a world heritage and that it's our business too."

Sources

International Wildlife, July-August 1989; September-October 1992.
Library Journal, October 15, 1992.
People, October 10, 1988; February 1, 1993.
Sports Illustrated, December 17, 1990.

—*Sharon Rose*

Christopher Patten

AP/Wide World Photos

Governor of Hong Kong

Born May 12, 1944, in Blackpool, Lancashire, England; married Lavender Thornton, 1971; children: Kate, Laura, and Alice. *Education:* Attended Balliol College, Oxford. *Religion:* Catholic.

Addresses: *Office*—Government House, Upper Albert Rd., Hong Kong.

Career

Joined Britain's Conservative Party, worked in research division, beginning in 1966; served in Cabinet Office of party, beginning in 1970; director of party research division, beginning in 1979; Member of Parliament from Bath, beginning in 1983; Under-secretary for Northern Ireland, beginning in 1986; Minister for Overseas Development, beginning in 1989; Environment Secretary, beginning in 1990; named Conservative Party Chairman, 1992; governor of Hong Kong, 1992—.

Sidelights

As the 28th and last governor of Hong Kong, Christopher F. Patten has had a sometimes violent effect on the British colony's stock market. When Patten announced his plans for a limited extension of democracy for Hong Kong, not long after his arrival in 1992, the market slumped badly. Later, when the media reported that Patten had received a coronary angioplasty, the market shot up, presumably because the premature report of Patten's impending demise was good for business. It seems like an overreaction to the man who has claimed:

"My goal is simply this—to safeguard Hong Kong's way of life." Britain has agreed to return Hong Kong to Chinese control in 1997. History makes this more easily written in a treaty than actually carried out: Hong Kong's role as an economic powerhouse on the coast of still-communist China, colonial ambitions by Britain, and China's fear that democracy might be contagious have turned the transition—and Patten's prospects—into a very uncertain process.

Hong Kong has been part of Britain since the First Opium War of 1842. The actual island of Hong Kong was ceded to Great Britain in perpetuity. Adjacent islands and part of the Chinese mainland were added in 1860 and in 1898, when Britain obtained a 99-year lease for their control. With the end of the lease looming, former British Prime Minister Margaret Thatcher visited Beijing in 1982 for talks on the future of the colony. As Ray Clancy wrote in the London *Times*, "The Chinese government made it clear that the issue [of ending the lease] was not negotiable." After two years of talks, the resulting Sino-British Joint Declaration, Clancy wrote, "proclaimed that there would be a democratic government to oversee the continuation of Hong Kong's present way of life for the 50 years after 1997. But worries were voiced that the human rights and freedoms guaranteed in the declaration would not be honored."

Enter Patten. He arrived in Hong Kong on July 9, 1992. He was a popular (if unusual) governor, mostly devoid of controversy, until he gave his now-famous speech of October 7, 1992, in which he called for increased democracy for Hong Kong and proposed concrete steps for achieving that. The Chinese were caught off guard, horrified at the prospect of inheriting a new territory raging with democracy—something discouraged with bullets and jail on the mainland. According to the *New Yorker*, the Chinese leadership called Patten a "clown," an "immature politician," and a self-styled "god of democracy." The plan, according to *New Yorker* writer John Newhouse, was seen by the Chinese as "nothing more than a sneaky, backdoor attempt to destabilize China by democratizing a corner of the country which other corners would see as a model." *Time* magazine wrote that a columnist for *Wen Wei Po*, a pro-Beijing Hong Kong daily, said, "His politician's style of being perfidious is completely incompatible with Oriental values and morals."

"China," wrote Sheryl WuDunn in the *New York Times*, "was outraged by [Patten's] speech. China has argued that Britain made no attempt to bring democracy to Hong Kong during its past century of rule so that there is no need to do so now." Patten's answer to this has varied over the months following his appointment as governor. According to Kelly McParland in the *Financial Post*, Patten "says Foreign Secretary Douglas Hurd tried hard to win agreement for an increase in directly elected seats in Legco (Hong Kong's legislative body), and when that didn't work a different approach became necessary." But Patten told Newhouse that the Chinese "argument is a bit of a cop-out. There is rarely a right time in politics. Letting this problem hang around longer would have made it even less manageable. Why should we conduct the argument entirely on Chinese terms? They always set the terms of the debate and box you into their agenda." And Patten told *Business Week*: "The position of the United Kingdom was that there should be an increase in the number of directly elected seats. The position of China was there shouldn't be . . . I took the view that we were inevitably going to have an argument, so we were better off having it as far ahead of 1997 as possible."

Britain's newly found concern for Hong Kong democracy may have several roots. There was the perception that Britain was abandoning a former colony to an ugly fate. This feeling only increased after China crushed the democracy movement in Tiananmen Square in 1989, five years after Britain

and China signed the Joint Declaration on the future of Hong Kong. With that background, the job of closing out British rule in Hong Kong was a role that required a politician such as Patten, and not the imperial grandees or Sinologists who had been sent by London in the past.

The role is an odd one for Patten, since there had been no real indication that his career would lead to Hong Kong until virtually the day he was appointed by British Prime Minister John Major (see *Newsmakers 91*). On the other hand, Patten needed to get out of town. "The most gifted politician of his generation went to Hong Kong, it seems, because he had run out of good political options," Newhouse wrote in the *New Yorker*.

Patten's first real brush with politics came after graduating from Oxford University's Balliol College in 1965 and receiving a Coolidge Traveling Scholarship to the United States, where he worked with John Lindsey's mayoral campaign in New York. The

> "I want to see the Chinese economic revolution succeed. That would be good for all of us."

experience convinced him to drop plans for a career in journalism and to pursue politics. After returning to England the next year, Patten's first political job was in the Conservative Party's research department. In 1970 he took a job in the Cabinet Office and later became private secretary to Lord Carrington.

Patten was never part of the conservative branch of the Tory party, which was the architect of England's economic revolution of the 1980s. When Margaret Thatcher became prime minister in 1981, she dumped him from what had been the Tory's shadow cabinet while Labor ruled. Patten had always been held suspect by strict conservatives. By 1983, though, Thatcher rehabilitated Patten, and returned him to her government as junior minister in Northern Ireland, a position considered political "Siberia" by a certain class of British politician, but one at which Patten performed admirably. He told the *New Yorker*, "I loved it. And I became obsessed with Irish poetry and literature." That posting was followed by more important positions in the education ministry, as minister for overseas development (where he earned a reputation for innovation), and in 1989 as environmental secretary, all at the behest of Thatcher.

Thatcher, despite potential ideological misgivings, respected Patten as a speechwriter and political strategist. Patten told the *New Yorker,* "We always had a brisk relationship. She never held our differences against me. It's untrue that she doesn't brook dissent." It was as environmental secretary that Patten had the job of implementing the hugely unpopular poll tax, which became Thatcher's biggest albatross. "I was trying to get the government to see how suicidal it was. The poll tax was the most unpopular measure ever introduced in Britain," Patten told the *New Yorker.*

In 1990 Patten became party chairman. In the run-ups to the general election, he first backed Foreign Minister Douglas Hurd. But when John Major became the Tory candidate, Patten waged an all-out campaign on his behalf. Major, according to most polls and predictions, was supposed to lose the April 1992 election. Patten's campaign, though, kept the government in Tory hands, beating back a Labor challenge and he got much of the credit. But Patten, during the same election, lost his own parliamentary seat in Bath. And while he may have made his peace with Thatcher, when his defeat was broadcast on television on election night, a loud cheer went up from the conservatives watching in Tory headquarters. Patten may have lost his own seat because he devoted so much time to Major's national campaign, which was as bitter and unsubtle as any American election. A Tory slogan: "You can't trust Labour."

Nicholas Hills wrote in the *Vancouver Sun,* "In his role as election campaign chairman, [Patten] assumed a particular and effective brutishness which had no connection with his effusive, humorous nature. Only the west country liberals of his Bath constituency were really offended by his play-acting, and threw him out of his beloved riding." The *Guardian* newspaper, nominally friendly, headlined a story about Patten "The Cuddly Beast" and asked, "Is he, at heart, still a Thoroughly Decent Chap obliged by the Tory tradition to lower himself to doing a Thoroughly Dirty Job? Is it simply that, faced with a choice between career and conscience, he has quietly jettisoned all that made him seem Thoroughly Decent in the first place?" Still, Hugo Young, a biographer of Thatcher, told the *Sun,* "He has a human decency and intellectual breadth that survive his incumbency [as party chairman]. He remains a paragon in British political life." Young, in the *New Yorker,* added, "Chris could say things to Major that no one else could say without being misunderstood or arousing distrust. And he had the vision thing, which none of

the rest of them have. He has always had a grasp of gritty detail combined with this broad view of issues. And he has a lot of self confidence for one who had no reason to have it. He went to a minor Catholic school. There wasn't much money." Patten's loss of the Bath seat left him with several options, none particularly appealing to him. Major, grateful to Patten for saving his own campaign, offered to allow Patten to run for a safe seat in a by-election. A second option was to go to the House of Lords, considered in British political life as a place to retire to. Instead, the day after the election, Major offered and Patten accepted the position as governor of Hong Kong.

The London *Times* described his initial press conference after arriving in Hong Kong "typical of the affable erudition which has been the Patten hallmark as a politician. When asked about his political prospects five years hence, he quoted Cardinal Newman's hymn "Kindly Light": "I do not ask to see the distant scene, one step enough for me." About the loss of his Bath seat, he quoted from *As You Like It:* "Sweet are the uses of adversity." The *Times* added, "Equally typically, he was careful to call [on] a Hong Kong journalist for the first question."

Patten's proposal for more democracy outlined in the October 7 speech seemed simple. He called for a modest increase in the number of Hong Kong legislators who are elected rather than appointed and for an increase in the number of people eligible to vote. For this, wrote *Time* magazine, "China has put the Governor in the deep freeze. On his first official trip to Beijing in October [1992], no high-level authority would see him.... Perhaps what really infuriated Beijing's gerontocrats is that Patten has managed to foil them at their own game. Chinese officials are adept at being faithful to the letter of an agreement while squeezing out maximum advantage between the lines." In retaliation, China has also refused to commit any money to a new Hong Kong airport hoped for by the British. Without Chinese approval, private capital for the project has dried up.

Patten, with rare exceptions, remained stoic in the face of the attacks. "The abuse and insults are neither here nor there," he told the *New Yorker.* "It doesn't compare with going to constituency surgeries [when Members of Parliament meet their constituents] and listening to elderly couples who do not know how to cope. It is different from being in the Cabinet, where there is a collective sense of responsibility. What is different about this job is the loneliness. It is the nature of the job here, and being perched on the edge of China, instead of [being in England], increases the pressure. It is also dealing with such massive and brute irrationality, which may go on remorselessly." "I'm keen on cooperation," Patten said during an interview with *Business Week*. "I do think that Hong Kong wants a modest increase in its ability to shape its life, its future. It's not part of some great elaborate plot or threat to the mainland."

There is good reason for Patten to hope for cooperation and an agreement with China pre-1997. As the *Economist* wrote, "There is a flaw in Mr. Patten's view of the protections more democracy can offer Hong Kong. How can democracy protect anything if China, as it threatens, tears the system up in 1997? That is why the governor still hopes for a deal with China." Patten says his bottom line is simple. He told *Fortune* magazine, "I want to see the Chinese economic revolution succeed. That would be good for all of us."

Patten, a professional politician, may have sensed the mood among Hong Kong's population. Christine Lo, an appointed legislator and small–business owner, told *Forbes*, "If China declines to accept the Patten proposals, it can only be because China is determined to rule Hong Kong entirely as it pleases. If that's China's attitude, we have nothing to gain by appeasement." "Doubtless the governor will end up pleasing no one," wrote the *Economist*. "China will be allergic to any reform; Hong Kong's liberals will want more democracy and so more directly elected legislators; and Hong Kong's conservatives will worry that any change risks upsetting China to the colony's detriment."

The political drama has made Patten a genuine personality. After his October 7 speech, the South China *Morning Post* conducted a survey in China's Kwangtung Province, which borders Hong Kong to the north, and found that Patten had a 97 percent name recognition, compared to 67 percent for the governor of the province. In Hong Kong, Patten has maintained a low-key style that extends to a certain reluctance to wear the traditional ceremonial garb of the governor. Lavender Thornton Patten, his wife, told the London *Sunday Telegraph*, "Um. We're slightly ambivalent about the feathered hat." So when Patten first ferried into Hong Kong harbor it was in a business suit and not the swan-feathered pith helmet, starched white uniform, and sword. The length (short) of a skirt worn by one of his daughters got more attention. Still, the perks of the job aren't bad. Patten, as governor, receives a tax-free annual salary of about $400,000, a yacht, three cars including a Rolls Royce, and an entertainment allowance.

Forbes wrote that "his political style is akin to Bill Clinton's"—Patten seems to honestly enjoy pressing the flesh, appearing on television talk shows and being a kind of elevated policy wonk. There is a common touch. "The closest most people got to [the previous governor David] Wilson," wrote McParland of the *Financial Post*, "was when they handed in petitions at the front gates of the governor's colonial mansion." W. M. Sulke, a British businessman with 40 years in Hong Kong, told the *New Yorker*, "Without speaking a word of Chinese, he has established a rapport with people here that none of his predecessors had." Unlike previous governors, Patten is not a China expert and does not speak the language.

Can he really be so enthusiastic? Apparently so. Patten told the *New Yorker:* "This job struck me as one of the most interesting and imposing in the world. Closing the last chapter of British empire, and the huge challenge that was posed. And Hong Kong is an exciting place, with a real buzz. It was quite a leap, but politics isn't the whole of life. There is a lot of life beyond Westminster."

Political analysts in Britain still wonder what Patten will do next. Robin Oakley wrote in London *Times*, "He will be 52 when the governship ends with the Chinese takeover in July 1997 and will then once again have to consider his future. Chris Patten is a political animal. What he enjoys most is making political decisions and mobilizing consent for them and he cannot envision a life outside public service even when he returns from Hong Kong." He professes to have no grand plan other than finishing the job in Hong Kong. Patten told the *New Yorker:* "A number of political decisions had to be made. There was a feeling that the last person should be someone who kept the lights on rather than turning them off."

Sources

Associated Press wire service, April 24, 1992; July 11, 1992.
Business Week, December 21, 1992.
Economist, July 11, 1992; September 19, 1992; November 14, 1992.
Financial Post, November 7, 1992.
Fortune, March 8, 1993.
New Yorker, March 15, 1993.
New York Times, October 8, 1992; October 24, 1992.
Sunday Telegraph (London), May 3, 1992.
Sunday Times (London), May 3, 1992.
Time, January 4, 1993.
Times (London), April 25, 1992.
Vancouver Sun, April 30, 1992.

—*Harvey Dickson*

Judit Polgar

AP/Wide World Photos

Chess master

Born in Hungary in July, 1976; daughter of Laszlo (a retired psychologist and teacher) and Klara (a language teacher) Polgar; older sisters are Zsuzsu and Zsofia.

Addresses: *Home*—Budapest, Hungary.

Career

Began playing chess with father and sisters at age 4; participated in the Women's Chess Olympiad in Greece, 1988; ranked the youngest international chess master in history, 1989; ranked a grandmaster, the fourth woman ever to hold this rank, by the International Chess Federation, in 1991; ranked number-one woman chess player in the world, 1992.

Sidelights

Sixteen-year-old Judit Polgar may look like a typical teenager, dark-haired, small, ready with a smile, and fidgeting slightly in her chair, but the men who face her across a tournament chessboard will attest to her difference. She became the youngest international chess grandmaster ever by intimidating a flock of mostly male, middle-aged grandmasters with an aggressive playing style the *New York Times* called "ferocious." The title and accolades come as no surprise to her parents and two sisters who have groomed her for just such feats since birth.

Judit's father, Laszlo, a psychologist and teacher in Budapest, began plotting his strategy for outstanding children even before they were born. His study of the

lives of the world's great intellectuals led him to the conclusion that environment could override heredity as an influence toward achievement. "Miss Klara," he recalled telling his future wife, for *People*, "we both agree that the school system produces the gray average mass. But give me a healthy newborn and I can make a genius."

Validation of his premise are the careers of Judit and her older sisters, Zsuzsu and Zsofia, who are also ranked as chess masters. Laszlo, whose own chess game is only adequate, consulted experts and launched his plan systematically by educating his girls at home and scheduling an organized and intense curricula of chess, math, and languages. The sisters were playing the demanding board game by age four, and speaking Hungarian, Russian, and English by age five.

Laszlo's educational experiment was not without its detractors. He battled the former Communist government in Hungary for the right to keep the girls out of traditional schools, and then tackled the staid and chauvinistic Hungarian chess federation for the right to place the sisters in competition with men, rather than in women's ranks. Traditionally, chess competitions and rankings are segregated by sex, and women are considered inferior players. Laszlo believed that his daughters' chances for fame were better if they always competed in the tougher men's divisions. He allowed the girls to compete with women only once, in 1988, so they could represent Hungary in the Women's Chess Olympiad in Greece. The Polgar sisters gained a national following when they helped beat out the Soviet favorites for the team gold medal. Judit, who came in first, considered the level of play rather weak.

The Polgar sisters work on their games six or seven hours a day with the aid of professional coaches and an enormous home library of chess textbooks. "When my father started with Zsuzsu," Judit told the *New York Times*, "ninety-nine percent of the people were against him, and the fact that he still succeeded made it doubly painful for them." His popularity didn't increase with demands for high fees in exchange for exhibition tournaments and interviews. Tough negotiation has paid off for him, though. He's retired from work, manages his daughters' careers, and is building a country home on the Danube River, not far from their Budapest apartment.

Judit's star continues to rise in the world of chess. She has played in tournaments all over the world, and in 1989, at age 12, she was ranked No. 1 in the World Chess Federation's women's rankings. In 1991 she smashed another barrier by achieving the status of chess grandmaster by the International Chess Federation. She is only the fourth woman to hold this rank (one is her sister, Zsuzsu), and the youngest person ever, at age 15—male or female—to nab the title. In the age category, she beat out American chess prodigy Bobby Fischer, who also became a grandmaster at age 15, in 1958, by one month. She earned the ranking by systematically defeating ten grandmasters at the Super Championship of Hungary in Budapest.

Chess master players and followers consider Judit a genuine contender for the world championship, typically citing her sex as her only real drawback. Despite her aggressive style, traditionalists adamant-ly maintain that females are just not capable of domination in the game. Russian Gary Kasparov, the present world champion, told *Sports Illustrated*, "It's inevitable that nature will work against her, and very soon. She has fantastic chess talent, but she is, after all, a woman. It all comes down to the imperfections of the feminine psyche. No woman can sustain a prolonged battle. She's fighting a habit of centuries and centuries and centuries, from the beginning of the world. She will be a great grand master, but she will never be a *great* grand master."

Despite the prejudice against her gender, no one has anything negative to say about Judit personally. She is considered to be modest, sweet-natured, and polite, with an age-typical tendency to giggle a lot. Thankfully, the killer instinct only takes over at tournament tables. Meanwhile, the teenager from Budapest is having a great life and insists that she doesn't miss hanging out in a high school. Her talent has made her a world traveller with a variety of interests, if not the time to indulge them. She enjoys tennis, swimming, classical music, and television.

In February 1993, Judit defeated former world chess champion Boris Spassky, 56, in a ten-game exhibition match staged in Budapest. She pocketed $110,000 for her efforts. The *New York Times* deemed her methods "daring" and "skillful." It will be interesting to see if she carries the same intensity and aggressive, risk-taking style into other endeavors. So far, she's proven herself the chess equal of any man.

Sources

People, May 4, 1987; August 10, 1992.
Newsweek, March 27, 1989.
New York Times, February 4, 1992; February 8, 1993; February 13, 1993; February 15, 1993; February 17, 1993.
Sports Illustrated, February 6, 1989; February 12, 1990.

—*Sharon Rose*

Sheik Omar Abdel-Rahman

Islamic cleric

Born 1938 in Daqahliya Province, Egypt; married to two or three wives; children: one daughter and nine sons. *Education:* Cairo University School of Theology, master's degree; Al Azhar University (Cairo, Egypt), doctorate degree. *Religion:* Islamic.

Career

Cleric in Egypt and abroad; activist in the Islamic fundamentalist movement.

Sidelights

Sheik Omar Abdel-Rahman of Egypt (he has lived in the United States since 1990) "causes chaos wherever he goes," wrote Robert I. Friedman in the *Village Voice.* Abdel-Rahman, as of yet in name only, has been linked to the cataclysmic 1993 bombing of the World Trade Center in New York; the 1990 assassination of Rabbi Meir Kahane and murder of Mustafa Shalabi, who worked with Abdel-Rahman in providing aid to Afghan rebels, both also in New York; and the 1981 assassination of Egyptian President Anwar Sadat. Abdel-Rahman has been to Pakistan to coordinate aid for the Afghan rebels and may have been involved in an assassination attempt in Baghdad, Iraq, on an Egyptian government minister. Yet the only crime he has been convicted of: forging a smallish check, one of the infractions for which the United States is trying to have him deported. One of Abdel-Rahman's major talents, besides tapping a huge underclass of poor and disenfranchised Muslims, is remaining just far enough above the frays he apparently creates to avoid long prison terms. In proving a connection between Abdel-Rahman and the Trade Center bombing, a *Newsweek* reporter remarked, "the odds are stacked against the [U.S.] government."

Newsday wrote that Abdel-Rahman "is a man so charismatic that he can easily move an audience to tears. But at the same time his views are so extreme that most of those who hear him, even pious Muslims, are eventually repelled by his message." Yet, the magazine added, "His brand of militant fundamentalism has shaken political and social life in the Islamic world as violently as the explosion in the World Trade Center."

The breadth of his appeal is unclear. *Newsday* estimated that he may have 2,000 followers in the U.S. and Egypt, but that "active adherents ready to do his bidding may number only in the dozens." Even if that was so, there remain millions of potential converts to his brand of extremism in Egypt and abroad. James Bill, an expert on Islamic populism at the College of William and Mary, told *Newsweek*, "This is a movement of the alienated, the crippled and the dispossessed. They feel they're at the bottom of the social structure and on the receiving end of some terrible things." Rashid Khalidi of the University of Chicago told *Newsweek,* "They're angry about poverty, inequality in wealth. They're angry about what they perceive as the subservice of Egypt to the United States. They are people who are pretty angry at the rest of society."

Born in a small Egyptian town in Daqahliya Province in the Nile Delta, Abdel-Rahman has been blind since childhood, either from diabetes, or from a parasite commonly found in the Nile and transmitted to humans, according to various sources. "He had few options besides Islamic studies, which were based on learning by rote," Mary Anne Weaver noted in the *New Yorker.* "By the age of eleven, he had memorized a Braille copy of the Koran." Alexander Bardosh, an Islamic scholar at Queens College in New York, told the *Tribune* that Abdel-Rahman's disability adds to his appeal as an Islamic radical cleric: "The fact that he's blind has something to do with it. In the Islamic religion there's a great deal of tolerance for blind people who are thought to have special prophetic abilities."

Abdel-Rahman's early life as a cleric was undistinguished. Then, after the Arab nations were embarrassed by Israel during the Six Day War in 1967, Abdel-Rahman changed. A sheik who studied with him at Cairo's Al-Azhar University told the *New Yorker,* "Perhaps it was there all the time but [after the war] he showed a violence of language that I had never seen before. He had always been vastly intelligent and vastly ambitious, and now he was vastly radicalized." Abdel-Rahman focused his radicalized attention, though, not on Israel, but on the lay government of Egypt, which he saw as too secular. He was first arrested in 1969—twice—and again in 1970, by the government of Egyptian President Gamal Abdel Nasser. Weaver wrote in the *New Yorker:* "As Nasser lay dying, in 1970, Sheikh Omar, in what was in effect a door-to-door campaign, traversed the villages of Faiyum [in Egypt] admonishing people not to pray for their President, who was still popular."

The cleric spent much of the 1970s in Islamic universities, galvanizing a growing Islamic political movement. By 1976, however, the Egyptian government felt threatened enough to move against the growing fundamentalist movement. Abdel-Rahman fled the country, first to Saudi Arabia, and later to points throughout the Middle East, returning to Egypt only in 1980.

The following year, Egyptian President Anwar Sadat was assassinated in a fusillade of automatic weapons fire during a military parade. Egyptian officials investigating the slaying, according to *Newsweek,*

reported that followers of a radical Islamic group had asked Abdel-Rahman: "Is it lawful to shed the blood of a ruler who does not rule according to God's ordinances?" What they sought was a "fatwa," a pre-signed death warrant against Sadat (much as former Iranian leader Ayatollah Khomeini issued a fatwa against writer Salman Rushdie, author of *The Satanic Verses,* which Khomeini and followers denounced as blasphemous). When Abdel-Rahman answered affirmatively, he was reportedly asked specifically about Sadat, but said, "I cannot say that he has definitely crossed the line into infidelity." Still, Abdel-Rahman was tried but acquitted for the murder. He told the *New Yorker,* "It was Sadat himself who issued the fatwa to be killed, by moving away from his religion and imprisoning his people. And it was his own people who killed him, and this will be [current Egyptian President Hosni] Mubarak's fate as well."

The cleric by the early 1980s was considered a real menace to secular Egypt. He faced trial at least five

> *"It was his own people who killed Anwar Sadat, and this will be Hosni Mubarak's fate as well."*

times for various offenses and spent seven years in jail or under house arrest, according to the *New Yorker.* Clearly, Abdel-Rahman felt the pressure and again decided to leave Egypt and work to overthrow the Mubarak government from abroad.

Abdel-Rahman slipped past a U.S. State Department watch list—on which he was listed as an undesirable—to enter the United States in 1990. U.S. officials said Abdel-Rahman was able to acquire a visa in the Sudanese capital of Khartoum, according to the *New York Times,* because his name was not spelled correctly at the consulate. The Immigration and Naturalization Service said it committed a second error, the paper reported, by granting him permanent resident status as a religious leader in 1991. But later that year, he was stopped while re-entering the country, his Green Card was revoked, and Abdel-Rahman was ordered deported, according to the *New York Times.* Abdel-Rahman was appealing that decision in 1993. Weaver wrote in the *New Yorker* that the repeated bungling of his case by U.S. officials made some neutral observers skeptical, "especially since Sheikh Omar had at one time helped the United States interests by supporting the anti-Soviet mujahedin [so-called holy warriors, or Muslim guerrillas] in Afghanistan." Friedman wrote in the *Village Voice* that a law enforcement source told him, "My gut feeling is that we are protecting the sheikh. We got him a visa as a reward for his help in Afghanistan."

"His three great passions," wrote Weaver in the *New Yorker*, "were the civil war in Afghanistan, the spread of Islam, and the overthrow of the Egyptian government." Ironically, he could accomplish more in New York, safe from an increasingly hostile Egyptian government. To help accomplish the latter two goals, cassette tapes of his sermons were made and sent back to the Middle East and Egypt. To aid Afghanistan, there was the Alkifah Refugee Center in Brooklyn, New York, established in the mid-1980s by Mustafa Shalabi. Shalabi adopted Abdel-Rahman following the cleric's rival in the United States, and they worked at the center together. Weaver noted in the *New Yorker* that they recruited fighters, trained them, and sent them to Afghanistan. In March of 1991, Shalabi was found murdered in his apartment. Abdel-Rahman has denied knowing anything of the attack, and has sometimes denied even knowing Shalabi.

But Mike Dorning and Michael McGuire wrote in the *Chicago Tribune*, "Letters under the cleric's name had been posted in area mosques shortly before the murder of the electrician, Mustafa Shalabi, instructing worshippers he was a bad Muslim and should be spurned." M. T. Mehdi, an associate of the sheik, told the *Chicago Tribune* that the cleric's words have been "really taken out of context." For example, Mehdi said that when Abdel-Rahman uses the term *jihad,* he "means self-defense, the struggle for sustenance, the struggle for self-improvement. But in the American language, they have translated jihad to mean a holy war . . . All wars are ugly and unholy."

Abdel-Rahman likewise denied involvement in the World Trade Center bombing. He told the *New Yorker*, "I had no connection at all, and the bombing of the Trade Center was absolutely contrary to Islam. Yet every time I pick up the newspapers, or turn on the TV, there I am—there is the [new Jersey-based] Al-Salam mosque, which is described as a headquarters of terrorists! This is pure hypocrisy on the part of the press. Look at this man in Texas [cult leader David Koresh]—the one who claims to be Jesus Christ. Have Christian churches been blamed for what he's done?"

The sheik's appeal may be hidden to Americans, but it's clear to Arabic speakers. As'ad Abu Kahlil, of the Middle East Institute in Washington, told *Newsday*, "I was attracted by the language he uses. He does not disguise his intentions . . . . All those who look for his fingerprints will look in vain. He is not as clumsy and stupid as Mohammed Salameh [a suspect who has been charged in the Trade Center bombing] is being made out to be." But Kahlil told the *Chicago Tribune*, "He is somebody who speaks on the fringe of the fringes of Islamic fundamentalism, so not only is he unrepresentative of Islam, but he's also unrepresentative of Islamic fundamentalism."

Ibrahim Elgindy, a Chicago businessman who has heard Rahman preach, told *Newsweek* that the sheik is "about average" as a speaker. "He didn't tell people, 'Go and kill somebody,'" Elgindy told the magazine. But *Newsweek* wrote: "That's not always the case. 'Hit hard and kill the enemies of God in every spot to rid it of the descendants of apes and pigs fed at the tables of Zionism, communism and imperialism,' Rahman reportedly has preached." A U.S. counter-terrorism official told the magazine, "He doesn't say, 'Go out and hit number-6 bus.' But he creates a climate which his followers interpret as authorizing the attacks. He's smart enough to know that it keeps him from being convicted."

It is an effective strategy. Cherif Bassiouni, a Middle East expert and law professor at Loyola University in Chicago, told the *Chicago Tribune* that the cleric's teachings are "oversimplification of problems and solutions, playing on the anger and frustration of people, emphasizing the corruption of government . . . and the use of unsophisticated language, studded with not only colloquial language but also profanity, which amuses people." Abdel-Rahman does simplify his vision of a post-secular Egypt. Asked by the *New Yorker* what he imagined an Islamic Egypt to look like, he said, "What we want is a true Islamic state. We want a state where there will be no poverty, where freedom is guaranteed."

Newsweek reported in March of 1993 that Iran had been funneling money to Abdel-Rahman through one of his wives in Cairo. The frequency and size of the payments were not specified, although Rahman's American lawyer, Barbara Nelson, denied the allegation entirely. He has also been linked to—and denied any responsibility for—a terror campaign waged against tourists and the government of Egypt. Much of it may be backed by Iran, according to media reports. "The Iranians are behind Sheik Rahman," Vincent Canistraro, a former CIA counterterrorism analyst, told *Newsweek*.

In interviews with Western media, it is difficult to judge whether Abdel-Rahman is a great dissembler or just has an inaccurate grasp of the world outside the mosques where he preaches. Asked in an interview with *Newsweek* what specific arguments he has with U.S. foreign policy, Rahman said America "doesn't intervene between the Bosnians [who are Muslim] and the Serbians. Instead, American and other Western countries are helping the Serbians with money and weapons"—a view that does not correspond to the United Nations arms embargo against Serbia or any other known reality. Asked in the same interview what the West's position should be toward the Islamic movement, the sheik answered, "If the West is serious about human rights, freedom and democracy, the West should not fear Islam but rather love Islam, because Islam established the principles of freedom and democracy 1,400 years ago. So why is the West the enemy of Islam? Why has the West knocked down Islamic movements in Algeria, Tunisia and Egypt? The West is doing its best to destroy Muslims all over the world."

Because of his effectiveness in coordinating a radical Islamic movement from exile, he has been compared to Iran's Ayatollah Khomeini, who spent long years in Paris before returning triumphantly to the capital city of Teheran. It is a comparison Rahman appreciates. He told an interviewer from *Insight* magazine: "I just want to serve Islam by all my strength and power. Khomeini led a revolution and beautified his country, made it clean of the shah, who was so unjust. What Khomeini did was a real success." But asked if he would like to head a new government in Egypt, Rahman has said, simply, "No." Some observers feel he really means "yes."

Sources

Chicago Tribune, March 7, 1993.
Insight, January 9, 1993.
Newsday, March 14, 1993.
Newsweek, March 15, 1993; March 22, 1993; March 29, 1993.
New Yorker, April 12, 1993.
New York Times, March 14, 1993; March 28, 1993; April 24, 1993.
Village Voice, April 6, 1993.

—Harvey Dickson

Janet Reno

AP/Wide World Photos

Attorney General of the United States

Born July 21, 1938, in Miami, FL; daughter of Henry and Jane (Wood) Reno; not married; no children. *Education:* Cornell University, A.B. in chemistry, 1960; Harvard University, LL.B., 1963.

Addresses: *Office*—United States Department of Justice, Tenth St. and Constitution Ave. N.W., Washington, DC 20530.

Career

Admitted to Bar of State of Florida, 1963. Joined Brigham & Brigham as associate, 1963-67; partner, Lewis & Reno, 1967-71; staff director, Judicial Committee, Florida House of Representatives, Tallahassee, 1971-72; consultant to the Florida Senate Criminal Justice Committee for Revision of Florida's Criminal Code, spring, 1973; administrative assistant to state attorney, 11th Judicial Circuit, Florida (Miami), 1973-76; partner, Steel, Hector & Davis, Miami, 1976-78; Dade County, FL, state attorney, 1978-93; chairman, Florida Governor's Council for Prosecution of Organized Crime, 1979-80; U.S. attorney general, 1993—.

Member: American Bar Association (served on Juvenile Justice Standards Committee, 1973-76), American Law Institute, American Judication Society, Dade County Bar Association, Florida Prosecuting Attorney Association (president, 1984-86).

Awards: Herbert Harley Award from American Judication Society, 1981.

Sidelights

Janet Reno, a veteran prosecutor from Miami, made history in 1993 when she was appointed by President Bill Clinton as the nation's chief law enforcement officer. Reno, 54, brings impressive law-enforcement credentials to the post of United States Attorney General, having served four terms as the Dade County, Florida, prosecutor. Her selection as attorney general, she told *People* magazine, doesn't faze her in the least. "My mother always told me to do my best, to think my best and to do right—and consider myself a person," she said after President Clinton announced her nomination.

In her 15 years as a prosecutor for Dade County—which includes Miami, the city that provided TV's *Miami Vice* with so much prime-time fodder—Reno has become known for her toughness and her delicate handling of cases involving political corruption and racial violence. A pro-choice Democrat who still managed to win elections in a strong conservative community, Reno has also vigorously prosecuted child abuse cases and has been an advocate of children's rights. In her capacity as state attorney, Reno supervised a staff of 900 employees that brought to trial 40,000 felony cases a year, according to *Newsweek*. "In a criminal-justice cesspool [Miami],

Janet Reno is as pure as the driven snow," said James K. Green, president of the Florida ACLU, in *Newsweek*.

Among Miami lawyers, Reno has a reputation as a fair but very demanding, outspoken, and—at 6 feet, 1-1/2 inches tall—a physically imposing boss, published reports said. As an example of her willingness to speak her mind, according to the *New York Times*, Reno once told a group of juvenile court judges they were "dunderheads," and walked out of the convention they were holding. She also brings with her to Washington a reputation for accessibility and integrity. In Florida, *People* reported, Reno refused an official car, preferring to drive a battered Chevrolet Celebrity; she kept a listed home phone number; and she consistently refused pay raises and returned unused campaign contributions.

"This is a truly experienced big city prosecutor, a front-line warrior who has fought all the battles and faced all the slings and arrows," said Seymour Gelber, the former judge and prosecutor who hired Reno to the state attorney's office in Miami and is now mayor of Miami Beach, in the *New York Times*. "She is a tough, tough lady. She has a soft, genteel way about her, but she is an adversary of steel." Reno's first major test of her mettle came almost before she'd had a chance to get the key in the door of her new Washington office. Near the end of a 51-day stand-off between self-proclaimed messiah David Koresh and the Bureau of Alcohol, Tobacco, and Firearms (ATF) and the FBI—during which Koresh and his Branch Davidian followers barricaded themselves inside the cult's Waco, Texas, compound with an impressive arsenal, killing four agents and injuring 15—Attorney General Reno was called upon to take decisive action and bring the situation to a close. She "had to balance conflicting reports about whether the Davidians were prepared for a mass suicide, the one finale she hoped to avoid at all costs," according to *Time*. After conducting extensive interviews and briefings with the embattled experts who had been at the Waco site for close to two months, Reno gave the nod for tanks to close in on the compound, with the hoped-for result of driving the Davidian men, women, and children out—alive.

Koresh had other intentions, however; the carefully constructed ATF-FBI-Reno plan turned into a spectacle of horror. As tanks continued to roll into the compound, cult members set the buildings ablaze; the area quickly became an inferno, fanned by 30-m.p.h. prairie winds. In the end, Koresh and 85 Davidians died, with little left to identify them other than scattered bones and ashes. In this decisive end,

the questions came fast, with most of them directed at Reno and her role in the disaster. As *Time* put it, "Reno drew herself up tall . . . and went on national television to say, The buck stops with me, I take full resposibility, it was my decision, I approved the plans . . . . She was everywhere on the evening news and the talk shows, declaring that after hard thought she had reached the best judgment she could and that 'based on what we know now, obviously it was wrong.'"

There were heard rumblings of her resignation, or public outcry for it; eventually these ceased as the media analysis progressed. Perhaps the harshest criticism in the Waco aftermath was leveled at Reno's boss, President Clinton, who, it was generally agreed, distanced himself entirely from the situation. According to *Time*, "After the smoke cleared, Clinton, never camera shy, remained in the shadows. The White House released a statement one paragraph long. 'The law-enforcement agencies involved in the Waco Siege recommended the course of action pursued today,' it said. 'I told the Attorney General to do what she thought was right, and I stand by that decision.'" Since the event, however, most of the focus has been on the cult and its mysterious leader, David Koresh; Reno's job appears intact.

Reno comes from a family long regarded as one of the most colorful in Miami. When she was a child, her father, Henry Reno, a Danish immigrant who for more than 40 years was a police reporter for the *Miami Herald*, moved the family onto a remote 21-acre homestead not far from the Florida Everglades, where they settled in a rustic home they built themselves. Her mother, Janet Wood Reno, also a newspaper reporter for the now-defunct *Miami News*, hunted and wrestled alligators and was made an honorary princess by the Micosukee (Florida) Indians. "When Janet Reno wants to go out and reflect on life, she will get in a canoe and paddle 30 or 40 miles," Gelber told the *New York Times*. "She is an outdoorswoman who is at home with nature. She has lived most of her life way out in the country, in a house that still doesn't have locks on the doors."

Reno remains close with her three siblings, whom *People* magazine reported have taken to calling her "General Janny Baby." Reno's brother Robert, 53, is a columnist for New York's *Newsday*; Maggy, 52, is one of five commissioners of Martin County, Florida, and Mark, 51, is a boat captain in an oil field off Nigeria. Together, the siblings "have dived, sailed or canoed almost every wet inch of their home state," said *People*. And Reno can be an animated storyteller in the best of Southern traditions, reported *News-*

week. "The [Reno home] is right out of 'Tobacco Road,'" said Madelyn Miller, a friend from Reno's undergraduate days at Cornell, and who spent time with the family. And when not enjoying outdoor sports like boating, camping, or hiking, Reno is most likely to be found delivering speeches to any community group or social organization that invites her to a social gathering or dinner, the *New York Times* reported.

Reno, a state debating champion while in high school, studied chemistry at Cornell University and served as president of the women's student government. Reno subsequently attended Harvard Law School, graduating in 1963 as one of only 16 women in a class of 500. She returned to Miami to pursue a career in law, working in both private practice and as staff director of the Florida House Judiciary Committee. In 1978 she was appointed Dade County state attorney, and was reelected four times. Even after attaining that post, Reno continued to live in her family's home with her mother, who died in December, 1992, at the age of 79.

> *"When Janet Reno wants to go out and reflect on life, she will get in a canoe and paddle 30 or 40 miles."*
> *—Sydney Gelber, mayor of Miami*

As Dade County state attorney, Reno was the first Florida prosecutor to assign lawyers to collect child-support payments from deadbeat fathers. Reno also crusaded for children's rights and established the progressive Miami drug court (where First Lady Hillary Rodham Clinton's brother Hugh works as a public defender). "[Reno] was dogmatic in her determination to get to the truth," Buddy McKay, lieutenant governor of Florida, told *People* magazine. "But she also showed great compassion for those who were victims of crime."

Reno's career as chief Dade County prosecutor was not all smooth sailing. In May of 1980, just two years into her tenure, four Dade County police officers prosecuted by Reno on charges of beating to death Arthur McDuffie, a black insurance man, were acquitted by an all-white jury, touching off riots in the Liberty City section of Miami. Reno's relations with the city's black community were stretched to the breaking point. "In the early 1980s, Janet Reno was probably the public official most criticized in the black community," said H. T. Smith, a prominent Miami lawyer, in the *New York Times.* "She was the focal point of the dissatisfaction, disillusionment and almost the disintegration of this town. But I have gone from being one of her strongest and most outspoken critics to a strong supporter. There may be a better choice for Attorney General, but I don't know that person."

In the *New York Times,* Smith further explained that Reno won back public confidence by "opening up her office to blacks, Latins and women in all positions," and becoming the "most accessible politician in the state." Reno also began a personal tradition of marching in the annual Martin Luther King, Jr. Day Parade. Smith noted that blacks in particular have been impressed that Reno refocused the priorities of her office, and has been "aggressive and consistent in making absent fathers pay up" financial support to their abandoned children.

Reno is known for setting strict standards of accountability for her staff and aides. Lawyers and investigators who worked for Reno in Dade County told the *New York Times* that Reno keeps a little black book with a detailed record of the progress—or lack thereof—on every case that interests her. "Everybody hated that little black book," Wayne Black, one of Reno's former investigators, was quoted as saying in the *New York Times.* "She would ask you to brief her, and then two or three weeks later she'd call you in and refer to the black book and what you had told her you would be doing. She was very big into checking up" on how an investigation was proceeding. "No matter how much she has to adjust [to Washington], I'm sure she will keep a pretty strong hand on things and will definitely demand to be made aware of every important decision," said Jose Quinon, a former assistant state attorney now in private practice in Miami, in the *New York Times.* "She's a hands-on type of person, no matter what the type of system or the number of individuals she will be supervising. She has a need to control things."

Despite Reno's penchant for the smallest details, former associates told reporters that Reno was unusually accessible and welcomed suggestions so long as they were well-reasoned. "She was surprisingly open and forthright, and always willing to discuss all the ramifications of a case openly," as the *New York Times* quoted Wendell Graham, a lawyer who spent five years on Reno's staff before going into private practice in Miami. "You could talk about any problem, no matter how sensitive it was. I learned that when you went in, she wanted you to give it to her straight. Period."

By putting public concerns ahead of her private beliefs, *U.S. News & World Report* said Reno was consistently able to win reelection. Reno has sought the death penalty against dozens of defendants, for example, even though she personally opposes executions on principle. It is the kind of balance that Reno supporters believe won her the nod from President Clinton. "Clinton has positioned himself on both ends of criminal justice," noted political scientist Cornell Clayton of Washington State University in *U.S. News & World Report*. "He favors more police protection and capital punishment but also wants to look at crime's root causes."

Although Reno has a reputation for dealing aggressively with crooked cops and judges, *Time* magazine reported that Reno has been criticized for passing off to federal prosecutors the difficult job of pressing corruption charges against local officials. Reno defenders, however, insist that this strategy makes it easier to get convictions, since federal trial procedures give the accused fewer advantages in court than they get under Florida law, according to *Time*.

Reno's experience in Dade County should help Clinton enact his crime-fighting strategy, as Randy Berg of the Florida Justice Institute observed in *U.S. News & World Report*. "She has looked at Dade County's problems from the bottom up," he said. Reno arranged for a prosecutor to help residents of an impoverished housing project open a convenience store to create jobs and boost community spirit; she helped set up a court devoted to handling narcotics cases, as well as a computer program that has earned a national reputation for assessing the costs and benefits of streamlining the justice system, the magazine reported.

Reno has on occasion expressed regret that she never married or had children, saying, "I am just an awkward old maid with a very great attraction to men," *People* magazine reported. Instead, most of her career has been devoted to public service. Over the years, Reno has been offered or encouraged to seek other judicial posts, including a seat on Florida's Supreme Court. In the meantime, however, she'll continue to serve in one of the nation's most powerful offices.

Sources

Newsweek, February 22, 1993.
New York Times, February 12, 1993; April 16, 1993.
People, March 29, 1993.
Time, February 22, 1992; March 22, 1993; May 3, 1993.
U.S. News & World Report, February 22, 1993.

—*Laurie Freeman*

Keith Richards

AP/Wide World Photos

Guitarist, singer, and songwriter

Born December 18, 1943, in Dartford, England; son of Bert Richards (a factory laborer) and Doris Dupress; married Patti Hansen (a model and actress), December 18, 1983; children: (by Anita Pallenberg) Marlon and Dandelion (later Angela); (by Hansen) Theodora and Alexandra. *Education:* Attended art college in Sidcup, England.

Addresses: *Agent*—Raindrop Services, 1776 Broadway, New York, NY 10019. *Record company*—Virgin Records, 338 N. Foothill Rd., Beverly Hills, CA 90210-3608.

Career

Musician, songwriter, and singer, 1960—. Recording and performing artist and member of the Rolling Stones, 1962—; solo performer, 1988—. Appeared in and acted as musical director of film *Hail! Hail! Rock 'n' Roll* and produced soundtrack album, 1987.

Awards: 1989 inductee into the Rock and Roll Hall of Fame.

Sidelights

Much has been made of Keith Richards's reputation as rock's ultimate bad boy; his weathered face and checkered past are legendary. As the guitarist and primary musical force behind the Rolling Stones, one of the most influential bands in rock and roll history, Richards may have been less visible than flamboyant frontman Mick Jagger, but

he provided an example of cool that other musicians have imitated for decades. In the words of author Mark Leyner, who interviewed him for *Spin* magazine, "any one of a thousand Keith Richards photographs could serve as the defining totemic image of the rock 'n' roll life." Yet Richards's drug history and onstage attitude have overshadowed his remarkable focus and seriousness as a musician. Influenced by a variety of roots-based musical forms, primarily the blues, he has helped the Stones branch out continually as a vital creative unit. Since 1988 he has released two critically-acclaimed solo albums with a versatile backup band called the X-Pensive Winos; though he long avoided recording apart from the Stones, his work without them indicates he has lost none of his fire. As he noted in one of many candid interviews with *Rolling Stone* magazine, his intention has long been to "grow this music up"—to leave behind the teen appeal and theatricality of rock's past and invest it with maturity and honest feeling.

Richards also demonstrated in the wake of his renewed solo effort that he had reached a state of happy grace in his life. "The impression Richards gives is of someone perfectly content to be who he is and do what he does with no evident regard for external judgments or objections," noted Ira Robbins in *Pulse!*. The guitarist confirmed this perception in numerous interviews: "To me, the main thing about living on this planet is to know who the hell you are and be real about it," he told *Rolling Stone*. "That's the reason I'm still alive." Content in his second marriage, with several children of various ages, he showed he'd put aside the youth-obsessed sentimentalism exemplified by a classic line in "My Generation," a 1960s standard by Stones contemporaries The Who: "Hope I die before I get old." *People* quoted an interview in which the musician declared, "Getting old is a fascinating thing. The older you get, the older you want to get."

Richards was born in 1943 in Dartford, England. His father Bert worked in a factory, struggling to feed the family. "We just about made the rent," the guitarist recalled in a *Rolling Stone* interview. "The luxuries were very, very few." Keith knew early on that he didn't have his father's discipline—"that's the hardest work of all, bein' lazy," he quipped to Kurt Loder in 1987—and he was expelled from the Dartford Technical School for truancy at age 15. He spent a little time at art school before discovering the guitar and blues music. Rock and roll was brand new in the late 1950s, and its arrival, Richards told Loder, signaled the advent of "a new era. Totally. It was almost like A.D. and B.C., and 1956 was year 1, you know? The world was black-and-white, and then suddenly it went into living color. Suddenly there was a reason to be around, besides just knowing you were gonna have to work and draggin' your ass to school every day. Suddenly everything went *zoom*—glorious Technicolor."

Richards always understood—and is at pains to explain to contemporary rock fans—that rock and roll derived in large part from blues music, an African-American art form. And the work of black artists in ensuing years, from soul and rhythm and blues to the pioneering rock of Richards idol Chuck Berry, would provide basic musical compass points for the guitarist and his band. Richards met Jagger in 1960; the singer was then attending the London School of Economics. They shared a love of R&B and ended up jamming together with a handful of other musicians. The Rolling Stones—named after a song by blues legend Muddy Waters—formed in 1962 and featured a shifting roster of musicians as they coalesced, though always Jagger and Richards. The rhythm section of Bill Wyman and Charlie Watts stabilized their sound and they released their first single, a Chuck Berry cover, in 1963. Although they were often touted as "London's answer to the Beatles," and at first sported a clean-cut look, the group's gritty, sexy sound and attitude had a unique appeal. Their 1965 single "(I Can't Get No) Satisfac-

tion" was a monster hit and one of the defining songs of the era. *Newsweek* later called Richards's signature "Satisfaction" guitar riff "five notes that shook the world."

The Stones unleashed a string of hit singles—among them "The Last Time," "Time is On My Side," "19th Nervous Breakdown" and "Get Off My Cloud"—before the tide of the decade turned to "album-oriented" rock. Late-1960s and early-1970s Rolling Stones LPs such as *Beggar's Banquet, Let it Bleed, Sticky Fingers* and *Exile on Main Street* have become hallmarks of committed, adventuresome rock. The Stones also saw a tragic watershed of the hippie age: at a 1970 concert at Altamont Speedway, members of the Hell's Angels motorcycle club—the band's erstwhile security force—killed an unruly fan as the Stones played their hit "Sympathy for the Devil."

Richards, during this tumultuous period, became something of a poster boy for excess. While many

> *"This is a job. It's a man's job, and it's a lifelong job. And if there's a sucker to ever prove it, I hope to be the sucker."*

rockers—including Jagger and the Beatles—championed mysticism and psychedelia, Richards was laying low and shooting up. He admitted to Bryan Appleyard of *Vanity Fair* that during his heroin days in New York he carried a gun and "I got used to getting shot at." At the same time, however, his status often bestowed a strange immunity upon him; would-be muggers waved him through and "cops [gave] me lifts when [it was] raining." In Toronto in 1977 he was arrested on a serious possession charge and—faced with stringent penalties—underwent treatment and played a 1979 charity concert.

Living on this particular edge, he told *Spin*'s Leyner, was in part a way of dealing with stardom's distorting effect on one's self-regard: "I've tried to keep my feet on the ground—sometimes almost six feet under—in order not to stay up there in that stratosphere [of fame]. Maybe the whole dope thing was some way of negating that—'cause that put me down in the gutter. One minute I'm operating as a superstar and the next I'm shooting up with some guys on the Lower East Side. I'll never know really what that was all about—just an experiment that went on too long, I guess." Richards told Kurt Loder in 1981 that "the problem is not how to get off of it, it's how to *stay* off of it." By 1980 Richards's long-term relationship with Anita Pallenberg had come to an end, and in 1983 he would marry actress and model Patti Hansen.

Jagger served as best man at their wedding in Mexico; by the time Richards and Hansen had their two daughters, his two children by Pallenberg, Marlon and Dandelion, were in their teens. In 1982 the guitarist also reunited with his father, with whom he hadn't met in many years; their newfound closeness became another constant in Richards's life.

The Rolling Stones sustained their success through the 1970s—releasing such hit albums as *Goat's Head Soup*, *It's Only Rock 'N' Roll* and *Some Girls*—and played in more and more massive arenas. By the 1980s their tours had become events of elephantine proportions, and though he still felt firmly committed to the band, Richards was keenly aware of the intimacy and directness lost in the fanfare. But in 1985 Mick Jagger decided to release a solo album, *She's the Boss*, and announced in 1986 that he would not tour with the Stones in support of their most recent record, *Dirty Work*. Richards and Jagger traded barbs in the press; "To me, twenty-five years of integrity went down the drain with what he did," the guitarist told Anthony DeCurtis of *Rolling Stone*. Speculations about the band's imminent dissolution flew about, and were not quelled by Richards's decision to ink a deal with Virgin Records and put out his own solo album.

In addition to assembling a band, Richards served as musical director for director Taylor Hackford's *Hail! Hail! Rock 'N' Roll*, a film biography of Chuck Berry. "He's a loner," Richards said of the senior rocker in his interview with DeCurtis. "That's why I could work with Chuck Berry, because he's very much like Mick." But not working with Mick—or Ron Wood or Wyman or Watts—was Richards's imperative for the moment. He decided to collaborate with drummer Steve Jordan, who had played in the "World's Most Dangerous Band" on television's *Late Night With David Letterman*, and assembled a stellar ensemble that included bassist Charley Drayton, guitarist Waddy Wachtel, and keyboardist Ivan Neville.

An air of mutual admiration and camaraderie pervaded the sessions for *Talk is Cheap*, the first album by Keith Richards and the X-Pensive Winos. "Every drummer's dream is to play with Keith," Jordan declared to *Newsweek*. "He's the Time Machine, right?" Jordan wasn't referring to a nostalgia trip;

Richards's rhythmic accuracy as a guitarist—what musician's call "time" is legendary. Wachtel confirmed this, adding "it's due to his right hand. Magic. When he plays rhythm, it's like a room full of the best drummers in the world." *Talk is Cheap* featured guest musicians like funk superstars Bootsy Collins and Maceo Parker, and soulful vocals from Sarah Dash. Yet Richards's own singing, only an occasional feature on the Stones' records, was the biggest surprise for many listeners and critics. *Guitar Player* rated the album the best by the Rolling Stones—even though Richards is the only Stone on it—in nearly two decades. Richards and his group also released a live album taken from a performance at the Hollywood Palladium in December of 1988.

The Stones reassembled for their highly successful 1989 album *Steel Wheels*, which spawned a huge tour. "The songs just tumbled out," the guitarist told the *New York Times* of the recording sessions in Barbados. "First, we just screamed and yelled at each other. We needed to clear the air, which, as old mates, we're very good at. Then, when we got into that room and sat down with our guitars, something entirely different took over." Richards and Jagger were admitted into the Rock and Roll Hall of Fame that year as well. In a 1992 *Guitar Player* interview, Richards noted that the imbalance produced by frenzied playing and idle downtime had been a root cause of the tension within the group. "And that's what the Stones had to live with from the early '70s until the middle '80s: Constant work for a year and half, and then nothing for two years. And that stopping and starting was fraying. That was the underlying force of what all of that s—t was about."

1992 saw the publication of Victor Bockris's largely panned Poseidon Press book *Keith Richards: The Biography*, which Gene Santoro attacked in *Pulse!* as a collection of "recycled press clips" interlaced with pretentious analysis and pop clichés. More importantly, late in the year Richards released his second solo studio album, *Main Offender*. Once again employing the versatile X-Pensive Winos—who this time around traded instruments during the sessions—Richards explored more emotional territory this time around. *Entertainment Weekly* awarded the album a "B+" and closed its review with a cheeky "Your move, Mick." *Spin*'s Leyner called *Main Offender* "the finest 'Rolling Stones' album in years. It's stripped down and full of gorgeous songwriting—sinewy and poignant." *Musician* was a trifle more critical, calling it perhaps "the best mediocre album of the year" because it conveys a pleasantly raw feel with no obvious effort: "Exile on Easy Street." Richards claimed in an interview with

Rolling Stone's Kim Neely that "This band is very new and fresh for me. In a way it reminds me of working with the Stones in the early days."

The Stones were set to regroup for a new record in 1993, despite the departure of bassist Wyman, which was apparently in the works for some time. Richards had joked about scaring Wyman into remaining by threatening to replace him with a woman, but this macho gambit failed. Richards had articulated to Neely his feeling that "I think there's a possibility of another golden period in the Stones somewhere," and this projection was apparently undimmed by Wyman's exit. As Richards told Anthony DeCurtis in 1988, "I played with Muddy Waters six months before he died, and the cat was just as vital as he was in his youth. And he did it until the day he died. To me, that is the important thing. I mean, what am I gonna do now, go for job retraining and learn to be a welder? I'll do this until I drop. I'm committed to it and that's it."

As a Rolling Stone and as a solo artist, Keith Richards has demonstrated that it is possible to "grow up" in rock and maintain the spark and intensity required to keep it fresh. "To me, it's important to prove that this isn't just teenage kids' s—t and you should feel embarrassed when you're over forty and still doing it," he remarked to DeCurtis. "That's not necessary. This is a job. It's a man's job, and it's a lifelong job. And if there's a sucker to ever prove it, I hope to be the sucker."

Selected discography

With The Rolling Stones; on ABKCO Records:

The Rolling Stones (England's Newest Hitmakers), 1964.
12 X 5, 1964.
The Rolling Stones Now!, 1965.
December's Children, 1965.
Big Hits (High Tide and Green Grass) (includes "(I Can't Get No) Satisfaction," "The Last Time," "Time is On My Side," "19th Nervous Breakdown" and "Get Off My Cloud"), 1966.
Aftermath, 1966.
Got LIVE If You Want It!, 1966.
Between the Buttons, 1967.
Flowers, 1967.
Their Satanic Majesties Request, 1967.
Beggar's Banquet (includes "Sympathy for the Devil"), 1968.
Through The Past, Darkly (Big Hits, Vol. II), 1969.
Let it Bleed, 1969.

Get Yer Ya-Ya's Out, 1970.
Hot Rocks, 1964-1971, 1971.
More Hot Rocks (Big Hits and Fazed Cookies), 1972.
The Rolling Stones Singles Collection: The London Years, 1989.

On Rolling Stones/Columbia Records:

Sticky Fingers, 1971.
Exile on Main Street, 1972.
Goat's Head Soup, 1973.
It's Only Rock & Roll, 1974.
Made in the Shade, 1975.
Black and Blue, 1976.
Love You Live, 1977.
Some Girls, 1978.
Emotional Rescue, 1980.
Sucking in the Seventies, 1981.
Tattoo You, 1981.
Still Life, 1982.
Undercover, 1983.
Rewind (1971-1984), 1984.
Dirty Work, 1986.
Steel Wheels, 1989.
25 X 5, 1990.
Flashpoint, 1991.

With the X-Pensive Winos (All on Virgin Records):

Talk is Cheap, 1988.
Keith Richards and the X-Pensive Winos Live at the Hollywood Palladium, December 15, 1988, 1988.
Main Offender, 1992.

Sources

Books

Loder, Kurt, *Bat Chain Puller: Rock & Roll in the Age of Celebrity*, St. Martin's Press, 1990.
The Rolling Stone Interviews: The 1980s, edited by Sid Holt, St. Martin's/Rolling Stone Press, 1989.

Periodicals

Entertainment Weekly, November 6, 1992.
Guitar Player, December 1992.
Musician, May 1992; December 1992.
New York Times, June 4, 1989.
Newsweek, October 24, 1988.
People, November 9, 1992.
Pulse!, November 1992.
Rolling Stone, November 26, 1992; February 4, 1993.
Spin, January 1993.
Vanity Fair, December 1992.

—Simon Glickman

George F. Smoot

AP/Wide World Photos

Astrophysicist

Full name, George Fitzgerald Smoot III; born February 20, 1945, in Yukon, Florida; son of a geologist and a science teacher. *Education:* Massachusetts Institute of Technology, B.S. (mathematics), B.S. (physics), 1966; Ph.D. (physics), 1970.

Addresses: *Home*—10 Panoramic Way, Berkeley, CA 94704.

Career

On the faculty of University of California, Berkeley, since 1971, and researcher at Lawrence Berkeley Laboratory since 1974.

Member: International Astronomical Union, American Physical Society, American Astronomical Society, Sigma XI.

Sidelights

When astrophysicist George Smoot was asked to describe his feelings after his history-making scientific presentation on April 23, 1992, he replied, "If you're a religious person, it's like looking at God." Smoot's memorable response referred to the discovery, by the research team he heads, that helps explains the very dawn of the universe. His group at the Lawrence Berkeley Laboratory in Berkeley, California, detected minute ripples in cosmic microwave radiation thought to be the afterglow of the Big Bang. The ripples were detected in data sent to Earth by the Cosmic Background Explorer satellite, or COBE, which Smoot helped to design.

According to the Big Bang theory of creation, a cataclysmic explosion 15 billion years ago spewed high-energy radiation into the early universe and began a process of expansion that continues today. Not until 300,000 years later, when the temperature had cooled enough so that atoms could join together, did matter begin to form. Echoes of that distant radiation can still be detected in the universe. And what Smoot's team found were long-sought ripples in the cosmic radiation, a key missing link in the Big Bang theory.

Smoot's announcement was greeted with excitement throughout the world's scientific community. Noted physicist Stephen Hawking (see *Newsmakers 90*), of England's Cambridge University, author of the best-selling book *A Brief History of Time,* called the finding "the discovery of the century—if not of all time." *Scientific American* said the discovery ushers in "the golden age of cosmology"—the study of the nature of the universe.

George Smoot was born in 1945 in Florida. As a child, Smoot wanted to be a scientist like his father, George, a geologist with the U.S. Geological Survey. Smoot's mother was a science teacher. "Both my parents instilled an interest in science and mathematics," Smoot told *People Magazine.* "I played football and ran track in junior high, but by high school I was getting serious about my studies."

Smoot earned his doctorate in physics from the Massachusetts Institute of Technology (MIT) and ventured to the University of California, Berkeley, in 1971. He studied under the guidance of particle physicist Luis W. Alvarez. Smoot soon began studying cosmic background radiation, the very low energy microwaves coursing through the universe.

The first evidence of cosmic background radiation was announced in 1964. Two scientists with the AT&T Bell Telephone Laboratories, Arno Penzias and Robert Wilson, discovered the radiation, which is believed to be whispers of the tremendous blast that began the expansion of the universe some 15 billion years ago. Their work, which earned Penzias and Wilson the Nobel Prize, gave rise to the Big Bang Theory.

However, there was a flaw in the theory. The cosmic microwaves appeared to be smooth. Scientists were at a loss to explain how particles would have clumped together to evolve into the vast variety of structures that make up our world and our galaxy today. "The theory says that the universe started from conditions that were extremely hot and extremely dense," Smoot told *Maclean's*. "The big mystery was that when we observe the universe, we see all these [stars and galaxies] that are clumps of matter with empty regions between them. Up until now, when we look at the relic radiation from the Big Bang, which gives us a picture of what the universe looked like 300,000 years after the Big Bang, or 15 billion years ago . . . it was uniform."

For 27 years, scientists searched for wrinkles in the cosmic radiation that would be physical evidence to explain why the cosmos became differentiated and not uniformly smooth. In 1974 Alvarez, Smoot, and their colleagues proposed using a satellite to measure cosmic microwave radiation. The National Aeronautics and Space Administration (NASA) accepted the project in 1982 and combined the idea with proposals from the Goddard Space Flight Center and the Jet Propulsion Laboratory. The result was COBE, a $240 million satellite now in orbit some 560 miles above the Earth.

Smoot headed a team responsible for designing a specialized device called the Differential Microwave Radiometer, which is capable of measuring variations in the temperature of space to one one-hundred-thousandth of a degree. It was one of three sensitive instruments to be loaded on COBE. Smoot went on to study cosmic radiation using instrumentation

housed in a U2 aircraft, and reported in 1977 that the cosmic background was hotter in one area of space than in the other. NASA planned for the COBE satellite to be launched in an unmanned rocket. Later COBE was scheduled to go up on a space shuttle. But the project was nearly scrapped in 1986 after the Challenger space shuttle exploded, killing all seven astronauts on board.

The 20-foot tall COBE was again redesigned for an unmanned Delta rocket. The satellite was finally launched in November 1989 from Vandenberg Air Force Base. As COBE circled 560 miles above the Earth, Smoot's team and other researchers analyzed the millions of measurements radioed back from the satellite. Like piecing together a giant jigsaw puzzle, Smoot's team processed more than 360 million pieces of data from the satellite.

"Given the scale of everything, you have to believe there are other living things out there....When people really understand the Big Bang and the whole sweep of the evolution of the universe, it will be clear that humans are fairly insignificant."

In just over a year, the scientists finally detected minute variations of one thirty-millionth of a degree in the cosmic background radiation. "They are the imprints of tiny ripples in the fabric of space-time put there by the primeval explosion," Smoot told *Newsweek*. Then Smoot's team spent another year rechecking all the calculations looking for a mistake. Smoot went so far as to offer round-trip air fare to any of his colleagues who could find a mistake in the calculations. No one claimed the tickets.

Smoot told *Discover:* "Toward the end, people were still not focusing on finding the mistake. Everyone wants to be in on the discovery part, and discovery is like an archeological dig. You're scraping away layers—you start to expose the pyramid, and it's getting bigger and bigger. That's exactly how it was at this time." At last, Smoot announced his findings in April of 1992 at the meeting of the American Physical Society.

"We knew there had to be ripples," Smoot told *Maclean's.* "The ripples become changed variations in matter, and those are the seeds that were going to clump the matter together and make it cooler so stars and galaxies formed and the primordial material condensed into planets." He explained further in *Maclean's:* "These small variations are the imprints of tiny ripples in the fabric of space-time which were put there by the primeval explosion process. Over billions of years, the smaller of these ripples have grown into galaxies, clusters of galaxies and the great voids of space." The breakthrough may be only the beginning of discoveries from COBE, according to Smoot and his team. They have another year's worth of information to analyze.

Despite the acclaim echoed through the scientific community, some scientists are waiting for further proof. John P. Huchra, of the Harvard-Smithsonian Center for Astrophysics, raised the question that the variations might be the result of previously unknown types of astronomical objects rather than variations caused by the Big Bang. But most researchers were enthusiastic about the discovery. Joel Primack, physicist at the University of California, Santa Cruz, told *Maclean's* that the ripples are "as close as we are ever going to get to seeing the conditions at the start of the universe."

Richard Bond, a professor of physics at University of Toronto, said in *Maclean's* that the results of Smoot's research are fantastic, if they can be validated. "Now we have a window back to very early time . . . . This is why there is so much excitement. They have built a very strong case that the fluctuations they detected are primordial, that they are from the edge of time."

The wrinkles reported by Smoot are some 15 billion years old and up to 59 billion trillion miles across, making them not only the oldest relic, but also the most gigantic structure ever seen. Smoot calls the variations the "big brothers of the galactic seeds," as reported by *Newsweek.* The ripples that went on to form the Milky Way and other galaxies are smaller than COBE can pick up, he explained. "Whatever caused the rapid expansion of the universe following the Big Bang—the same forces caused the tiny ripples," Smoot said in *Maclean's.* "If you try to do something too fast, you shake a little. God might be the designer."

Although Smoot says he is not religious, he sees cosmology as the place where "science and religion meet." He serves on a committee at the University of California at Berkeley, designed to "give better public appreciation of science and show that scientists are real people—that's why I try not to be too stiff," he told *Scientific American.* The astrophysicist believes the findings will help people understand how the universe evolved and will ultimately enrich human life. "People are excited by knowing where they came from and knowing how they fit in the universe," he told *Maclean's.* "Think of how people felt when they saw the pictures from the moon of Earth. They saw the blue-and-green glow with clouds around it, and they realized that is where we live. Now, we are going to give people perspective about how our solar system, our galaxy and everything else fit together, and how we conceive of how the whole universe was born and how it developed, the phases it went through and how it came to have a structure in it."

As Smoot said in *People:* "It really is like finding the driving mechanism for the universe. Given the scale of everything, you have to believe there are other living things out there . . . . When people really understand the Big Bang and the whole sweep of the evolution of the universe, it will be clear that humans are fairly insignificant."

A man not used to being in the public spotlight, Smoot told *Discover:* "I would be terribly embarrassed by the publicity if it weren't for the fact that I thought I was doing some good. Here's a story about science, about good science, that doesn't offend religion, that doesn't offend a lot of things, that's not going to be used to trash the environment. I already heard from one of my cousins that her kids want to be scientists now because you get to be famous and you get to discover the universe."

Smoot told *Maclean's* about the motivation behind his work. "When I got to Lawrence Berkeley Laboratory, there were six Nobel Prize winners, and some of them had fire in their bellies. I never felt that I had quite that same fire, but maybe I do. What drove me . . . was that I wanted to know the answer. I know the secret of the universe. I have the key."

Sources

Discover, October 1992.
Maclean's, May 4, 1992.
Newsweek, May 4, 1992.
People, May 25, 1992; December 28, 1992.
Scientific American, July 1992.
Time, December 28, 1992.
Wall Street Journal, April 24, 1992.

—*Donna Raphael*

Howard Stern

AP/Wide World Photos

Radio disc jockey

Born January 12, 1954, in Roosevelt, Long Island, NY; son of Ben (a radio engineer) and Ray Stern; married Alison Berns (a social worker), 1978; children: Emily and Debra. *Education:* Boston University, B.S. in communications, 1976.

Addresses: *Home*—Long Island, NY. *Office*—c/o WXRK Radio, 600 Madison Ave., New York, NY 10022.

Career

Worked as a student disc jockey at Boston University, Boston, MA; disc jockey with WRNW Radio, Briarcliff Manor, NY, 1976-78; WCCC Radio, Hartford, CT, 1978-79; WWWW Radio, Detroit, MI, 1979-80; WWDC Radio, Washington, DC, 1980-82; WNBC Radio, New York City, 1982-85; WXRK Radio, New York City, 1985—, with a show subsequently expanded to air in eleven markets nationwide. Hosted weekly *Howard Stern Show* on cable's WW0R-TV, 1990-92. Hosted weekly *The Howard Stern Interview* on cable's E! Entertainment Television, 1992.

Sidelights

Howard Stern was once fired for referring to station management as "scumbags" on the air during a salary dispute. He was suspended for a comedy bit about a video game called Virgin Mary Kong in which men chase Mary around a singles bar. He angered civil rights groups by telling in-studio guests the Pointer Sisters that he wished there were slavery so that he could be their "Massa Howard" and have his way with them. He even enraged his own wife by joking about her miscarriage on the air, and routinely tells attractive female guests that his wife has been killed in a car accident. His employers had to apologize when he said he prayed for the death of the chairman of the Federal Communications Commission (FCC), which had levied fines against some stations carrying his show.

More often than not, descriptions of Howard Stern come in the superlative form. Fans and some critics have called him the funniest disc jockey on the air waves. His disparagers have labeled him the most obscene. The FCC considers him the most notorious and most threatening of the industry's current crop of "shock jocks." And his millions of loyal listeners across the nation make him the most popular morning voice in many of the eleven radio markets he reaches. His widening audience is anchored by young males, drawn by his low-brow humor and quick, warped wit.

After angry listeners provided the FCC with transcripts from Stern's show about masturbating to a picture of Aunt Jemima and having rough sex with actress Michelle Pfeiffer, the commission fined

Stern's ownership, Infinity Broadcasting, $600,000 in December of 1992. The FCC also levied a $105,000 fine on Greater Media, which carries his show on KLSX-FM in Los Angeles. Stern replied by remarking about FCC Chairman Alfred Sikes' prostrate cancer treatments—"I pray for his death"—and added that he hoped the cancer would spread through the FCC. Both fines were quickly appealed, and despite pressure, Stern offered no apologies for his remarks. In the meantime, Stern began a weekly celebrity interview show on cable's E! Entertainment Network and proceeded with his plans to make a Hollywood film called *The Adventures of Fartman.*

Characterized as an easygoing straight-arrow off the air, Stern doesn't drink, smoke, or dabble in drugs, and practices transcendental meditation each morning in the limo ride to work. While sitting in traffic

---

"Whenever I ran into bosses who tried to tell me my kind of show wouldn't work, I always thought of that one miserable bastard on the parkway in his car. And I just knew if I could make him happy, I'd be all the rage."

---

with his father as a youth, Stern first began his road to morning radio. "I've had the same concept since the beginning," Stern told *Rolling Stone.* "I'd watch my dad commute, and when he was stuck in the car, he'd just sit and listen to CBS news. And I thought, 'Wouldn't it be great if he was laughing? If he heard a deejay say something funny, something that made him glad he was there?' Whenever I ran into bosses who tried to tell me my kind of show wouldn't work, I always thought of that one miserable bastard on the parkway in his car. And I just *knew* if I could make him happy, I'd be all the rage."

Stern's father, Ben, ran a successful recording studio in Manhattan. Stern remembers going there as a boy and seeing actors Don Adams, Larry Storch, and Allen Swift record the voices for the *Tennessee Tuxedo* cartoon show. "I thought they had the coolest job in the world," he told *Rolling Stone.* By junior high, Stern's Roosevelt neighborhood on Long Island

was mostly black, so he tried to fit in by speaking black dialect. "I remember for the longest time wanting to be black," he was quoted as saying in *Esquire.* "I hated being white. You want to be with the majority. Being white, I stuck out like a sore thumb. I'm sure that did something weird to my mind." He rejects all racist labels. "I love it when I get called a racist for doing black dialect," he told *Rolling Stone.* "The fact is that some people do talk like that. *I* talked like that."

While at Boston University in the early 1970s, Stern majored in communications and worked at the student radio station. He invited social work student Alison Berns to be in a movie he was making on transcendental meditation, and ended up marrying her in 1978. He took a $96-a-week job as deejay at WRNW-FM in Briarcliff Manor, New York, upon his graduation, and worked there for two years. "I was the world's worst straight disc jockey," he told the *Washington Post.* From there he went to WCCC, an AM/FM station in Hartford, Connecticut, leaving after a year when he was refused a $25-a-week raise. In 1980 he became the morning man at WWWW-FM in Detroit, a venerable rock station that suddenly one morning went country without prepping its staff. Stern had strong ratings and a $50,000 salary in Detroit, but country was not his gig. "I have no tolerance for country music," he told *Rolling Stone.* "The Judds remind me of Nazi women. I feel they would kill me." So Stern took a pay cut in 1980 and moved to Washington, D.C., where he hooked up with longtime sidekick Robin Quivers, who's still on the air with him, providing the female and black viewpoints between sycophantic giggles. (Quivers is a former Air Force nurse and radio reporter.)

In D.C., Stern drew a maelstrom of criticism for calling Air Florida two days after the fatal crash of a jet into Washington's 14th Street Bridge to inquire about one-way fares from the airport to the bridge. Management looked the other way that time, but fired him after the fateful "scumbags" comment directed at his bosses. Then Stern began his assault on Big Apple airwaves, signing as the afternoon drive man on WNBC-AM in August of 1982. In one of his first broadcasts, he aired a delivery room tape of the birth of his daughter, and followed up with bits about the Gay Lone Ranger and his sidekick, Homo Sabi, and "Hasidic West Side Story." The station was concerned with its corporate image, according to *New York,* and told him to lay off sex and religion, which, of course, he didn't. The station rewarded him with a $1 million contract anyway, but mysteriously fired him in 1985, despite his top-rated show. Stern believes it was because the chairman of RCA, then owners of NBC, heard Stern's crew playing "Bestiality Dial-a-Date" one afternoon, he told *New York.*

By 1986, Stern ruled New York's morning air waves on WXRK-FM, and his show was also being simulcast in Philadelphia, the beginning of the satellite-driven empire, which has since spread to Los Angeles, New Orleans, Cleveland, Baltimore, Buffalo, and Las Vegas, among others. He brought along his whole crew to WXRK, including Quivers, writer Fred Norris, producer Gary "Baba Booey" Dell'Abate, and intern "Stuttering John" Melendez (whose trademark shtick is to show up at celebrity press conferences and ask outlandish questions—which Stern later broadcasts on his show. He once asked baseball Hall of Famers Ted Williams, Carl Yastrzemski, and Reggie Jackson if any of them had accidentally passed gas in a catcher's face.)

The FCC inquiries and reprimands built momentum in Philadelphia. One of Stern's major problems with the FCC is the vagueness of its indecency statutes. "In the good old days, you just couldn't say the seven dirty words," he told *Rolling Stone.* "But now they've updated that by saying you can't 'discuss sexual or excretory matters in a patently offensive way.' What the f––– does that mean? All I'm saying is, don't give me a speeding ticket unless you can tell me what the speed limit is." In his later troubles with the law, he was chastised for saying offensive things at times when children may be listening, to which Infinity responded with expensive research that showed that very few children listen to Stern's show. Mel Karmazin, Infinity's president, further defended Stern by saying that the topics broached by Stern & Co. are regularly covered on TV talk shows and in magazines. The only difference, Karmazin said, is that Stern is joking. "You may not like the humor," he told *Time,* "but that is why every radio has an on-off button."

Stern has refused media interviews about the FCC, but regularly comments on the air. He summed up his views the day after Bill Clinton's victory on Election Day, 1992: "Hey, FCC, kiss my ass!" After taking WXRK from 21st to first in the New York market, Stern was rewarded in 1990 with a five-year contract believed to be worth $10 million. That same year he launched *The Howard Stern Show,* a weekly hour of raunchy comedy broadcast on cable's WWOR-TV. At eleven o'clock every Saturday night, Stern and his radio crew went on the air with a cast of goofball guests, like the Kielbasa Queen who swallowed foot-long sausages, and dozens of bikini-clad spokesmodels to pitch sponsors' products. Skits included "Bobbing for Tampons" and "Lesbian Love Connection." Some stations dropped the show after advertisers threatened to pull out. One was WFXT-TV, the Fox station in Boston, whose program director, Jim Byrne, explained with "three words: the Kielbasa Queen. We got a call from an elderly man . . . who said he and his wife fell asleep watching *Cops,* and his wife awoke during the Kielbasa Queen and couldn't sleep the rest of the weekend." The show was cancelled in 1992. "It was strictly a financial decision," WWOR president and general manager Michael Alexander told *New York.* Stern later said he would arrange to have Alexander and another WWOR executive sent on a fishing trip and stranded at sea so they "would be forced to drink their own urine."

Stern's multi-media empire also includes a booming mail-order video business. His three choice titles include "Howard Stern's U.S. Open Sores," "Howard Stern's Negligee and Underpants Party," and "Howard Stern's Butt Bongo Fiesta," in which men play women's buttocks like percussion instruments to a salsa beat. The video also includes a one-minute tribute by Jessica Hahn—once linked to notorious TV evangelist Jim Bakker—to her private parts. "Far and away the funniest, greatest, most groundbreaking, taboo-shattering program ever," say the promos. "Takes spanking to a new and exciting level."

Sketches like those on his TV show and prurient remarks heard daily on his radio program have catapulted Stern into the public eye, even in markets where he's not heard, and vaulted him into the forefront of First Amendment conflicts. His critics have singled him out as the repugnant representative of all that is disgusting and unwholesome on the public airwaves. American Family Association leader Rev. Donald Wildmon has spearheaded numerous letter-writing campaigns and consumer boycotts against Stern's advertisers. The National Organization for Women has called for a boycott of the E! Entertainment Network for providing Stern with yet another forum. Bloomfield Hills, Michigan, activist Terry Rakolta, who heads Americans for Responsible Television, has led petition drives to the FCC. Her group, which has had success fighting sex and violence on television, most notably against Fox's "Married . . . With Children," has threatened to lead advertiser boycotts if Stern's show is not moved to a latenight slot, a time change that would certainly cut Infinity's ad profits. "Stern wants to be in 200 markets," Rakolta told *USA Weekend,* "truly national every day, where tens of millions of kids can hear him. Is that really in the public interest?"

Defenders have said that Stern's humor appeals to more people than it offends, and that even when offensive, most admit Stern is still funny. Wrote Barbara Kruger in *Esquire:* "From a generalized fascination with bodily functions (his advice on bathroom etiquette, 'You should always flush twice. I believe in a courtesy flush') to explicit sexual descriptions, from silly pontifications on current events ('how can [serial killer] Jeffrey Dahmer get a fair trial unless there are more guys who want to have sex with dead men on the jury?') to incessantly jokey put-downs of both friends and enemies, he takes us back to another place and time—junior high school. Stern is no Morton Downey Jr., Rush Limbaugh or Andrew Dice Clay. Stern is funny. Really funny. And that's where things get complicated." Stern's humor is juvenile and "junior high," rarely politically oriented, though he loudly proclaimed his turnabout in support from the Republican presidential ticket of Reagan/Bush to the Democratic Party of Bill Clinton, largely because of the antiabortion stance of the Republicans. He told women that if they voted for George Bush in 1992, they may as well put their vaginas in envelopes and mail them to the White House.

A quick listen on any given morning reveals why critics find Stern so offensive. About a televised interview with Amy Fisher (who was convicted in 1992 of killing her alleged lover's wife): "I wanted her to take her clothes off." On the premature death of Chuck Connors, TV's "The Rifleman:" "I never liked him. Hated that show." To talk-show host Maury Povich, husband of newswoman Connie Chung: "For an Oriental woman, she has got big breasts." On Roseanne and Tom Arnold: "She's a big fat blob and he's the Rickey Ricardo of the '90s." On Arsenio Hall: "Malcolm X would throw up if he saw him. I've never seen such an ass-smoochio." But Stern "is a smart enough broadcaster to know that

his irreverence has practical limits: he does many commercials live and never makes fun of them," wrote Richard Zoglin in *Time*.

Those who know Stern best say he is a doting father and a nutrition nut who works out with a personal trainer. "Howard is almost like [the multi-personality figure] Sybil," fitness guru Richard Simmons told *Esquire*. "The Howard Stern you hear on the radio is not what he's really like. He's a very sensitive, brilliant, compassionate man, but very calculated. Everything he does is planned out." Stern feels that all he does is tell the truth, and is punished for it. He "feels he's controversial because he tells the truth and that his brand of honesty is the secret to his success," wrote *Rolling Stone*'s David Wild. "The truth is funny because we lie all day long," Stern said. "We have to smile at the right time. We have to act like we care what other people say. We have to pretend we like our asshole boss. I lie, too, but on the radio I say what I want."

Sources

Broadcasting, June 22, 1987; October 12, 1992; November 16, 1992; November 30, 1992; January 4, 1993.

Esquire, May 1992.

Fortune, January 11, 1993.

New York, April 18, 1988; November 23, 1992.

New York Times, December 18, 1992; December 19, 1992; December 20, 1992.

Newsweek, November 17, 1986.

Rolling Stone, June 14, 1990.

Time, November 9, 1992; November 30, 1992.

U.S. News & World Report, April 27, 1987.

USA Weekend, March 5-7, 1993.

Washington Post, December 26, 1983; October 2, 1985; April 21, 1987.

—*John P. Cortez*

Elizabeth Taylor

AP/Wide World Photos

Actress and activist

Full name, Elizabeth Rosemond Taylor; born February 27, 1932, in London, England; daughter of Francis (an art dealer and historian) and Sara (an actress; maiden name, Sothern) Taylor; married Conrad Nicholas Hilton, Jr., May 6, 1950 (divorced, 1951); married Michael Wilding (an actor), 1952 (divorced, 1957); married Michael Todd (a producer), February 2, 1957 (died, March, 1958); married Eddie Fisher (a singer), 1959 (divorced, 1964); married Richard Burton (an actor), 1964 (divorced, 1974); remarried Burton, 1975 (divorced, 1976); married William John Warner (a politician), 1976 (divorced, 1982); married Larry Fortensky (a construction worker), 1991; children: (second marriage) Michael, Christopher; (third marriage) Elizabeth Frances; (fifth marriage) Liza.

Addresses: *Agent*—Chen Sam & Associates, Inc., 315 East 72nd Street, New York, NY 10021.

Career

Actress, 1943—; founder and chairperson, American Foundation for AIDS Research, 1985—; founder, Elizabeth Taylor AIDS Foundation, 1991—. Fundraiser for other charitable causes, including Variety Clubs International.

Major motion pictures include *Lassie, Come Home,* 1943; *National Velvet,* 1944; *Life with Father,* 1947; *Little Women,* 1949; *Father of the Bride,* 1950; *A Place in the Sun,* 1951; *Ivanhoe,* 1952; *The Last Time I Saw Paris,* 1954; *Giant,* 1956; *Raintree County,* 1957; *Cat on a Hot Tin Roof,* 1958; *Suddenly Last Summer,* 1959; *Butterfield 8,* 1960; *Cleopatra,* 1963; *The Sandpiper,* 1965; *Who's Afraid of Virginia Woolf?,* 1966; *Reflections in a Golden Eye,* 1967; *The Taming of the Shrew,* 1967; *Hammersmith Is Out,* 1972; *Night Watch,* 1973; *Ash Wednesday,* 1974; *The Blue Bird,* 1976; *A Little Night Music,* 1977; and *The Mirror Crack'd,* 1980. Principal television appearances include *Victory at Entebbe,* 1976; *North and South,* 1985; *Malice in Wonderland,* 1985; and *Sweet Bird of Youth,* 1989.

Selected awards: Academy Award nomination, 1957, for *Raintree County;* Academy Award nomination, 1958, for *Cat on a Hot Tin Roof;* Academy Award nomination and Golden Globe Award, both 1960, both for *Suddenly Last Summer;* Academy Award, 1960, for *Butterfield 8;* Academy Award and British Academy Award, both 1966, both for *Who's Afraid of Virginia Woolf?;* Hasty Pudding Woman of the Year Award from Harvard Hasty Pudding Theatricals, 1977; Tony Award nomination, 1981, for *The Little Foxes;* Cecil B. DeMille Award, 1985; named Commander des Arts et Lettres (France), 1985; French Legion of Honor, 1987; Onassis Prize, 1988; special humanitarian award from Academy of Motion Picture Arts and Sciences, 1993.

Sidelights

Everything about Elizabeth Taylor is larger than life. From her legendary beauty and dazzling jewels to her celebrated marriages, award-winning film roles, and work on behalf of important charities, Taylor has held international attention for half a century. *New York Times* correspondent Stephen Harvey called Taylor "the ultimate celebrity," a superstar whose tumultuous private life overshadows an "exceptionally intriguing career on screen." In recent years Taylor has actually capitalized on her notoriety to become co-founder and spokesperson for the American Foundation for AIDS Research. Since 1985 she has brought millions and millions of private dollars into the scientific fight against the deadly virus. As Nancy Collins put it in *Vanity Fair*, "The world's most famous movie star is now the world's most famous AIDS activist. And once again she is center stage."

"After age 10 I didn't have a childhood. I didn't date. I had no friends my age except for other child actors at MGM."

Taylor's never-mundane life has included pinnacles of joy and depths of despair. Twice she has nearly died of pneumonia. She has had seven husbands, four of whom died prematurely. On more than one occasion she has sought treatment for alcohol and drug abuse. Through it all, her every move has been chronicled in the popular tabloids and the mainstream press. To judge by the amount of publicity she receives, she is the closest thing to royalty America has to offer.

Taylor has demonstrated a ceaseless ability to rebound from blows to her health and well-being. She has turned her fame to good use and has sought to stabilize her private life, all the while clinging to the extraordinary beauty that assured her worldwide fame. Taylor told *Good Housekeeping:* "The ups and downs, the problems and stress, along with all the happiness, have given me optimism and hope because I am living proof of survival. I've come through things that would have felled an ox. That fills me with optimism, not just for myself but for our particular species."

Elizabeth Rosemond Taylor was born in London in 1932 to American parents. Her father was a prosperous art dealer who had his own gallery in a fashionable part of London. Her mother was an actress who had been successful prior to marriage under the stage name Sara Sothern. Taylor and her older brother grew up in comfortable affluence. Some of Taylor's privileges included dancing lessons with Madame Vacani—instructor to the royal family—as well as riding lessons and visits to the vast property of her godfather, Victor Cazalet. "My happiest moments as a child were riding my Newfoundland pony, Betty, in the woods on 3,000 acres of my godfather's estate near the village of Crambrook, in Kent," the actress told *Good Housekeeping.* "Our family lived in the hunting lodge. I was given the pony when I was three. The very first time I got on her back, she threw me into a patch of stinging nettles. But I soon became an accomplished horsewoman. I'd ride bareback for hours all over the property."

The outbreak of World War II brought an end to Taylor's idyllic childhood. The family moved back to America and settled in California. There, Sara Taylor encouraged her beautiful young daughter to seek work in the motion picture industry. Elizabeth enthusiastically agreed, and in 1941 she obtained a contract with Universal Pictures. The following year she went over to Metro-Goldwyn-Mayer and quickly landed the part of an English heiress in *Lassie Come Home.* The film was a hit, and offers for further work poured in. Today Taylor expresses some regrets about her youth, much of which was spent on the MGM lot making movies. "After age 10 I didn't have a childhood," she remembered in *Good Housekeeping.* "I didn't date. I had no friends my age except for other child actors at MGM. I rode horses and acted."

Those dual passions won Taylor consideration for the lead in *National Velvet,* the story of a young woman who wins a horse in the lottery and eventually rides it in England's Grand National Steeplechase. At 12 Taylor was slightly young and small for the part of Velvet Brown, but she was so determined to do the film that she dieted and exercised rigorously for four months. The regimen worked—she added three inches to her height and won the role. During filming she was thrown from a horse and suffered a broken back, but she finished the project. *National Velvet* was both a critical and commercial success when it was released in 1944. Since then it has become a children's cinematic classic.

Under contract at the MGM studio, Taylor made several movies each year throughout the late 1940s.

She graduated gracefully to ingenue roles, including that of Amy in the 1949 remake of *Little Women*. She also had leading roles in *Life with Father, Cynthia,* and *Julia Misbehaves*. Taylor told *Vogue* that she felt like a misfit during those years. "When I tried to blend in, I stuck out like a sore thumb," she said. "I was famous and I looked much older than I was. When I was fifteen I was playing eighteen-year-olds and going out with men in their twenties or more."

In 1950 Taylor played a bride-to-be opposite Spencer Tracey in *Father of the Bride*. That same year she became a real bride when she married Nicky Hilton, heir to a hotel fortune. The marriage lasted only a year. Meanwhile she continued to appear in MGM movies, including *Ivanhoe, A Place in the Sun, Beau Brummel,* and *The Last Time I Saw Paris*. After divorcing Hilton she married English actor Michael Wilding, with whom she had two sons.

The mid-1950s found Taylor in several romantic films that paired her with two lifelong friends, Rock Hudson and Montgomery Clift. She starred with Hudson in *Giant*, a 1956 movie based on the story of a Texas rancher and his wife. The next year she appeared opposite Clift in *Raintree County*, a strange, melodramatic Civil War-era epic set in the South. Taylor's portrayal of a mentally disturbed woman in *Raintree County* earned her the first of four Academy Award nominations. Taylor told *Good Housekeeping:* "The highlight of my teens was getting to know Montgomery Clift.... Acting had been a game to me. He taught me acting was more than just performing on camera. Monty showed me it was an art form."

Taylor's marriage to Wilding ended when she became involved with the handsome and dynamic producer Michael Todd. They were married in 1957, just as Taylor became one of America's top box-office performers. Only thirteen months later, Todd was killed when his private plane crashed. Devastated, Taylor was forced to endure a crush of press and fans at the funeral—and then return to the set of the film *Cat on a Hot Tin Roof,* in which she played the emotionally-wrenching part of Maggie. Taylor admitted in *Vogue* that she nearly suffered a nervous breakdown during that difficult time. "I developed an awful stutter, and the only way I could talk straight was in Maggie's voice, with that Southern accent," she said. "Any other time I would just *ug, ig, um,* like that; my jaw would jerk."

Cat on a Hot Tin Roof was an enormous hit in 1958, making superstars of Taylor and Paul Newman. Taylor received a second Academy Award nomination for her portrayal of Maggie. The next year she

was nominated again for her work as Catherine in the melodrama *Suddenly Last Summer*. Even then her performances caused less sensation than her personal life. The tabloids had a field day in 1959 when she married singer Eddie Fisher soon after his breakup with actress Debbie Reynolds. In 1961 Taylor again made headlines when she was hospitalized with severe pneumonia. Her condition became so desperate that the physicians performed a tracheotomy so she could breathe. "I had a near-death, out-of-body experience," Taylor told *People,* "but nobody talked about that 30 years ago, because you felt crazier than a bedbug if you did. I saw the light and the tunnel. And there was somebody who was deceased and making me go back. It's extraordinary. So vivid.... I was fighting to hang on to the brink of consciousness with all my life. Maybe it was just obstinacy, but I did *not* want to die."

By the spring of 1961 Taylor had recovered sufficiently to attend the Academy Award ceremonies in Hollywood. There she earned her first Oscar for her performance as a prostitute in *Butterfield 8*. That same year she became the highest-paid actress in America, and she remained among the top ten money-makers throughout the decade. Taylor was the first star ever to be paid $1 million for a screen appearance. She received the fee for the lead in *Cleopatra*, a lavish costume drama about ancient Rome and Egypt. The film was released in 1962 to critical sneers, but it earned enough at the box office to cover the vast production costs.

Cleopatra marked the first on-screen pairing of Taylor and Richard Burton, a noted British actor. Their romance as Cleopatra and Mark Antony soon spilled over into their private lives, and they divorced their respective spouses and wed in 1964. Upon their engagement, Burton gave Taylor the 33-carat Krupp diamond—Taylor has had a lifelong fondness for precious gems. After their marriage Taylor and Burton teamed in a number of popular films, most notably *Who's Afraid of Virginia Woolf?* in 1966. That movie, based on the scathing play by Edward Albee, was a daring departure for Taylor. At the height of her beauty she deliberately gained weight and mussed her hair to appear as the frumpy, older, and foul-mouthed Martha. The film earned Taylor her second Oscar and numerous other acting awards.

The Taylor-Burton romance provided grist for the tabloid mills for years. The couple lived like royalty, with their own yacht and an international agenda. Their relationship was stormy but passionate. They divorced in 1974 after ten years together, remarried the following year, and divorced again in 1976.

"Richard enriched my life in different ways, internal journeys into feelings and thoughts," Taylor remembered in *Good Housekeeping*. "He taught me poetry and literature, and introduced me to worlds of beauty. He made me laugh. He made me cry. He explored areas in me that I knew existed but which had never been touched. There was never a dull moment . . . . I loved Richard through two marriages and until the day he died."

By the early 1970s Taylor was earning an average $1.25 million per picture. A combination of ill health and her troubled marriage to Burton began to take a toll on her productivity, however. She appeared in more than a dozen movies in the 1960s but completed only a handful in the 1970s, never again contending for an Academy Award. Highlights of the period include leads in *Night Watch, Ash Wednesday, A Little Night Music,* and *The Mirror Crack'd.* In 1981 she moved to Broadway for the first time in a well-received staging of *The Little Foxes,* a drama about a greedy Southern family.

Soon after her final divorce from Burton, Taylor married Virginia politician William John Warner. The alliance was an unlikely one from a professional standpoint, but Taylor soon rose to the occasion by campaign-stumping the state during her husband's senatorial race. After Warner won a Senate seat, Taylor stayed close to the nation's capital, venturing north occasionally for her stage work in New York City. Her career in feature films was all but over as she opted for television work or—more often—to donate her time to charitable causes. Taylor recalls the years with Warner as the most difficult of her life. "I had been a very unhappy, self-destructive person the whole time I lived in Washington," she said in *Good Housekeeping*. "It's a difficult city for women anyway, and so ego-oriented it makes Hollywood look like chopped chicken liver. I wasn't allowed to express my opinions or even wear my favorite color, purple, because Republicans didn't like that color . . . . For five years in Washington, D.C., I was the loneliest person in the world. I didn't have a friend. I rarely saw my husband. My children were grown and had their own lives. I began drinking out of loneliness. It got out of hand and for a while I lost my identity. I had nothing to do. I was in a vacuum. It was a death sentence. There aren't many things in life I've missed, including despair so black I hit bottom."

Finally, in 1983, Taylor signed herself into the Betty Ford Clinic in California for treatment of her alcohol addiction. The tabloid press followed her there and—after her discharge—chronicled her weight gain and her love affair with financier Victor Luna. Her only major acting work during the period came in television films, the drama *Malice in Wonderland,* ironically about Hollywood's celebrated gossip columnists, and the Civil War mini-series *North and South.*

More troubles plagued Taylor by 1985. Recurring back trouble brought her severe pain. She began drinking again and used pain killing medication to an alarming degree. Additionally, a number of her close friends—Rock Hudson among them—became ill with AIDS. Even though her own health was poor, Taylor became determined to do what she could to fight AIDS. She became the first Hollywood actress of any stature to speak out about the need for research on the virus, and her 1985 "Commitment to Life" benefit was the first major fund-raising gala staged by the Hollywood community in support of AIDS research. The same year Taylor became co-founder and chairperson of the American Foundation for AIDS Research, a private, nonprofit enterprise with the goal of raising money for AIDS research.

As the 1980s progressed, Taylor lost some of her best friends to the deadly virus—Hudson, the fashion designer Halston, and Malcolm Forbes, as well as her private press secretary. On the other hand, her persistent crusading against AIDS helped to stem misconceptions about the disease. "When I first started doing the work I did for AIDS, it was very unpopular," she told *People*. "A lot of people told me I'd be badly burned by it, that it was very undignified. And I didn't give a hoot what people thought about it then, and I don't now. It's just that there has to be something done about it. I want to do all I can because I have to live with me."

Taylor faced yet another personal crisis, and returned to the Betty Ford Clinic in 1988 for additional addictions therapy. There she met a 40-year-old construction worker, Larry Fortensky, who was battling his own substance abuse. They became friends during group therapy and continued their friendship after they left the clinic. Taylor helped Fortensky deal with the death of his mother, and he provided support to her through yet another near-fatal attack of pneumonia in 1990. The two were married in 1991 at the home of Taylor's close friend, Michael Jackson.

Taylor told *Vanity Fair* that she wanted to retire completely even before her 60th birthday, but the tabloids would not allow her the luxury of a private existence. She has therefore continued to blaze through the mass media regularly, this time on behalf of AIDS awareness. As Nancy Collins wrote: "When you're as famous as Elizabeth Taylor, when a single utterance can command worldwide media attention, you are, almost by definition, political. And . . . Elizabeth Taylor has proved herself a political force to be reckoned with." Taylor told *Good Housekeeping:* "For the first time in my life I am making my fame work for me in a positive way . . . . This [AIDS] work means more to me than anything I've ever done as an actress."

In 1993 the Academy of Motion Picture Arts and Sciences honored Taylor with a special humanitarian award for her years with the American Foundation for AIDS Research. Looking radiant as ever, Taylor was present to accept the award and to thank all the other Hollywood stars who have helped her promote AIDS awareness. Taylor is now past 60—and grandmother to several adult grandchildren—but she has no plans to ease herself from the limelight. As photographer Herb Ritts (see *Newsmakers 92*) put it in *Vogue,* Taylor's "creamy public demeanor masks the will of steel—the boxing gloves behind the satin slippers—that has brought whole studios to their knees." Ritts added: "Whenever she set her heart on a man or a film role, a diamond or a racehorse, it was to be the only one in the world, for ever and ever.

Once she had it in her sights, her hold on it was total and irreversible."

Asked about her future in *Good Housekeeping,* Taylor laughed. "So far, I've lived a tremendously full life," she said. "I don't know how I could have crammed more into it. I've been asked to write my memoirs. Hell, no—I'm still living my memoirs. I can't stop to spend time in the past when I'm living each day to the fullest. To me, every new day is as important as yesterday."

Sources

Books

Contemporary Theatre, Film, and Television, Volume 7, Gale, 1989.

Periodicals

Good Housekeeping, February 1992.
Newsweek, May 7, 1990.
New York Times, June 16, 1985.
People, March 13, 1989; December 10, 1990; December 30, 1991.
Vanity Fair, November 1992.
Vogue, June 1991.

—*Anne Janette Johnson*

Jack Welch

Courtesy of General Electric

Chairman and CEO of General Electric Co.

Full name, John Francis Welch, Jr.; born November 19, 1935, in Peabody, MA; son of John Francis (a railroad conductor) and Grace (Andrews) Welch; married Carolyn Osburn, November 1959 (divorced, 1987); married Jane Beasley, April 1989; children: Katherine, John, Anne, Mark. *Education:* University of Massachusetts, B.S., 1957; University of Illinois, M.S., 1958, Ph.D., 1960.

Addresses: *Office*—3135 Easton Turnpike, Fairfield, CT 06431-0001.

Career

With General Electric Co., 1960—; engineer, 1960-68; general manager of worldwide plastics division, 1968-71, vice-president, 1972; vice-president and chief executive, components and materials group, 1973-77; senior vice-president, consumer goods and services division, 1977-79; vice-chairman and executive officer, 1979-81; chairman and chief executive officer, 1981—.

Sidelights

As a young, rising star at General Electric (GE) in the 1960s and 1970s, Jack Welch proved himself equally at home discussing the condensation in nuclear reactor steam systems and the backward business practices at one of America's largest corporations. By straddling the often warring worlds of science and management, Welch was perfectly posi-

tioned to see the waste and ineffectiveness spawned by a bloated corporate hierarchy that encouraged executive managers to stifle the inventiveness and spirit of the engineers and production staff. So impractical and overwhelming was the bureaucracy that, at one point, the GE light bulb division, in a pitch to high-level managers, spent $30,000—where a conversation should have sufficed—on a slick film demonstrating the efficiency of equipment that the division wanted to buy.

In 1981, when Welch became the youngest chairman and CEO in GE's much-storied history, his most pressing assignment was to redraw the business organizational chart that, he believed, would invariably frustrate the company's competitiveness in the future. He laid off more than 100,000 workers, an action of austerity that earned him the nickname "Neutron Jack," referring to the atomic bomb that theoretically kills people while leaving buildings intact. But Welch's business vision quickly delivered record growth and productivity to GE, and critics who had railed against his management style conceded that it had worked. Welch's image was further softened in the late 1980s and early 1990s, when he implemented new policies illustrating his firm belief that workers on the floor and engineers in the lab— rather than meddlesome executives in corner offices—are often a company's best decision makers. "You want to open up the place so people can flower and grow, expand, hit the home run," he was quoted as telling *Business Week*. "When you're tight-bound, controlled, checked, nitpicked, you kill it."

John Francis Welch Jr. was born November 19, 1935, in Peabody, Massachusetts, the only child of John Sr., a conductor on the Boston & Maine Railroad, and the former Grace Andrews. As his father was often away from home, much of Welch's moral, emotional, and intellectual support came from his strong-willed mother, who cheered her son on the sports fields and fostered in him the self-confidence he would bring to later academic and business challenges. She assured him that his serious stammer was not a speech impediment, but the result of a hyperactive brain working too fast for his mouth. Welch studied chemical engineering at the University of Massachusetts at Amherst, from which he graduated with honors in 1957, and won a graduate fellowship to the University of Illinois, where he earned his masters and doctorate degrees.

In 1960 Welch came to work at GE's engineered materials plant in western Massachusetts, where his skills as a scientist were quickly complemented by a business acumen that enabled him to understand not just a product's design, but the sales techniques and production steps required for that product to find a market niche. An increasingly prominent and respected voice in management decisions, Welch developed a reputation for abrasiveness, but his successes eclipsed skepticism about his management style. In one case, Welch sold to a competitor a new plastic that GE had developed but refused to use in its own housewares division. Only after this tactic of Welch's did GE also begin to use the plastic.

Within three years of his appointment as general manager of GE's worldwide plastics division, Welch turned the fledgling division into a $400 million-a-year powerhouse. Promotions followed rapid-fire; he was named vice-president in 1972 and in 1977 was appointed to head GE's consumers goods and services division. A vice-chairman in 1979, Welch achieved his signal success with GE Credit Corporation, which he turned from a small-time financier of refrigerators into a multibillion-dollar financial services colossus, making venture capital deals and, pivotally, serving as a shelter by which GE could avoid paying federal income taxes on its enormous income. In 1981 Welch's "Midas touch" was rewarded with his appointment to replace Reginald Jones as chairman of GE, the company that Thomas Edison had founded a century earlier and now, as the tenth largest industrial concern in the nation, made everything from 65-cent light bulbs to 400,000-pound locomotives to billion-dollar nuclear weapons.

The company to which Welch brought his maverick management style had, for more than 50 years, been the pacesetter for management in corporate America. In the 1950s GE led major American businesses in splitting into profit centers, and, in the 1970s, was in the vanguard in hiring huge staffs of strategic planners. In delivering a new management formula to GE, Welch, in the eyes of many observers, could either strengthen the entire field of U.S. businesses or, if he failed, take corporate America down with him.

While GE enjoyed sales of $25 billion, and under Jones had seen its profits tripled in eight years, Welch, joining a growing chorus of market analysts, feared that the company's size and bureaucracy

> *"You want to open up the place so people can flower and grow, expand, hit the home run. When you're tight-bound, controlled, checked, nitpicked, you kill it."*

would cast it as an out-of-focus, lumbering giant. Wielding the corporate equivalent of a surgeon's scalpel, Welch divided GE into winning divisions, those that were number one or number two in their markets, and losing divisions, mostly the company's older, slower-growing manufacturing concerns. Some criticized Welch for relying so singularly on market share, pointing out, for example, that Mercedes Benz and BMW, while not number one or two, consistently rank among the most profitable car makers in the industry. But others defended the criterion, arguing that a company as large as GE often needs to work with broad brush strokes; management, in deciding where to cut, must on occasion accept general and imprecise categories of winners and losers, lest it suffer the consequences of inaction.

Welch's winners, 16 of GE's almost 40 businesses, were further organized into three groups: manufacturing, services, and high technology. Managers of the losers were told that their divisions faced sale or shutdown unless business improved. Over the next five years, Welch closed 73 plants and facilities, sold 232 businesses and product lines for $5.9 billion, and laid off more than 132,000 workers—more than a quarter of the company's labor force. Nicknamed "Neutron Jack" for these firings, which hit managers as well as factory workers, Welch struggled to apply spin control, saying the former employees had been offered job-replacement help, retraining, and generous severance benefits. But at a company long perceived as offering lifetime security, Welch, as job killer, displayed what for many amounted to greed, arrogance, and a costly contempt for his employees. "Loyalty here is 24 hours deep," a GE executive was quoted as telling *Business Week*. "Welch has lost the dedication of a couple of hundred thousand people. He's done a remarkable job changing the emphasis of the company. But is the price bigger than the company should be paying?"

In the bottom-line world of investors and market analysts, the price was well worth it. By cutting its work force and by reorganizing divisions in such a way that management was encouraging rather than inhibiting product development, Welch fashioned a conglomerate that in no way resembled the slow-moving, reactive behemoth some feared it would become. Despite a modest start—by 1984 sales were still only about $28 billion, and annual growth rate in labor productivity was a meager 1.9 percent in Welch's first five years—GE, by the end of the first Welch decade, recorded sales of $58.4 billion, an annual growth rate of over eight percent, a third better than inflation. Although Welch's management philosophy put a premium on business focus, the chairman did not buy into the conventional wisdom that said small, nimble companies, at a time of increased global competition, would necessarily fare better than large ones. GE sold $10 billion worth of companies, stopped making television sets, and pulled out of mining and consumer electronics. But Welch bought $25 billion worth of new companies, including RCA, the New York investment bank Kidder Peabody, the Borg-Warner chemicals business, and Hungary's Tungsram lighting company. The 1986, $6.4-billion acquisition of RCA, whose crown jewel is the National Broadcasting Company (NBC), amounted to the largest merger in business history outside of the oil industry. Importantly, it proved to analysts that Welch could not only trim his company down, but boost its sales dramatically as well. The acquisition also broadened GE's base within the services and technology industries, the

two hot growth areas that Welch had expected to dominate the future business landscape.

But the high-profile purchases, while initially cheered by Wall Street, brought headaches in tandem with profits. At the time of the RCA deal, NBC was running strongly in the lead spot among the three major networks, but in the following years, it lost market share among the networks, all of which began to lose an increasing share to cable television. John H. Taylor wrote in *Fortune*, "This slippage must be galling for Jack Welch, an intensely competitive man, who has nearly tripled GE's profits since he took over ten years ago." Entertainment, Taylor wrote, is perhaps too wild an animal for GE, which is better equipped to handle the tamer specimens of manufacturing and money managing. But even the latter provided a setback, when, after GE's purchase of Kidder Peabody, the firm's top deal-maker was jailed for insider trading. Two other scandals, each involving fraudulent sales of GE military equipment, further eroded the company's standing in corporate America.

More than scandals, however, several questionable business decisions have revealed Welch's human side, and shaken his image as a corporate Messiah. In the early 1980s he pumped $500 million into the development of factory automation equipment to be sold to other companies, but the market failed to materialize and GE suffered a $120 million loss. In another case, GE did not pursue research into magnetic levitation technology for railroads—a technology seen by many as the next wave of public transportation—even as it boosted its investment in the manufacturing of conventional locomotives, whose revival Welch had optimistically and incorrectly predicted.

Despite these lapses, Welch is routinely listed among America's preeminent business gurus, even as his managerial image has undergone a dramatic transformation. The man who in the early 1980s used the corporate ax with ferocity and perceived remorselessness is, a decade later, embracing a fuzzy, feel-good approach to crafting a corporate atmosphere. "Neutron Jack" waxes on the advantages of a "boundaryless" workplace in which the traditional lines separating workers and departments are blurred in order to expedite the delivery of services and products. In an interview with *Fortune*, Welch was quoted as saying that he wants to one day leave behind "a company that's able to change at least as fast as the world is changing, and people whose real income is secure because they're winning and whose psychic income is rising because every person is participating."

The cornerstone of Welch's New Age management is the Work-Out, an intense forum in which rank and file GE employees and managers brainstorm about ways to make production more efficient in factories and other facilities. The idea came to Welch after attending a similarly rigorous, rough-and-tumble session of GE executives, and he believed the informal exchange would reap equally fruitful benefits if it included representatives from throughout GE ranks. The result, according to observers, has not only been an increased sense of inclusion among GE's labor force, but the adoption of significant cost-cutting policies that managers alone had never considered. Savings from Work-Outs have run into the millions, according to Welch, and have covered topics as far afield as reducing waste in GE polycarbonates, cutting paperwork by half in the aerospace division, and lessening the time it takes a new customer to open a credit card account at a mail-order store.

"The companies that have the technological skills and the manufacturing expertise are the ones that are going to come out ahead," a research analyst was quoted as telling *Kiplinger's Personal Finance Magazine*. "That is probably the most impressive area of GE—its ability to constantly drive down the cost structure and improve productivity. And for that, Welch is the key."

Sources

Business Week, December 14, 1987.
Economist, March 30, 1991.
Forbes, March 4, 1991.
Fortune, August 12, 1991.
Kiplinger's Personal Finance Magazine, August 1991.
New York Times, May 13, 1990; March 4, 1992; July 30, 1992.
Wall Street Journal, March 3, 1992.
Working Woman, December 1992.

—*Isaac Rosen*

Wynonna

AP/Wide World Photos

Singer and guitarist

Born Christina Claire Ciminella; name changed to Wynonna Judd; born May 30, 1964, in Ashland, KY; daughter of Michael Ciminella (a video producer) and Naomi Judd (a singer and songwriter).

Addresses: *Office*—MCA Records, Inc., 70 Universal City Plaza, Universal City, CA 91608.

Career

Country singer and guitarist since 1983; part of country duo the Judds, with mother Naomi; recorded and toured extensively, 1983-91 (Naomi forced to retire in 1991 due to chronic active hepatitis); Wynonna launched solo career with 1992 album and tour.

Awards: Four Grammy Awards and more than 60 country music awards.

Sidelights

Wynonna started out in the music business with her mother Naomi by her side; together they became one of the most popular country music duos ever—the Judds. When Naomi was sidelined by illness, Wynonna marched on as an extremely successful solo artist, selling a million copies of her initial album in its first week. Early in her career, Alanna Nash of *Stereo Review* wrote that Wynonna "is probably the most important new female country voice of the last twenty years." When her first solo album was released, David McGee of *Rolling Stone* noted, "It's easily the most important release by a

country artist so far this decade." Despite the heady praise, along with sold-out concert dates and continued strong record sales, Wynonna still feels insecure and greatly misses performing with her mother. "I go between one minute feeling like I can conquer the world," she told Steve Dougherty and Jane Sanderson of *People*, "and the next minute wanting to call my mom and have her come get me."

Wynonna was born in 1964 in Ashland, Kentucky. Her given name was actually Christina Claire Ciminella. Her mother Naomi (then known as Diana) had married at the age of 17 to childhood sweetheart Michael Ciminella. Wynonna was born during her mother's high school graduation week. In 1968 Michael finished college and took a job in California, moving his family with him. Settling in Los Angeles, a second daughter, Ashley, was born that year. The marriage, however, became rocky and by 1972, when Wynonna was eight, her parents divorced.

Naomi and the girls moved to Hollywood after the breakup. The single mother worked a variety of jobs to support her daughters, including managing a health food store, working as a secretary, and doing some modeling. Once the divorce was final, Naomi decided to restore her maiden name, Judd. She also determined that she would change her first name too and make a fresh start. She changed from Diana to Naomi, taking her name from the Bible story about Ruth and Naomi. Daughter Christina hated the fact that her parents divorced and decided to start over as well. She chose the name Wynonna from the lyrics of the pop song, "Route 66."

Naomi soon began to feel that Hollywood was not the best place to raise her children. "The girls were starting to think Hollywood was normal," Naomi said to Holly Gleason of *Ladies' Home Journal*. "I've always said there's more swimming pools in Los Angeles than there are Bibles. That's not what I wanted for my children." In 1976 Naomi moved the family back to Kentucky into a small house in the tiny, rural town of Morrill near Ashland. It was the true rural South. The house had no phone and no electricity, thus no television. "We went from having three TVs, two refrigerators and four phones to having none of the above," Wynonna told Gleason.

Naomi began nursing-school studies at Western Kentucky College as well as working to pay the bills. Wynonna, now 12 years old, discovered a plastic-string dime-store guitar that had been given to the family. She started teaching herself how to play the guitar and sing, and became engrossed in music. Listening to her daughter, Naomi began to join in. "I started singing and Mom'd be doin' chores and she'd start singing lower harmony," Wynonna said to Lisa Russell of *People*. "We'd sit around the supper table and sing just to pass the time."

In 1978 Naomi decided to complete her nursing studies at the College of Marin, near San Francisco, and moved the family to California. By the next year, Naomi had her degree and was a registered nurse. She then settled with her daughters in Nashville and pursued a nursing career.

Meanwhile Wynonna's teen years were rebellious and difficult. "I was very lazy, just lying in my room playing my guitar and singing," she related to Dougherty and Sanderson. "Mom worried about me. She'd try to cow-prod me to get out and do things, and I rebelled against that." When Wynonna did go out, her mother was very protective. "She was always asking me where I was going, who with, what time I'd be home, all the time," Wynonna said to Laura Fissinger of *McCall's*. The teen would break her curfew, leave her room messy, and talk back. Mother and daughter would then have some real battles. "One time I walked out in anger, and Mom locked me outdoors in my slip for a couple of hours," Wynonna recalled to Fissinger. "There were times when we really hated each other." The fighting became so intense that on a couple of occasions

Naomi sent her daughter packing. Once Wynonna stayed with friends for a while until her mother cooled down. Another time she spent a month living with her father in Florida.

Since Wynonna had won a high school talent show at the age of 16 and was consumed with music, Naomi decided to encourage that interest. She practiced singing with Wynonna and recorded some homemade tapes with her, singing harmonies to Wynonna's lead. In 1982, fate stepped in. The daughter of record producer Brent Maher was injured in an automobile accident and Naomi was assigned as her nurse at a Nashville hospital. After the girl's recovery, Naomi gave one of the Judd duet tapes to Maher and he listened to it. He was very impressed. Along with samples of bebop, bluegrass, and blues, "there was this Indian lullaby on it that Naomi had written....It just tore your heart out," Maher stated to Nash.

> *Being forced into close quarters on with her mother on their tour bus, according to Wynonna, was like "tying two cats' tails together and throwing them over the clothesline."*

Maher then worked with the Judds to turn them into professional singers, teaming them with guitarist Don Potter. Wynonna and Naomi defined and developed their style and the interplay of their voices with Potter's acoustic lead guitar. After several months of rehearsals, Maher was able to arrange a rare live audition for the Judds with RCA. Within an hour, the Judds had landed recording contract. "Things happened so fast, it was almost overwhelming," Wynonna said to Nash.

The Judd's first single, released in 1983, was "Had a Dream (For the Heart)." "Propelled by Wynonna's soulful lead vocals and Naomi's sweet-as-Moon-Pie harmonies," wrote *People*, that song broke into the country music Top 20, and their second single, "Mama He's Crazy," went right to the top of the charts. Their first album, *Why Not Me*, was released in 1984 and it too became a hit, eventually selling more than a million copies.

As the initial album was finished, the Judds prepared to go on the road and tour. But despite their newfound success, the duo still had a very rocky relationship. "Music was the only thing we agreed on," Naomi remarked to Fissinger. Being forced into close quarters on their tour bus, Wynonna told Kathryn Casey of *Ladies' Home Journal*, was like "tying two cats' tails together and throwing them over the clothesline." Some nights mother and daughter were refusing to speak to each other just moments before going onstage.

After months on the road, however, they finally reconciled. "Being on that bus together with nothing to do but communicate was the best thing that could have happened to us," admitted Wynonna to Casey. She and her mother were "in each other's faces twenty-four hours a day. We *had* to work it out," she noted to Fissinger. Slowly, the duo became close friends. "We've been comrades in the trenches," Naomi said to Gleason. "We both know we'll be there for each other."

Naomi Judd, left, and daughter Wynonna, perform at their farewell concert in Murfreesboro, Tennessee, in December of 1991. AP/Wide World Photos.

When the Judds went out on the road, some family members were afraid of the kinds of places they would be playing. "They thought we'd be singing in honky-tonks and drinking beer," Wynonna told Nancy Anderson of *Good Housekeeping*. "My grandfather decided everything was all right when he saw me on [the musical variety-comedy television show] *Hee-Haw.*" The Judds' second album, *Rockin' with the Rhythm*, was released in 1986. In reviewing the record, Nash, in another *Stereo Review* article, wrote that the Judds' influences are "diverse and eclectic, ranging from individual artists, such as Bonnie Raitt [see *Newsmakers 90*] and Joni Mitchell [see *Newsmakers 91*], to entire genres, including folk, urban and Mississippi blues, commercial pop, rock-and-roll, Western swing, gospel, and bebop." But their "hearts were in country," and especially noteworthy was Wynonna's "lusty, drop-dead pipes." The album, Nash stated, "has a world of wonderful things going on . . . . Whether you are a city or a country dweller, I cannot imagine your not liking this record. Good music, no matter what name you want to put on it, will always sound sweet." Jay Cocks of *Time* wrote that *Rockin' with the Rhythm* "shows the Judds off at their finest." The record "comes alive from adept musicianship and vocals that ease around, then animate the lyrics like a spring breeze blowing a window curtain." This album also sold over a million copies. The next Judds' album, *Heart Land*, came out in 1987. Fissinger, this time writing in *Rolling Stone*, noted that the Judds are "pushing themselves out" into new territory, taking on a jazz song, Ella Fitzgerald's "Cow Cow Boogie," a mountain hymn, and Elvis Presley's "Don't Be Cruel." Jimmy Guterman of *Musician*, however, found the album's songs disappointing. Although he called Wynonna "the most striking country-and-western singer today" who can turn "the most banal tune into a delight," on *Heart Land* "there are enough banalities to keep that voice busy." Guterman concluded: "The Judds' singing gets stronger every record—why can't the same thing happen to their songs?" Despite being a "middling" album, it went gold.

The Judds released two more albums in 1988, *Talk About Love* and *Greatest Hits.* Their albums continued to sell well and they continued to rack up No. 1 country singles. They were already reaching double-figures in hit singles, and in 1989 they added two more No. 1's. The Judds put out another album that year, *River of Time*, and had their own CBS television special. The busy year also saw Naomi remarry and Wynonna become engaged to singer/songwriter/musician Tony King.

The year 1990 was an unfortunate turning point for the Judds. On New Year's Day, Naomi woke up ill. After a couple months of lethargy, she saw a doctor. The eventual diagnosis was chronic active hepatitis, a serious, incurable, life-threatening disease. In October of that year, Naomi and Wynonna called a press conference to announce that they would end their career together at the completion of their 1991 concert tour. Naomi would retire and Wynonna would go solo. The Judds released their final studio album in 1990, called *Love Can Build a Bridge*, and it soared into the Top 20 on the country charts. To help her mother through her illness, Wynonna decided to postpone her wedding.

In 1991 a second compilation of Judds' hits was released, *Greatest Hits, Volume Two*. In mid-1991 Wynonna began recording her first solo album for release in early 1992. The Judds then prepared for their final road tour. In eight years, the duo had collected six gold records and registered 18 No. 1 country singles. For their finale the Judds scheduled a number of dates and, according to Alan Light *Rolling Stone*, "took a lot of heat for the seemingly endless farewell tour." Light noted, "The tearful TV appearances and medically detailed magazine stories risked putting them squarely back into country-kitsch territory." Wynonna was not surprised by the criticism. "I knew that at some point people were going to say, 'Oh, great, they're going to cry again,'" she told Light. "But on a personal level and a spiritual level, what that tour did for Mom far outweighs any critics' backlash."

The 1992 release of *Wynonna*, her debut solo album, was a spectacular success. The album, a collection of rock, blues, and country songs, took off like a rocket, entering the pop charts at No. 4 and challenging Bruce Springsteen, as well as knocking Garth Brooks (see *Newsmakers 92*) off the top of the country music charts for the first time in six months.

Wynonna received a number of glowing reviews. Besides labeling the album the "most important" country release, McGee wrote that it explores its "fully developed portraits with style, insight, nuance and a heart laid bare." He added, "*Wynonna* is an album informed by integrity and wisdom, begging no classification save that of powerful, stirring, ennobling music." Karen Schoemer of *Mademoiselle* remarked that "Wynonna's new album proves that she was more than ready to strike out on her own. Where the Judds always had the faint reek of home-sweet-home sentimentality, *Wynonna* is brash and confident." Schoemer continued, "No matter what end of the emotional spectrum she's exploring, Wynonna

brings each incident to life." James Hunter of the *New York Times* wrote that *Wynonna* is "an album without an extraneous note or languid moment." It is "a faultless 90's country album" that "demonstrates that a country performer can explore vibrant pop, deep gospel and straight-forward rock and still make sense to country traditionalists."

Not all critics praised the album, however. John Leland of *Newsweek* wrote: "Neither country nor pop, with tinges of gospel and blues, *Wynonna* ...dissipates in its ambiguities. Her ballads are syrupy, without the Judds' overwhelming conviction in syrup." Leland proclaimed, "Wynonna has yet to find her balance."

During her nine-month 1992 tour to promote the album, Wynonna was determined to fight her long-standing weight problem. She installed an exercise bike on the tour bus and brought along a physical trainer. "We all have our indulgences," she told Dougherty and Sanderson, "and mine aren't alcohol or drugs, and I don't smoke. But food has been my reward and, frankly, I've rewarded myself a lot."

During breaks in her busy schedule, Wynonna relaxes on her 22-acre farm near Franklin, Tennessee, just down the road from her mother's place. And she spends much of her free time alone at home with her horses, dogs, and cats. Her engagement to Tony King was broken, with wedding plans postponed indefinitely.

Sales of her first album continued to be strong and, by 1993, Wynonna became only the second solo female artist to sell more than two million copies of a studio album. Early in 1993 she went back to the studio to begin work on her second album. Producer Tony Brown told Brian Mansfield of *Country Song Roundup*, "Basically, we're taking the last album and stepping it up a little bit....We can't be scared to expand. That's the thing Wynonna has to do—create her own sound."

Wynonna's second album, called *Tell Me Why*, was released in May of 1993. Jean Calmen of the *Detroit Free Press* noted in her review of the album that "if her first solo left any doubt about what kind of audience Wynonna Judd would go after, this one clears it up: a broad one. She again pursues a wide range of styles that includes pop, country, blues and gospel, with mostly good results." Tony Scherman of *People* wrote, "On first listen, *Tell Me Why* may seem another bland crossover cocktail, that Nashville syrup of pop, rock and country. But there's an earthiness, a kick, to Wynonna's singing that gets more satisfying with each push of the play button.

Arriving just 14 months after *Wynonna*, her surprisingly self-assured solo debut, *Tell Me Why* establishes her as one of the finer pop voices of the young decade."

Wynonna insists that she never would have gone solo if Naomi had not become ill. "I could never have just left my mother. It just wasn't in my makeup," she said to *People*. "Mom and I were happiest singing together." Now standing in the spotlight all alone, Wynonna continues to have mixed feelings about her solo career. "Sometimes I'm excited about it all," she told Dougherty and Sanderson. "Other times I go, 'Oh, crap, this is what they all meant when they said someday you'll be on your own.'"

Selected discography

With the Judds

Why Not Me, RCA, 1984.
Rockin' With the Rhythm, RCA, 1986.
Heart Land, RCA, 1987.
Talk About Love, RCA, 1988.
Greatest Hits, RCA, 1988.
River of Time, RCA, 1989.
Love Can Build a Bridge, RCA, 1990.

Greatest Hits, Volume Two, RCA, 1991.

Solo albums

Wynonna, Curb/MCA, 1992.
Tell Me Why, Curb/MCA, 1993.

Sources

Country Song Roundup, May 1993.
Detroit Free Press, May 10, 1993.
Good Housekeeping, June 1988.
Ladies' Home Journal, November 1988; November 1991; November 1992.
Mademoiselle, July 1992.
McCall's, May 1986.
Modern Screen Yearbook No. 36, 1993.
Musician, April 1987.
Newsweek, April 20, 1992.
New York Times, May 24, 1992.
People, August 20, 1984; November 26, 1990; December 9, 1991; July 13, 1992; May 17, 1993.
Rolling Stone, July 2, 1987; May 28, 1992; June 25, 1992.
Stereo Review, February 1986; December 1986.
Time, January 13, 1986; April 20, 1992.

—*Greg Mazurkiewicz*

Jeff Zucker

Television news producer

Born c. 1965 in Miami, FL; son of Matthew (a cardiologist) and Arline (an English teacher) Zucker. *Education:* Graduated from Harvard University with a degree in history.

Addresses: *Office*—c/o NBC News, 30 Rockfeller Plaza, New York, NY.

Career

After graduating from Harvard, worked for NBC Sports as a researcher for the 1988 Summer Olympics; began working for NBC's *Today* show as a segment producer, became supervising producer, 1990; named executive producer, 1991. Also worked briefly as executive producer of *NBC Nightly News,* 1993.

Sidelights

Fans of the CBS sitcom *Murphy Brown* might draw a parallel between Jeff Zucker and the show's fictional news producer Miles Silverberg. Both came to fame as prodigiously young, urban-bred, Jewish go-getters, products of Harvard University and American popular culture. And according to those who know Zucker, the similarity doesn't end there. Where the sitcom Silverberg is a hypersensitive fly-off-the-handle type, Zucker is also notorious for his hair-trigger temper and bombastic reactions (a *Newsweek* article by Joshua Hammer depicted the young producer hunched behind a console screaming "Get the shot! Get the shot!" into the earpiece of a cameraman following Bill Clinton.) But even his critics admit that Zucker deserves some kind of an emotional outlet to handle the pressure of producing a live, two-hour daily broadcast that might cover a war one day, a presidential election the next.

Contrary to what his urbane image might suggest, Zucker was not born in New York City—although he may as well have been, as he refers to his native Miami as "the sixth borough." The son of a cardiologist and a high-school English teacher, Jeff Zucker showed early talent in both academics and athletics. In fact, he was an avid tennis player, who played "every day from the time he was 6 until he went to college, competing on the high-school team," as Tim Allis remarked in a *People* profile.

At the same time, Zucker devoted equal energy to his studies, editing his junior-high and high-school newspapers. By the time he graduated from Harvard in 1988, he had earned his degree in history while serving on of the university's well-known paper, *The Harvard Crimson.* There he wrote a sports column and used his own initials for its name: "All that JAZ." Hammer's *Newsweek* article quoted *Esquire* editor Michael Hirschorn's remark that Zucker proved "staggeringly competent" at Harvard. Zucker ended up winning editorship of the *Crimson,* beating out Hirschorn.

While as a youth he imagined himself "covering the Dolphins for the *Miami Herald,*" as he told *Newsweek,* a more grown-up Zucker had his eye on entering Harvard Law School. That his application was not accepted stung the young man, who had carried a B-plus average—though he later became philosophical about the rejection ("He figures [Harvard Law] probably had its quota of white, Jewish, Ivy League males," noted Edwin Diamond in *New York*).

Instead, Zucker, who had worked summers at ABC Sports, took a job for NBC Sports. He was hired in 1986, ostensibly as a researcher supporting the TV anchors at the 1988 Summer Olympics; he responded by spending two years compiling a massive 4,000-page historical opus on Olympic facts and background. Zucker eventually caught the eye of reporter Jane Pauley, who found him a "walking fact machine," as she recalled in the *People* piece.

> *Zucker admitted that after producing his first* Today *show he "went home and threw up."*

Pauley persuaded the NBC brass to hire Zucker for the venerable-but-struggling *Today* show. He joined the morning news-and-features show as a field producer in 1989. "His arrival coincided almost precisely with the start of the morning show's much publicized problems," Richard Zoglin pointed out in *Time.* "First was the infamous [Bryant] Gumbel memo, in which the anchor made disparaging remarks about some of his colleagues, notably weatherman Willard Scott. Then came the departure of longtime co-anchor [Pauley] and her replacement by [Deborah] Norville, the brittle blond who alienated both viewers and staff members."

When Katherine (Katie) Couric came on board as a national correspondent in 1990, "she spotted a callow-looking Zucker in a sweatshirt and jeans and remembers thinking 'he looks pretty darn cocky,'" as *People* reported. Cocky or not, Zucker was appointed *Today*'s supervising producer later that year. Acknowledging some skepticism among older staffers about a 25-year-old handling such a high-pressure job, Zucker admitted to Allis that after producing his first show he "went home and threw up."

Things began looking up when Norville went on maternity leave in 1991. Couric was named her replacement, and soon after was given the permanent post of co-anchor, opposite Gumbel (Norville subsequently surfaced first on network radio, then on CBS as a correspondent). For Zucker, the new, smooth-running *Today* heralded a year of advancement for him. He was promoted to executive producer of the show in December of 1991.

Television's latest *wunderkind* promptly set out to bring a fresh approach to a show that was older than he. As *Time* reported, Zucker booked up-to-the-minute musical acts (Color Me Badd, Curtis Steigers) for *Today* appearances; at the same time, he grew aggressive in his coverage of breaking news. When boxer Mike Tyson was convicted of rape, for instance, Zucker devoted almost a half hour of airtime covering the story, inviting several principals, including the trial's prosecuting attorney, as guests.

"Yet Zucker, defying the MTV-generation stereotype, has not turned the show into Short Attention Span Theatre," added Zoglin. "In fact, he is letting interview segments run longer—six to seven minutes, on average, compared to [just over four] to five minutes previously." ("I hate cutting people off," Zucker told Zoglin.)

Zucker has shown he can fly by the seat of his pants. That became evident when *Today* shows made headlines themselves. The Persian Gulf War was an early example of Zucker style. "We were originating from all over the world," he recalled in Diamond's *New York* article. "We began winging it; we just did it without checking with anybody." The war, added Diamond, "drove home for Zucker the most important lesson for the *Today* show: 'This is live TV. Let it roll.'"

Zucker "let it roll" again in late April 1992, the day after the Rodney King trial had ended in acquittal for the four Los Angeles officers accused of using excessive force. The ensuing demonstrations and riotous looting led the morning's *Today* coverage—and then Zucker "trashed the schedule to make room for live footage," as *Newsweek*'s Joshua Hammer noted. Later that year, independent presidential candidate H. Ross Perot was scheduled for an early interview. So compelling was Perot that Zucker ended up devoting almost the entire two hours to the candidate and his statements.

Not all of Zucker's new ideas proved successful—according to Zoglin, the show once tried "a series of daily call-in segments on such topics as sex, dieting and jobs; they seemed unfocused and pointless." But overall, the revised strategies seemed to work. *Today*'s ratings, while still nipping the heels of rival ABC's *Good Morning America*, rose under Zucker's tenure. Part of the credit can go to Couric, who helped revive the "family" atmosphere that had grown sour during the previous intra-show turmoil. Couric counts herself a fan of Zucker, and the feeling is mutual. In the *Time* article, the young executive also had words of praise for the much-maligned Bryant Gumbel, calling the moody anchor "very opinionated.... That's his greatest strength and it hurts him too. But you'd be hard pressed to find a better interviewer on TV."

As if the *Today* show weren't work enough, Zucker got yet another promotion in 1992. In a highly unusual move, he was made executive producer of NBC's *Nightly News—while* staying with the morning show. "This is probably nuts," said Zucker of the dual appointments, in a *Detroit Free Press* interview. Again, some wondered whether, at 27, Zucker was too young to appreciate the enormity of his responsibility producing two of NBC's major newscasts—and whether he was just too young, too lacking in history, to put the news in context. For his part, Zucker told the *Free Press*'s Marc Gunther that he vaguely recalled the first moon landing in 1969, and that the first major news event he remembers was President Nixon's resignation in 1974, when Zucker was nine. Yet his scholarly grasp of the past is considerable; he majored in history at Harvard. Tom Brokaw, the *Nightly News* anchor, expressed confidence in Zucker's ability: "He is mature way beyond his years," Brokaw told the *Free Press*. But in the same article, Gumbel admitted, "I don't think it's a good idea. I have my doubts that it can work." Likewise, an anonymous NBC veteran expressed doubt that anyone, no matter how talented, could competently hold down two stressful full-time-plus jobs, adding that Zucker could last "three months, tops" in this endeavor.

That last comment proved prophetic. In fact, Zucker lasted almost exactly three months at the helm of the *Nightly News* before resigning in mid-March of 1993 to work exclusively on *Today*. (The mistaken belief that one man could work on two shows was just one of the network news division's problems that year. The department also became the target of widespread criticism when General Motors proved that a magazine show, *Dateline*, had falsified a crash test during an investigation of a GM truck by planting small incendiary devices designed to produce a fire on impact. And in a later scandal, involving an environmental story, some stock film of fish was misleadingly presented as new. NBC News chief Michael Gartner resigned in early spring of 1993.)

But the man *New York* has dubbed the "wired wonder boy" has generally escaped this brand of controversy, emerging from the flack with his reputation intact. With his schedule, which includes leaving for work at 5:15 a.m., Zucker acknowledges that maintaining a social life is difficult. But "it's important that I have my friends and that I still date and go to screenings," he told Allis. "Otherwise, I would go nuts."

Sources

Detroit Free Press, January 29, 1993.
Newsweek, February 1, 1993.
New York, December 21, 1992.
People, August 17, 1992.
Time, March 23, 1992.

—Susan Salter

Obituaries

Arthur Ashe

Born Arthur Robert Ashe, July 10, 1943, in Richmond, VA; died of pneumonia resulting from AIDS, February 6, 1993, in New York City. Tennis player, author, and activist. One of the last times legendary American tennis player Arthur Ashe appeared in the news media before his death at 49, he was being arrested during a protest against treatment of Haitian immigrants carrying the AIDS virus. He suffered another of several heart attacks shortly thereafter. In a typically engaged fashion, Ashe had stayed as active and vocal as possible in the months following his 1992 press conference announcement that he was suffering from AIDS, which he contracted from a blood transfusion during open-heart surgery in 1983. He had been diagnosed in 1988 but opted for privacy, not assembling the press until four years later—only because someone close to him had leaked the fact of his illness to the media, and he wanted to avoid an undignified backdoor revelation. Soon thereafter he established the Arthur Ashe Foundation for the Defeat of AIDS, and joined the boards of the Harvard AIDS Institute and the UCLA AIDS Institute. In so doing he led the way for black American athletes and fought prejudice based on race or because of AIDS with grace and determination. As former competitor and perennial tennis favorite Jimmy Connors remarked, as quoted by the *Detroit Free Press*, "He didn't take it lying down, did he? He was out there doing things, taking care of business to the end."

Ashe was not only the first black man to win a singles title at Wimbledon, overcoming the tremendous odds and prejudices inherent in his sport as well as in his segregated home town of Richmond, Virginia, but he was an active social leader and the editor of a series of books on African-American athletic history, published in 1988. When his athletic career was cut short by his first heart attack at age 35, Ashe concentrated on other interests. In a way that foreshadowed his intense involvement in AIDS groups, Ashe served as campaign chairman for the American Heart Association.

As a young boy, Ashe spent much of his spare time in the Richmond public park designated for black use of which his father, Arthur Sr., was the superintendent. The caretaker's cottage there was the Ashe home. A bookish and introspective child, Ashe was rocked when his mother died in 1949. He became motivated and competitive in school and on the court. Ashe, quoted in *Contemporary Black Biography*, explained, "Books and sports were my way of bandaging the wound. I was too light for football and not quite fast enough for track, which left tennis as a logical choice." Many times the young tennis player fell victim to racist tricks and tactics when trying to break into the typically white country-club sport—sometimes he was barred from a match because he had "arrived late," which was nonsense. When allowed to play, however, Ashe was a cool competitor, gracefully making his way to a nationally ranked amateur status by age 14. Under the tutelage of Ronald Charity and Dr. Walter Johnson, Ashe won junior indoor singles titles in 1960 and 1961. He was then offered a tennis scholarship at UCLA, where he won many singles and doubles tournaments.

Ashe won his first international tournament in 1968 at the U.S. Open, and made regular appearances at the World Championship Tennis Finals until he beat Bjorn Borg in 1975. That same year, he surprised tennis fans worldwide by trouncing Jimmy Connors for the Wimbledon singles trophy. The *Times* of London recalled the match this way: "[Connors] was reckoned so formidable at that stage of his career that hardly anyone gave Ashe a chance.... But on that day Ashe played a very different match from the normal.... He broke up Connors's rhythm.... To the astonishment of Centre Court, Ashe took the first two sets 6-1, 6-1. Connors fought back strongly to take the third 7-5, but Ashe found new reserves of ingenuity to end it in the fourth, which he won 6-4."

Ashe was ranked in the top five players in the world when he began to experience health problems in 1977, the year of his marriage to Jeanne-Marie Moutoussamy, a photographer. Eye inflammations and heel injuries sidelined him for a year, at the end of which time he again astonished his fans by climbing back to the top. In 1979 he suffered his first heart attack, and retired for good after 33 tournament wins. *Contemporary Black Biography* recalled Ashe saying in the *Chicago Tribune* that "an athlete retires twice. The first time is when they don't renew your contract. But for a couple of years afterwards you still think you could get in shape again and play another season or two. Then one day you look in the mirror and the reality finally sinks in that it's time to find something else to do." Among those other things for Ashe was research into African-American athletic history, since existing material on the subject was scant. Using his own funds, Ashe threw himself into compiling a three-volume history titled *A Hard Road to Glory*, which was eventually adapted for television and earned an Emmy in 1988. Ashe worked as a tennis coach and television commentator as well as for his many charitable involvements.

Among the touching tributes after his death was a request to the spectators by Martina Navratilova for a moment of silence after a match in Tokyo, when she remembered "an extraordinary human being who transcended his sport, his race, religion and nationality and in his own way helped to change the world," reported the *Washington Post*. Of the many tributes to Ashe at the time of his death, President Bill Clinton remarked in a lengthy statement that "Arthur Ashe never rested with his fame. He used the strength of his voice and the power of his example to open the doors of opportunity for other African Americans, fighting discrimination in America and around the world . . . . He was a true American hero and a great example to all of us." Ashe is survived by his wife and their daughter, Camera Elizabeth. **Sources:** *Contemporary Black Biography*, volume 1, edited by Michael L. LaBlanc, Gale, 1992; *Detroit Free Press*, February 8, 1993; *Los Angeles Times*, February 7, 1993; *Oakland Press* (Michigan), February 7, 1993; *Sports Illustrated*, February 15, 1993; *Times* (London), February 8, 1993; *Washington Post*, February 8, 1993.

Thomas A. Dorsey

Born Thomas Anthony Dorsey in 1899 in Villa Rica, GA; died of Alzheimer's disease, January 23, 1993, in Chicago, IL. Gospel and blues composer, singer, pianist, and music publisher. Thought by many to be the father or the creator of gospel music, which merged religious lyrics with what had been secular rhythms, Thomas A. Dorsey was the author of some 1,000 gospel songs. Dorsey's songs are entwined with the history of the United States and the struggles of African-Americans therein. He was "the chief force in gospel's development, adding tabernacle song material and blues touches to the spiritual," according to the *New York Times*. The influence of Dorsey on gospel is so great as to almost make the man inseparable from the music. Jerry Adler of *Newsweek* did not exaggerate when he said, "From 30,000 churches across the land every Sunday, voices are raised in the music he put there," gospel hymns such as "Jesus is the Light of the World," "How About You," "Angels Watching Over Me," and "My Savior Carries Me Home." As Anthony Heilbut added in the *New York Times*, "Few composers dominate their genre so dramatically as Thomas Anthony Dorsey, father of the gospel song." "The lion's share of the most popular gospel compositions are his."

The T. A. Dorsey Gospel Chorus sang "Precious Lord, Take My Hand" at Dorsey's funeral; a Dorsey classic (eventually covered by Mahalia Jackson and Elvis Presley) that was a favorite of the Reverend Dr. Martin Luther King, Jr., it was sung at King's funeral as well. "In the anguished time following King's death, it was a prayer of healing and comfort," said Bernice Johnson Reagon, founder of the female gospel group Sweet Honey in the Rock, in the *Washington Post*. And yet, Dorsey also penned some 2,000 blues tunes in his earlier incarnation as "Georgia Tom," a pianist who toured with Ma Rainey. A blues chart hit in 1928, "It's Tight Like That," sold seven million copies. Some said that Dorsey, the son of a minister and his wife, experienced a moral conflict between the commercial music he played and his religious upbringing.

At the age of 12, Dorsey had begun playing the blues for money in movie houses and houses of prostitution. As such he gained "his first exposure to the blues and ragtime from the theater's piano players," said Reagon. He saved enough money to move north three years later, at the age of 15. Dorsey eventually attended the Chicago Music College and then began touring as Georgia Tom. He had already sampled some gospel arrangements with his five-piece band after hearing E.M. Nix sing "I Do, Don't You?" in 1922 at the National Baptist Convention in Chicago. "My inner being was thrilled. My soul was a deluge of divine rapture," Dorsey once said in an interview, according to the *Washington Post*. "My emotions were aroused; my heart was inspired to become a great singer and worker in the Kingdom of the Lord—and impress people just as this great singer did that Sunday morning."

Dorsey composed his first religious song in 1926 called "If You See My Savior, Tell Him That You Saw Me" after the death of a friend. Death was also the catalyst for his most popular song: in 1931, Dorsey's first wife died in childbirth. A day later, their newborn son followed her. *Newsweek* quoted Dorsey in the documentary *Say Amen, Somebody:* "People tried to tell me things that were soothing to me . . . none of which have ever been soothing to me from that day to this." But somehow in the face of such tragedy he wrote "Precious Lord," which has helped to soothe the entire world—it has been translated into 50 languages. The next year, Dorsey was transformed into a full-time, and very busy, gospel musician. He was made musical director of Pilgrim Baptist Church, a post he held until 1983. (The year of his retirement, the Chicago church created the T.A. Dorsey choir in his honor.)

At first there was a fair amount of resistance from the churchgoers to Dorsey's bluesy rhythms, which they associated with the South, and a life of deprivation they wished to leave behind. Some believe that without Dorsey, however, this wellspring of Southern life might have evaporated. Dorsey broke through to them by producing a disciplined and famously appealing choir. Dorsey wrote in 1949 that he had found some choirs "who do not possess enough spirit and others who have too many embellishments that are mistaken for spirit. Loud vociferous singing, uninspired gesticulations, or self-encouraged spasms of the body is not spirit . . . I don't believe in going to get the spirit before it comes," he said, according to the *Washington Post.*

In 1932 Dorsey formed the National Convention of Gospel Choirs and Choruses with blues singer Sallie Martin. By the 1940s he was touring with Mahalia Jackson. Dorsey soon discovered that there was money to be made in gospel music. As the first African-American to publish gospel music, Dorsey gave demonstrations and hired salesmen to spread his church music far and wide. In this way, Dorsey finally reconciled his potential for commercial success and his spirituality. Dorsey married his second wife, the former Kathryn Mosley in 1941, and the couple had a son and daughter; all three survive him. **Sources:** *Chicago Tribune,* January 25, 1993; *Jet,* February 8, 1993; *New York Times,* January 25, 1993; *Newsweek,* February 8, 1993; *Time,* February 8, 1993; *Washington Post,* January 25, 1993, January 31, 1993.

Clara Hale

Born Clara McBride, April 1, 1905, in Elizabeth City, NC; died of complications from a stroke, December 18, 1992, in New York City. Philanthropist, social activist, child care worker also known as "Mother Hale." No one could better qualify for the affectionate title "Mother" than Clara Hale of New York City's Hale House fame. The biological mother of three, adoptive mother of one, foster mother to 40 (and she considered herself grandmother to their 60 children), and provider of love, care, and nurturing to more than 1,000 under the auspices of Hale House, Mother Hale enfolded some of the most troubled children New York could produce into her arms. When newborn babies began appearing at the five-story brownstone in the early 1980s—addicted to crack or exposed to AIDS in the womb—Mother Hale only lavished more affection on them, often taking the babies needing the most care into her own bedroom. Doctors and other health care workers despaired of finding an effective treatment for these tortured children, but Mother Hale's method had a 90 percent success rate. When tiny infants would wake in the night with terrible drug withdrawal pains, Mother Hale would hold them and rock them for hours. In her later years, she complained that she had become too weak to bear them in her arms for very long. Mother Hale had not acquired any traditional training for her lifelong child care mission; as she said in the *Chicago Tribune,* "It wasn't their fault they were born addicted. Love them. Help one another, love one another."

Although a federal grant initially paid for Hale House at 145 West 122nd Street, and New York City monies supported Mother Hale's efforts for many years, she had to battle a city ordinance forbidding children under five to be raised in group care. She was made an exception to the rule, but Mother Hale was hobbled again in 1989 when the city withdrew funds, claiming that the crack baby epidemic had crested. Still, these babies came to Hale House, which Mother Hale and her daughter Lorraine then operated on private funds. Aided by such celebrities as singers Lena Horne, John Lennon, and Tony Bennett, Mother Hale eventually expanded her operation to include treatment programs for drug-addicted mothers, troubled young people, and AIDS-infected babies. Mother Hale was a pioneer in the firm belief that the only effective help for the disadvantaged was self-help; she was a tireless fundraiser for these bootstrap enterprises.

An orphan at 16 and a widow at 27, young Clara Hale cleaned houses and theaters until she became reluctant to leave behind her three children at home. Instead, she began taking foster children into her home for $2 a week. Caring for seven or eight children at a time, Mother Hale eventually taught each of her 40 foster children self-respect and self-preservation. Mother Hale had just retired at age 63 when an impulse of Lorraine Hale's changed both of their lives forever. Lorraine was driving through a poor neighborhood of New York City and saw a drug-addicted woman in a stupor almost drop her two-month old baby. She stopped her car and told the woman to take her baby to Mother Hale and seek drug treatment. The next day, Mother Hale called Lorraine to say, "There's a junkie at my door, and she says you sent her," reported the *New York Times.* Mother Hale cared for the child for free, and the word quickly spread. Within six months Mother Hale took in 22 drug-addicted babies.

In Hale House's first years, the program was to accept babies of drug-addicted mothers, no matter what their condition; and as long as the mothers sought treatment, they could be reunited with their children. The success rate was, and continues to be, unprecedented. Lorraine Hale, who earned doctorates in child development and developmental psychology, is the president of Hale House and its programs, which had a budget of $3.5 million in 1991. At the time of her mother's death, Lorraine Hale planned to continue the good works of Hale House and reach out to more people in need. A true role model and hero by any measure, Mother Hale was mentioned in former President Ronald Reagan's 1985 State of the Union address as an "American heroine," according to the *Los Angeles Times.* Mother Hale retorted that she was no hero, as recalled the *New York Times;* instead, she reiterated her loving philosophy: "We hold them and touch them. They love you to tell them how great they are, how good they are. Somehow, even at a young age, they understand that. They're happy, and they turn out well." **Sources:** *Chicago Tribune,* December 20, 1992; *Los Angeles Times,* December 19, 1992; *New York Times,* December 20, 1992; *Oakland Press* (Michigan), December 20, 1992.

Ferruccio Lamborghini

Born April 28, 1916, in Cento, Italy; died of a heart attack, February 20, 1993, in Perugia, Italy. Carmaker. In 1987 a Lamborghini sportscar fetched $125,000; surely the leopard-skin-upholstered model made for crooner Frank Sinatra in the 1960s would have an enormous price tag at an auction. Since its introduction to the car-buying public in 1963, the name Lamborghini has conjured up images of dashing Italian playboys driving impossibly fast, sexy-looking cars. The man behind the car, Ferruccio Lamborghini, was not encouraged in his native farming village to become a mechanic. In spite of this, he became an industrial engineer, which put him in good stead as a soldier when World War II swept over Europe. Lamborghini was working as a mechanic in the army's motor pool when he was captured and sent to a Greek prisoner-of-war camp. After his release, the future car magnate recycled deserted German tanks into tractors. Soon he could afford to build factories that produced heaters and auto parts as well.

It was in 1959, according to legend, that Lamborghini found a fault in the design of his Ferrari. That year, he designed and built his first sportscar, assisted by fellow engineer Paolo Stanzani. The 350 GT was intended to be a more reliable version of its temperamental European counterparts, which continue to be famous for their in-garage repair time. According to Burt A. Folkart of the *Los Angeles Times,* Lamborghini and Giotto Bizzarrini "created a four-cam, V-12 engine with six carburetors. The body was styled to resemble a melding of the Jaguar XK-E and an Aston Martin with a Ferrari-like profile.... Later models included a more complex Miura model and the Countach. It was powered by the 420-horsepower V-12s that had top speeds of 170 m.p.h." Among other original concepts, Lamborghini invented an air-cooled engine. Lamborghinis were made available to the public for the first time in 1963; the expensive, beautiful machines caught the eyes of many sportscar enthusiasts, including Princess Grace (Kelly) of Monaco, and Lamborghini was soon struggling to fill orders. The energy crisis of the 1970s hurt the automaker to the extent that he was forced to sell the majority of his holdings. By 1987, the giant American car company Chrysler Corporation took over the small Italian company, called Nuova Automobili F. Lamborghini. Lamborghini retired to Italy's Umbrian countryside, saying, "When a man gets old, only two things to do: Sell ice cream or go to the farm," as the *Los Angeles Times* reported. There he cultivated vineyards and collected his own sportscars. Lamborghini suffered a heart attack on February 5, and succumbed to its effects soon after. **Sources:** *Chicago Tribune,* February 22, 1993; *Los Angeles Times,* February 22, 1993; *New York Times,* February 22, 1993.

Reginald Lewis

Born Reginald Francis Lewis, December 7, 1942, in Baltimore, MD; died of a cerebral hemorrhage, January 19, 1993, in New York City. Attorney and chairman of TLC Beatrice International Holdings Corporation. Reginald Lewis may have been the most important African-American businessman in this century. His successes were unparalleled, and his company, TLC Beatrice International Holdings Corp. (better known as simply "Beatrice"), was the largest ever to be owned by a black American. (TLC stands for the "The Lewis Company.") Lewis's net worth at the time of his death was estimated by *Forbes* to be $400 million. Lewis was a world-class academic philanthropist, too. He contributed $1 million to Howard University, a predominantly black school, and he also gave $3 million to Harvard Law School in 1992—the largest ever lump-sum gift to the 175-year-old institution—which built an international law center in his name, the first Harvard building to be named after an African American.

Lewis rose from a large, tightly-knit Baltimore family to the upper echelon of law and business to ownership of Beatrice. Lewis was quoted as insisting, in the *Washington Post,* that his race did not affect his efforts in business: "It's understandable that [my race] is something people focus on. But what I focus on and what others focus on are two different things. I focus on doing a first-rate job on a consistent basis . . . . I would say my race hasn't been a factor one way or the other." He added in *Fortune,* "I'm very proud of the accomplishments of African-Americans, and I'm delighted that people feel this accomplishment [the Beatrice acquisition] adds to that list. But to dwell on race—to see that as something that becomes part of my persona—is a mistake, and I do everything I can to discourage it."

Lewis would probably credit his hardworking family for his drive and ambition. Pushing him to excel from boyhood on were his mother, a postal worker, his stepfather, a government worker, and his grandmother, who worked as a housekeeper; they raised him for higher things. His lifelong drive, intelligence, and curiosity were remembered with great fondness by his colleagues. The business world was stunned by Lewis's premature demise, though he had been diagnosed with brain cancer two months previous. New York City's Mayor David Dinkins said at Lewis's funeral service that "Reginald Lewis accomplished more in half a century than most of us could ever deem imaginable, and his brilliant career was matched always by a warm and generous heart." The list of performers attending Lewis's service is a testament to his fame: the entire Harlem Boys Choir sang, operatic soprano Kathleen Battle delivered a rendition of "Amazing Grace," and Leo Salonga of the Broadway hit *Miss Saigon* sang "The Quest," better known as "The Impossible Dream." These tributes were complimented by the attendance of many important business leaders. The crowning farewell was a videotaped biographical presentation about Lewis in which he charged his ambitious fellows to "Keep going on, no matter what!" according to the *New York Times.*

Lewis attended a series of private schools before being admitted to Virginia State University in 1961. After graduating with a degree in economics, he moved on to Harvard Law School, from which he graduated in 1968. Already fascinated by business takeovers, Lewis spent two years at a New York law firm before forming his own practice in 1970. He was joined by Charles Clarkson in 1973, and the pair's clients included General Foods and Aetna. A committed fundraiser for charities and for the presidential bids of the Reverend Jesse Jackson, Lewis was council for the National Association of Investment Companies—an organization concerned with directing investor monies to minority-owned businesses—from 1973 to 1981. Its chairperson, JoAnn Price, said of Lewis in the *Washington Post:* "There are people who grow up immediately and get on with it. He was someone who very early knew clearly what he wanted to do and where he wanted to go."

Lewis purchased the Beatrice food distributor in 1987 (in a leveraged buyout) for $985 million. The company's earnings in 1991 reached $1.5 billion, and within a year had increased by $.04 billion. Lewis and his family originally had $20 million worth of Beatrice shares. The value of the shares increased to $300 million. Vital to the acquisition of Beatrice were the profits made by Lewis through the McCall's Pattern Company. Lewis had purchased the down-and-out firm in 1984 for $1 million and $24 million in debt. By the time of the Beatrice purchase, Lewis had sold McCall's for $95 million. Beatrice announced on January 18, 1993, that Lewis had left the company in the hands of his half-brother, Jean S. Fugett, Jr. A former tight end for the Dallas Cowboys, and later, for the Washington Redskins, Fugett said in the *Washington Post* that "our goal will continue to be to maximize returns from each of our business units." Lewis is survived by his wife, attorney Loida Nicolas, and their two daughters. **Sources:** *New York Times,* January 26, 1993; *Newsmakers 88,* edited by Peter Gareffa, Gale, 1988; *Washington Post,* January 20, 1993.

Thurgood Marshall

Born July 2, 1908, in Baltimore, MD; died of heart failure, January 24, 1993, in Bethesda, MD. Supreme Court justice. The first African-American Supreme Court justice, Thurgood Marshall has often been compared to the great civil rights leaders of the 1960s, Rev. Dr. Martin Luther King, Jr., and Malcolm X. Marshall, too, fought to bring equal rights and treatment to American blacks, and he was not afraid to confront an entire system of government that tolerated, and ratified, racism. Like King and Malcolm X, Marshall regularly received death threats. Unlike them, however, he lived into productive old age, retiring from the supreme court of the land in 1991.

From the landmark victory for equal rights in *Brown v. Board of Education* in 1954, in which the Court ruled that segregation in the public schools is prohibited by the Constitution, to his steadfast defense of embattled affirmative action policies in the late 1980s, Justice Marshall worked from within the legal system to promote egalitarian rulings from the most powerful group of judges in the country. Some legal experts hail Justice Marshall as the author of opinions (essays from a justice that either express the views of the majority and explain the ruling or of dissention that challenge the ruling) that became examples to the world of the necessity of human rights preservation within the law. "It's my belief," said former NAACP head Benjamin Hooks in *People*, "that without Thurgood Marshall, we would still be riding in the back of the bus, going to separate schools and drinking 'colored' water." (Hooks referred to segregational practices that had to be challenged in court throughout the 1950s and 1960s.)

Justice Marshall was the great-grandson of a slave abducted from the African Congo; his paternal grandfather chose the name "Thoroughgood" when he joined the Union Army during the American Civil War. Namesake Marshall condensed this given name while in grade school. He was the son of William Marshall, a waiter, and the former Norma Williams, an elementary schoolteacher. A self-proclaimed "hell-raiser" in grade school, he was frequently punished by being sent to the basement to memorize a section of the Constitution. Marshall was encouraged by his parents to become a dentist, which was then thought to be a sure path to a prosperous future for a young black man, who would, it was understood, practice only for other African-Americans. Instead, the future justice attended Howard University Law School (after graduating from the predominantly black Lincoln University of Pennsylvania),

where he was greatly influenced by Charles Hamilton Houston, a vice dean who encouraged his students to become "social engineers," according to the *New York Times*. Marshall graduated first in his class in 1933, and was soon practicing law in Baltimore. He was eventually recruited by Houston, who was chief counsel for the NAACP at the time, to take on civil rights cases. Two years later, he became chief counsel himself. As such Marshall created the NAACP Legal Defense and Educational Fund, which he headed for 21 years. "Marshall was thus one of the first public interest lawyers," said biographer Mark Tushnet in the *New York Times*. "His commitment to racial justice led him and his staff to develop ways of thinking about constitutional litigation that have been enormously influential far beyond the areas of segregation and discrimination."

Throughout the 1950s, Marshall traveled the South, and alongside regional lawyers sympathetic to the civil rights cause, he pled some of the most important and influential cases in civil rights history. The most famous was *Brown v. Board of Education*, in which he argued against a 1896 ruling in *Plessy v. Ferguson* that allowed "separate [black/white] but equal" schools. ("In the year of Marshall's birth," noted *Newsweek*, "the Supreme Court ruled in *Berea v. Kentucky* that a state could outlaw even voluntary integration at a private college.") When the judge in the case challenged Marshall to define "equal" before the court, Marshall replied, according to the *New York Times*, "Equal means getting the same thing, at the same time, and in the same place." The London *Times* reported that the court eventually ruled that "Separate educational facilities are inherently unequal."

President John F. Kennedy named Marshall to the Federal Appeals Court in 1961, and in 1965 Marshall became the country's first black solicitor general under President Lyndon B. Johnson. President Johnson later said that placing Marshall on the Supreme Court was "the right thing to do, the right time to do it, the right man and the right place," as the *New York Times* recounted. Justice Marshall was sworn in as the first African-American Supreme Court justice on October 2, 1967. His 24 years of service to the court was characterized by the championing of liberal causes and the promotion of egalitarian society. Marshall was quoted in the *Washington Post* as having said, with typical eloquence, "At every point from birth to death, the impact of the past is reflected in the still-disfavored position of the Negro. In light of the sorry history of discrimination and its devastating impact on the lives of Negroes, bringing the Negro into the mainstream of American life should be a state interest of the highest order. To fail to do so is to ensure that America will forever remain a divided society."

Marshall was a fierce opponent of the death penalty to his last day in service of the Supreme Court. Often a gruff or sarcastic inquisitor of lawyers arguing such cases to the court and of his fellow justices, Marshall once snapped at Justice William Rehnquist's musings about the cost of life imprisonment to the taxpayer: "It would have been cheaper to shoot him right after he was arrested, wouldn't it?" the *New York Times* reported. The fact that black convicts are much more likely than whites to be actually executed always incensed him. "Death is irrevocable. Life imprisonment is not," Marshall stated in a ruling on the death penalty in 1972. "Death, of course, makes rehabilitation impossible. Life imprisonment does not. In short, death has always been viewed as the ultimate sanction . . . . In striking down capital punishment, this court does not malign our system of government. On the contrary, it pays homage to it . . . . In recognizing the humanity of our fellow beings, we pay ourselves the highest tribute."

The Supreme Court grew increasingly conservative through the appointments of Republican presidents in the 1970s and 1980s. More and more often, Justice Marshall saw civil rights progress erased, and his dissenting opinions grew more angry. Former President Ronald Reagan had amassed a substantial reputation as a foe of civil rights legislation by 1989 when Justice Marshall said, as quoted by the *New York Times*, "I wouldn't do the job of dogcatcher for Ronald Reagan." He added, "It's said that if you can't say something good about a person, don't say it. Well, I consider him dead."

Justice Marshall retired from the Court in 1991 citing health problems. Although he had vowed to stay in place until a Democratic president was elected to nominate a liberal replacement, Justice Marshall was plagued by glaucoma and suffered strokes and heart attacks. When he announced his retirement, Marshall remarked that he was not interested in whether or not his replacement was a black judge; he was primarily concerned, to the end, with the preservation of equal rights for all Americans. **Sources:** *New York Times*, January 25, 1993; February 8, 1993; *People*, February 8, 1993; *Time*, February 8, 1993; *Times* (London), January 26, 1993; *Washington Post*, January 25, 1993.

Steven J. Ross

Born Steven Jay Rechnitz, April 5, 1927, in New York City; died of complications from prostate cancer, December 20, 1992, in Los Angeles, CA. Chairman and co-chief executive of Time Warner Inc. An instinctive businessman who blended his business and personal life, Steven J. Ross experienced both heartbreak and elation in the upper realms of business deal-making. Working his way up from a family-owned funeral home business, Ross became one of the top operators in the high-stakes entertainment world. Although he suffered financially from the collapse of Atari (the company that produced the first home video games) and several scandals in the ranks of Warner employees, his early gambles on the burgeoning home entertainment field sustained him. Ross backed cable television in 1971, before it was even comparable to the big three networks, and he saw that Music Television (MTV), Home Box Office (HBO), and Nickolodeon would become preeminent. Ross felt that companies were mere building blocks for the real moneymakers, the conglomerates. The 1980s saw deals and mergers that set the curve for profits; the well-publicized merger of Warner Communications and Time Inc. of 1989 was the last of the big ones. Ross struggled throughout his career, sharing the company spotlight with other managers. In 1983, he had sold 20 percent of Warner shares to Chris-Craft Industries, thereby entitling its leader, Herbert J. Siegel, to a say in management. The pair battled famously, ending with Siegel's sale of his shares in 1989, realizing an enormous profit. Later, Ross fought with Nicholas J. Nicholas of Time Inc. Discordant management styles were once again at fault; Ross's friendly, congenial attitudes did not strike some as businesslike.

True to such a nature, his generosity was famous. Celebrity gossip columnist Liz Smith recalled at Ross's extravaganza funeral that when she asked for a printout of all of the charities that Ross patronized, the stack was so heavy she could not lift it. As Ross was a high-profile Democratic fundraiser, his family received personal condolences from President Bill Clinton and former president Jimmy Carter. Luminaries packed his funeral to attest to Ross's charisma and warmth, qualities that Ross did not abandon during the hard times.

Like so many businesspeople, Ross started his training early. The son of Jewish immigrants who lost all of their money in the Depression, Ross was encouraged to pursue his dreams by his father, who had been a builder and a heating oil salesman. Hoping to stump anti-Semitic employers, Ross's father had changed the family's name while looking for work, but he was to remain unemployed for a substantial period. At the age of 8, Ross began carrying groceries home or collecting laundry for pocket change. He attended vocational school for two years before joining the Navy. After his military stint, he joined his uncle in business in New York City's garment district. At 26, Ross met and married his first wife, Carol Rosenthal, and entered her family's funeral parlor business. The parlor's limosines were not being used at night, and Ross hit on the clever idea of renting them out in the evenings. Thus Abbey Rent-A-Car was founded, and Ross built it into a force to be reckoned with through mergers and acquisitions, including a chain of garages and an office cleaning service.

In 1962, when the firm's shares were offered to the public, its value was estimated at $ 12.5 million. This conglomerate bought the Warner film studio in 1969 for $400 million. The studio was then called Warner-Seven Arts, and soon after the purchase turned out the hit movies *Dirty Harry* and *Klute*. Besides changing the name to Warner Communications, Ross pioneered a new, disarming management style, one having both advantages and drawbacks. Warner executives were well paid and rewarded for good work with extraordinary perks, such as cosmetic surgery. Ross himself drew fire for his 1990 salary (including bonuses) of $78.2 million. Some insiders felt that Ross's trust in his employees was a detriment to the security of Warner and then Time Warner Inc. "Steve delegates a lot," said his friend and financier Felix G. Rohatyn in the *New York Times*. "That is his strength in dealing with talent and his weakness in dealing with adversity."

Throughout the 1980s, it seemed like "two steps forward, one back" for Ross and Warner. After introducing home video games, Atari flourished in the 1970s. Warner had purchased it in 1976, and by 1982, it accounted for half of Warner's profits. The bottom fell out of Atari soon after, partially due to competition, and Ross had to dump the holding in 1984. Insiders claimed that Ross should have been notified about trouble on the Atari horizon long before then; as it was, the collapse was a surprise, and Warner took a huge loss. The 1980s also saw several indictments at Warner's executive level for mob involvement and stock fraud and kickbacks, "with at least one federal prosecutor saying he thought Mr. Ross was a culprit too. Mr. Ross denied all charges of wrongdoing and was never charged with a crime, but analysts were suddenly critical of his loose corporate management and flamboyant lifestyle," reported the *Washington Post*. This lifestyle included a Park Avenue duplex and homes in East Hampton, Acapulco, and Los Angeles. Ross had divorced and remarried twice between 1978 and 1982. He maintained friendships with Hollywood's biggest names—Barbra Streisand, Dustin Hoffman, Steven Spielburg, Chevy Chase. Some felt that Ross could hardly be a serious businessman among these luminaries.

Throughout the troubled decade, however, Ross continued to pick up the pieces and acquire new companies. Warner itself had doubled its earnings between 1985 and 1988, when it was valued at $14 billion. The studio where hit 1980s films like *Batman*, *Driving Miss Daisy*, and *JFK* were made, Warner was viable but ailing. Ross engineered the merger with Time Inc. to form Time Warner Inc. in 1989, which encompassed the publications *Time*, *People*, *Sports Illustrated*; the Warner, Elektra, and Atlantic record companies; and Warner Books and DC Comics, among others. In 1991 Time Warner's revenues surpassed $12 billion. Sadly, just at the point when the tide of tough times was turning, and Ross had weathered the challenges of Siegel and Nicholas, he was diagnosed with prostate cancer. He succumbed to the disease after a battle of several years' duration. **Sources:** *Chicago Tribune*, December 21, 1992; *New York Times*, December 21, 1992, February 12, 1993; *Times* (London), December 22, 1992; *Washington Post*, December 21, 1992.

William Shawn

Born August 31, 1907, in Chicago, IL; died of a heart attack, December 8, 1992, in New York City. Magazine editor. William Shawn nurtured and taught some of the century's finest writers during his 35-year-tenure as the editor of the *New Yorker*. Shawn was as well-known a personality as a shy person could be: his politeness, formality, and taste for privacy was famous. A stickler for detail, Shawn nonetheless had firm ideas about the greater purposes and higher importance of writing that he was not afraid to defend, even to his last days on the magazine. He was given almost unlimited authority over the weekly, from the covers, drawings, and cartoons, to the advertisements. The separation of the editorial and commercial concerns of the magazine was, he felt, as essential to the freedom of the writers as that of the editors, who had to create and maintain the periodical's earnest tenor.

The consummate editor, Shawn edited on weekends to relax, he edited non-stop in his *New Yorker* offices, he encouraged new writers, and he maintained relationships with longtime contributors such as Dorothy Parker, Truman Capote, J. D. Salinger, John Updike, Rachel Carson, John Hersey, and James Baldwin. The testimonials from some of these authors at the time of Shawn's forced retirement from the *New Yorker* in 1987 compete with those at the time of his death for their sincere gratitude, admiration, and sadness. Jane Kramer said in the *New Yorker:* "He wasn't simply a genius—he was a genius at *your* disposal." John Updike added that "this shy man, in his buttoned vest, concealed a mental swashbuckler who constantly kept readers and writers on their toes." "What I found remarkable," writer Calvin Trillin recalled, "is not that he invariably put his finger on the flawed sentence but that as he read I often understood how to fix it." Roger Angell, a *New Yorker* editor, called Shawn "the greatest editor of our time," as quoted in the *Los Angeles Times.* And, "He read every piece of writing in every issue of the magazine at least three times: first when it was submitted, again when it had gone into galleys, and, finally in page proof," said the "Comment" section of the *New Yorker* following Shawn's death.

Shawn was not a native New Yorker himself; born in Chicago to Benjamin W. Chon (a prosperous cutlery merchant) and Anna Bransky Chon, Shawn changed his name as a young journalist, believing that he would have an easier time reaching an audience that didn't think he was Chinese. He was sent to the private Harvard School for Boys, where he was president of his freshman and senior classes, secretary of his junior class, president of the debating society, and editor of the senior yearbook. He attended the University of Michigan for two years before dropping out in 1927. Shawn then headed west to work on the newspaper *Las Vegas Optic* for $30 a week when the gambling mecca was still just a small town. On returning to Chicago, he met and married the former Cecille Lyon, a journalist; the newlyweds then experimented with the expatriate life. Shawn worked in Paris, France, as a jazz pianist in a bar and composed music for the ballet and theater. "My work was primitive," Shawn said in the *New York Times.* "I was an uneducated musician." Shawn continued to play the piano, though only privately, for the rest of his life. When the Shawns returned to the United States, they settled in New York City, where Shawn became a reporter for the *New Yorker* and wrote for the "Talk of the Town" column at a pay rate of $2 for each inch of copy.

Each distinct phase of the *New Yorker's* temperament was (and continues to be) dictated by its editor. Under founder Harold Ross, for example, it was a dry, educated, clique-ish humor magazine, and when it became Shawn's after 25 years, it became more sober, including many influential social-issues articles. Under Shawn the *New Yorker* still contained the best humorists of the day, but its tone was almost educational. Furthermore, Shawn wanted to create and maintain a forum for writers. He published Rachel Carson's "Silent Spring," subsequently published as a book warning of environmental catastrophes. James Baldwin wrote about racism in the United States. The magazine opposed the Vietnam War and published many biting antiwar editorials. *New York Times* critic John Leonard argued that "Shawn changed the New Yorker from a smarty-pants parish tip sheet into a journal that altered our experience instead of just posturing in front of it."

Simply, authors bloomed under his attention. For Shawn "the idea of a 'New Yorker School' of writers was more tangibly associated with a specific critique of the American ethic than it had previously been," wrote an obituarist for the London *Times.* "Under Shawn the employee directory of the *New Yorker* might have provided, year after year, a running nomination for the Pulitzer prizes in journalism, fiction and poetry." Shawn's contribution to excellence in American journalism and literature was eventually curtailed by financial concerns. Circulation of the *New Yorker* went from 485,000 in 1974 to 510,000 in 1983, but dropped back down to 500,000 the next year. In 1985, the magazine was sold to publishing magnate S.I. Newhouse for $142 million. Shawn had already tendered a resignation to previous owners Raoul and Peter Fleischmann in 1978, but had asked to stay on for an additional two years to break in a successor. In the end, Shawn got to stay on as editor through the transition in ownership, but those years were marred by what observers described as staff in-fighting, favoritism, and poor morale. Newhouse said at the time of the purchase that he respected Shawn and did not want to change the magazine's style, but Shawn published a minor manifesto in the "Notes and Comments" section anyway, saying: "We, the editorial people, knew by instinct that to be able to make the *New Yorker* the magazine we wanted it to be we had to separate ourselves from the business side of the venture . . . . In this atmosphere of freedom, we have never published anything in order to sell magazines, to cause a sensation, to be controversial, to be popular or fashionable, to be 'successful.'" This attitude did not jibe with what Newhouse wanted for the magazine, and Shawn was forced out in 1987, barred from choosing—or even stating his preference for—his successor. Robert Gottlieb of Knopf was named and took the job over the protests of many writers and editors on the staff, but served only five years of editorship before Newhouse fired him to hire former *Vanity Fair* editor Tina Brown in 1992. Her first issue appeared on October 5, 1992; advertisement numbers soon rose 16 percent, and circulation soared to 659,000 in the second half of 1992. Brown told the *New York Times* in April of 1993 that "we would like to see it turn a profit in five years." Of her many critics, including longtime subscribers who complain that she has "tarted up" the magazine, Brown replies, "Well, you know there is a lot of faux Puritanism out there. It's all part of the New Yorker fakery. Good taste in the prissy sense has never been of interest to me." Shawn's son Wallace was asked in the *New York Times* about his father's response to Brown's changes in the magazine. He replied that his father had not given him any indication, but had planned to have lunch with Brown, "and I know that he still wished everyone at the magazine very, very well." Tina Brown eulogized Shawn as "probably the greatest magazine editor who ever lived," reported the *Los Angeles Times*, "and one of the most important figures in American letters in this century." After leaving the *New Yorker*, Shawn worked as a consulting editor at Farrar, Straus & Giroux, editing some 20 books before his death.

Sources: Gigi Mahon, *The Last Days of the New Yorker*, McGraw-Hill, 1988; *Los Angeles Times*, December 9, 1992; *New York Times*, December 9, 1992, April 12, 1993; *New Yorker*, December 21, 1992, December 28, 1992/January 4, 1993; *Times* (London), December 10, 1992; *Washington Post*, December 9, 1992.

—Obituaries by Christine Ferran

1993 Nationality Index

This index lists newsmakers alphabetically under their respective nationalities. Indexes in soft-bound issues allow access to the current year's entries; indexes in annual hardbound volumes are cumulative, covering the entire *Newsmakers* series.

Listee names are followed by a year and issue number; thus **1988:3** indicates that an entry on that individual appears in both 1988, Issue 3 and the 1988 cumulation. For access to news-makers appearing earlier than the current softbound issue, see the previous year's cumulation.

AMERICAN
Acuff, Roy
  Obituary **1993**:2
Alexander, Jason **1993**:3
Allen, Tim **1993**:1
Altman, Robert **1993**:2
Arman **1993**:1
Arnold, Tom **1993**:2
Ashe, Arthur
  Obituary **1993**:3
Barber, Red
  Obituary **1993**:2
Bentsen, Lloyd **1993**:3
Bialik, Mayim **1993**:3
Bolton, Michael **1993**:2
Bonds, Barry **1993**:3
Booth, Shirley
  Obituary **1993**:2
Bowe, Riddick **1993**:2
Braun, Carol Moseley **1993**:1
Brown, Jim **1993**:2
Burton, Tim **1993**:1
Cage, John
  Obituary **1993**:1
Carey, Ron **1993**:3
Cher **1993**:1
Clinton, Hillary Rodham **1993**:2
Courier, Jim **1993**:2
Crawford, Cindy **1993**:3
Cyrus, Billy Ray **1993**:1
Daniels, Faith **1993**:3
Dorsey, Thomas A.
  Obituary **1993**:3
Douglas, Marjory Stoneman **1993**:1
Eastwood, Clint **1993**:3
Edwards, Bob **1993**:2
Ellerbee, Linda **1993**:3
Ephron, Henry
  Obituary **1993**:2
Feinstein, Dianne **1993**:3
Fenwick, Millicent H.
  Obituary **1993**:2
Fielder, Cecil **1993**:2
Forsythe, William **1993**:2
Gaines, William M.
  Obituary **1993**:1
Garrison, Jim
  Obituary **1993**:2
Gates, Bill **1993**:3
Gertz, Alison
  Obituary **1993**:2
Gillespie, Dizzy
  Obituary **1993**:2

Goldberg, Whoopi **1993**:3
Gore, Albert Jr. **1993**:2
Gund, Agnes **1993**:2
Hale, Clara
  Obituary **1993**:3
Healy, Bernadine **1993**:1
Hilfiger, Tommy **1993**:3
Iacocca, Lee **1993**:1
Jemison, Mae C. **1993**:1
Johnson, Jimmy **1993**:3
Johnson, Larry **1993**:3
Joyner-Kersee, Jackie **1993**:1
Kendricks, Eddie
  Obituary **1993**:2
King, Larry **1993**:1
Kinison, Sam
  Obituary **1993**:1
Kistler, Darci **1993**:1
Klass, Perri **1993**:2
Kopp, Wendy **1993**:3
Kordich, Jay **1993**:2
Krzyzewski, Mike **1993**:2
Laettner, Christian **1993**:1
Lansbury, Angela **1993**:1
Leary, Denis **1993**:3
Lewis, Reginald F.
  Obituary **1993**:3
Lewis, Shari **1993**:1
Little, Cleavon
  Obituary **1993**:2
MacKinnon, Catharine **1993**:2
Marky Mark **1993**:3
Marshall, Thurgood
  Obituary **1993**:3
McCloskey, James **1993**:1
McGowan, William G.
  Obituary **1993**:1
McKenna, Terence **1993**:3
McMillan, Terry **1993**:2
Miller, Roger
  Obituary **1993**:2
Monk, Art **1993**:2
Neiman, LeRoy **1993**:3
Newman, Arnold **1993**:1
Owens, Delia and Mark **1993**:3
Perkins, Anthony
  Obituary **1993**:2
Predock, Antoine **1993**:2
Priestly, Jason **1993**:2
Prince, Faith **1993**:2
Quindlen, Anna **1993**:1
Redford, Robert **1993**:2
Reno, Janet **1993**:3

Robbins, Tim **1993**:1
Ross, Steven J.
  Obituary **1993**:3
Rudner, Rita **1993**:2
Sagansky, Jeff **1993**:2
St. James, Lyn **1993**:2
Schuman, Patricia Glass **1993**:2
Sevareid, Eric
  Obituary **1993**:1
Shawn, William
  Obituary **1993**:3
Sirica, John
  Obituary **1993**:2
Smoot, George F. **1993**:3
Snipes, Wesley **1993**:1
Stern, Howard **1993**:3
Thomas, Dave **1993**:2
Thomas, Thurman **1993**:1
Truitt, Anne **1993**:1
Turner, Janine **1993**:2
Van Duyn, Mona **1993**:2
Walton, Sam
  Obituary **1993**:1
Washington, Denzel **1993**:2
Weicker, Lowell P., Jr. **1993**:1
Welch, Jack **1993**:3
Wells, Mary
  Obituary **1993**:1
Wenner, Jann **1993**:1
Williams, Willie L. **1993**:1
Wynonna **1993**:3
Zucker, Jeff **1993**:3

AUSTRALIAN
Allen, Peter
  Obituary **1993**:1
Humphries, Barry **1993**:1

BELGIAN
Hepburn, Audrey
  Obituary **1993**:2

BRITISH
Clapton, Eric **1993**:3
Diana, Princess of Wales **1993**:1
Elliott, Denholm
  Obituary **1993**:2
Faldo, Nick **1993**:3
MacMillan, Kenneth
  Obituary **1993**:2
Patten, Christopher **1993**:3
Richards, Keith **1993**:3

1993 Occupation Index

This index lists newsmakers by their occupations or fields of primary activity. Indexes in softbound issues allow access to the current year's entries; indexes in annual hardbound volumes are cumulative, covering the entire *Newsmakers* series.

Listee names are followed by a year and issue number; thus **1988**:3 indicates that an entry on that individual appears in both 1988, Issue 3 and the 1988 cumulation. For access to newsmakers appearing earlier than the current softbound issue, see the previous year's cumulation.

1993 Subject Index

This index lists newsmakers by subjects, company names, products, organizations, issues, awards, and professional specialties. Indexes in softbound issues allow access to the current year's entries; indexes in annual hardbound volumes are cumulative, covering the entire *Newsmakers* series.

Listee names are followed by a year and issue number; thus **1988:3** indicates that an entry on that individual appears in both 1988, Issue 3 and the 1988 cumulation. For access to newsmakers appearing earlier than the current softbound issue, see the previous year's cumulation.

Cumulative Newsmakers Index

This index lists all entries included in the *Newsmakers* series.

Listee names are followed by a year and issue number; thus **1988**:3 indicates that an entry appears in both 1988, Issue 3 and the 1988 cumulation.

Cumulative Newsmakers Index

DATE DUE
